Economic Valuation Techniques for the Environment

Contributors

Beta Balagot National Environmental Protection Council, Manila, Philippines
Cheng Shengtong Qing Hua University, Beijing, China
John A. Dixon East-West Center, Honolulu, Hawaii, USA
Siriwut Eutrirak Thammasat University, Bangkok, Thailand
Fu Guowei Qing Hua University, Beijing, China
Somluckrat Grandstaff Thammasat University, Bangkok, Thailand
Yuzuru Hanayama Tokyo Institute of Technology, Japan
Maynard M. Hufschmidt East-West Center, Honolulu, Hawaii, USA
Eric L. Hyman East-West Center, Honolulu, Hawaii, USA
David E. James Macquarie University, North Ryde, Australia
Sung-Hoon Kim Chung-Ang University, Seoul, Korea
Anton D. Meister Massey University, Palmerston North, New Zealand
Nie Guisheng Environmental Protection Institute, Beijing, China
Ikuo Sano Environmental Protection Agency, Tokyo, Japan
Ruangdej Srivardhana Kasetsart University, Bangkok, Thailand
Zhang Lansheng Qing Hua University, Beijing, China

Economic Valuation Techniques for the Environment

A Case Study Workbook

edited by
John A. Dixon and
Maynard M. Hufschmidt

The Johns Hopkins University Press
Baltimore and London

This book has been brought to publication with the
generous assistance of the East-West Center.

Published, hardcover and paperback, 1986
Second printing, paperback, 1990

The Johns Hopkins University Press
701 West 40th Street
Baltimore, Maryland 21211
The Johns Hopkins Press Ltd., London

The paper used in this publication meets the minimum requirements of American
National Standard for Information Sciences—Permanence of Paper for Printed Library
Materials, ANSI Z39.48-1984.

Library of Congress Cataloging-in-Publication Data

Economic valuation techniques for the environment.

 Includes bibliographies and index.
 Contents: The role of economics in valuing en-
vironmental effects of development projects / by
John A. Dixon—A hypothetical case study, the Lake
Burley Fishery Project / by David E. James—Time
horizons, discounting, and computational aids / by
John A. Dixon and Anton D. Meister—[etc.].
 1. Environmental policy—Cost effectiveness—
Addresses, essays, lectures. 2. Economic development
projects—Cost effectiveness—Addresses, essays, lectures.
I. Dixon, John A., 1946–   . II. Hufschmidt,
Maynard M.
HC79.E5E274 1986   363.7'05'0681   86-2730
ISBN 0-8018-3352-3 (alk. paper)
ISBN 0-8018-3308-6 (pbk.)

Contents

Figures

Tables

Foreword

This compilation of case studies is a companion volume to *Environment, Natural Systems, and Development: An Economic Valuation Guide* by Hufschmidt et al. (published in 1983 by the Johns Hopkins University Press). Both books result from a continuous, multinational collaborative study begun in 1979 under the auspices of the Environment and Policy Institute (EAPI), a unit in the East-West Center at Honolulu, Hawaii. The East-West Center brings together experts and practitioners from the United States and countries of Asia and the Pacific to work on problems of mutual concern and thereby, according to its charter from the United States Congress, "promote better relations and understanding." The economic development of natural resources and the environmental consequences of such technological changes form a rich field for cooperative research.

The writing of the first book, *Environment, Natural Systems and Development* (hereafter referred to as the *Guide*), was carried out during 1980 and 1981. At the same time case studies were being developed to illustrate the use of economic valuation techniques to place values on environmental and natural systems effects of existing development projects. The authors of the case studies were usually residents of the countries involved and in some cases were actively involved in the projects described.

By early 1982 the EAPI team had a complete draft of the *Guide* and a series of case studies ready for use in actual training courses. While the *Guide* was written as a text for instruction or self-teaching, the case studies were designed to illustrate practical applications of the approaches advocated in the *Guide*.

Interest in these materials led to a number of training workshops co-sponsored by host country governments and international development organizations along with the EAPI. These one- to two-week sessions have been held in the Philippines (1982), Thailand and Korea (1983), Honolulu and China (1984), and Sri Lanka (1985). Through these training sessions the case studies were reviewed and revised and additional materials developed to clarify certain points. The actual case studies and supporting materials used in this workbook were prepared by 16 experienced contributing authors from Australia, China, Japan, Korea, New Zealand, the Philippines, Thailand, and the United States. John A. Dixon and Maynard M. Hufschmidt led the training teams, directed the preparation of this case study workbook, and made major contributions to the writing. The result is a set of tested examples of applications of some of the valuation techniques presented in the *Guide*.

Another result of this effort is a network of trainers and economists in Asia and the Pacific who have come to know one another and have become familiar with the economic valuation approach. This approach is now beginning to be used in various countries in the region. The inclusion of economic externalities in the conceptual and prefeasibility stages of project analyses will help in avoiding adverse impacts on the environment and in revealing opportunities for more effective and sustainable development of each nation's endowment of renewable natural resources.

The next goal of our East-West Environment and Policy Institute project is to apply the techniques outlined in the *Guide* and the Case Study Workbook to a variety of actual development projects and resource management problems. These applications should further document the usefulness (and undoubtedly also the shortcomings) of the methods. Readers are invited to correspond with the authors about their own experiences and to collaborate with us in continuing to help development planners and decision makers with more complete economic analyses.

RICHARD A. CARPENTER
Program Area Coordinator

Preface and Acknowledgments

The seven case studies included in this book illustrate how the various economic techniques discussed in the companion *Guide* can be used to value environmental and natural systems effects of development projects. The case studies were originally commissioned in 1980 and substantially completed in late 1981. They were first used in a training workshop held in Quezon City, the Philippines, in January 1982. The case studies were revised in form and content as a result of their use in this and subsequent workshops in Thailand, Korea, China, Honolulu, and Sri Lanka. These workshops served as critiques of the *Guide* and the case studies in terms of the utility of the valuation techniques to actual planning situations in those countries.

Complementing the case studies are three introductory chapters. In Chapter 1, the role of economics in the valuation of environmental effects of development projects is briefly presented in a real world context. Chapter 2 consists of a hypothetical case study that takes the reader through both financial and economic analyses of a project, pointing out economic fallacies and errors to be avoided. In the final introductory chapter, the topics of economic time horizon and discounting are discussed and some computational aids are presented. These introductory chapters are designed to help the users of the case studies in working through the economic valuation exercises.

We wish to thank all of the 14 contributors to the case studies and the introductory chapters. Special thanks are due to Dr. Somluckrat Grandstaff, Research Associate at EAPI from 1981 to 1983, who played a major role in preparing several of the case studies and who was a key member of the EAPI team while she was in Hawaii.

Many people reviewed parts or all of the draft manuscript, and a number of very helpful suggestions for improvement were received. Useful feedback was also received from a number of professors who used the draft case studies in teaching. In addition, the training workshops yielded many valuable comments and suggestions for revision.

Our appreciation is extended to Professor Fred Hitzhusen, Department of Agricultural Economics and Rural Sociology, Ohio State University; Professor Shaul Ben-David, Department of Economics, University of New Mexico; Dr. Ferenc Juhasz, Environment Directorate, Organization for Economic Cooperation and Development; and an anonymous reviewer for their perceptive comments and suggestions for improving the manuscript. To Lou Fallon and Paul Sherman we owe special thanks for their meticulous review of the manuscript, including a check of the many calculations and the results as shown in the tables and figures. The dedicated work of East-West Center editors Helen Takeuchi and Sheryl Bryson in preparing the manuscript for final publication is deeply appreciated. Our special thanks go to Joan Nakamura who has worked on various drafts of the case studies and on this manuscript since 1981. The assistance of Ethel Tokuyama and Lucy Kamealoha is also acknowledged. The support and encouragement of Anders Richter, Editorial Director, and others at the Johns Hopkins University Press are gratefully acknowledged. Finally we wish to thank William H. Matthews, Director of the Environment and Policy Institute until October 1, 1985, for his consistent support of our work on economic valuation, which led to the preparation and publication of the *Guide* and this book.

I
The Approach to Valuation

1
The Role of Economics in Valuing Environmental Effects of Development Projects

John A. Dixon

Over the past two decades the interrelationship of the environment and the continuing production of goods and services that are extracted from our physical surroundings has become more accepted and better understood. The ideal of sustainable development has led to a search for ways in which development projects can be assessed in order that both direct project outputs and environmental effects can be included in the valuation process. This approach explicitly recognizes that there are trade-offs between development and the goods and services provided by the environment.

This search for ways to explicitly include environmental concerns into the project evaluation process has resulted in the publication of *Environment, Natural Systems, and Development: An Economic Valuation Guide* (Hufschmidt et al. 1983), hereafter referred to as the *Guide*, and this case study workbook. The *Guide* presents the theory behind and techniques for economic valuation of environmental quality effects. This workbook shows how some of the techniques have been used in assessing development projects in the Asia-Pacific region. Together, the documents are designed to assist the economist and planner in integrating environmental factors into project development and appraisal.

The interrelationship between the environment and development goals is expressed in the introduction to the *Guide:*

> Economic development in both industrialized and developing countries relies crucially on natural resources and on the productivity of natural systems. Economic development implies sustained increases in welfare derived from conventional goods and services, the production of which often requires natural resources and productive natural systems. Moreover, the environment directly provides services that contribute to increased welfare as implied by economic development.
>
> At the same time, economic growth often is accompanied by increasing stress on natural systems and significant adverse effects on environmental quality. The central issue, then, is to conduct development activities in a fashion that preserves the long-run productivity of natural systems for sustained development and that minimizes deterioration in environmental quality.

3

Unfortunately, experience in both the developed and developing worlds demonstrates that on many occasions economic development activities have not shown sufficient concern for maintaining natural systems and environmental quality. This is due in part to the view that economic growth and environmental quality are alternatives—deterioration in environmental quality is viewed as a necessary cost of rapid economic growth. This view is misleading. . . . Even when deterioration of environmental quality does not lead to reduced capacity to produce conventional goods and services, natural-systems services that are consumed directly, such as recreation, are affected and the objective of development—improved human welfare—is undermined. For these reasons, it is of utmost importance that the effects on natural systems of development projects and programs be carefully analyzed. Such analysis is not a luxury, but must become an essential part of project formulation and evaluation if protection is to be provided to the natural-resource base that sustains human welfare.

The *Guide* offers a comprehensive approach to the problem of incorporating the environmental quality effects of development projects into the process of economic analysis and evaluation. The first two chapters of the *Guide* provide a general introduction and an explanation of the institutional and planning context within which decisions are made. Chapter 3 outlines the principles and environmental quality extensions of benefit-cost analysis; this exposition is designed to highlight the major principles of welfare economics that underlie benefit-cost analysis as well as to introduce certain key concepts.

The processes of analyzing activities and the effect of these activities on natural systems and receptors are discussed in the next two chapters. This material is an essential component of the economic valuation approach presented in the *Guide:* before environmental effects can be included into an evaluation, the nature of the process or activity under consideration (a factory, an agricultural development, a housing project) must be understood. Once understood, the *effects* of this process or activity on the surrounding environment (natural, manmade) and on receptors (human and nonhuman) need to be analyzed. Only then can the valuation techniques be applied to place monetary values on these effects and consequently incorporated into the project evaluation process.

The actual valuation techniques are presented in the last three chapters and, for expositional reasons, are roughly divided into those techniques that measure environmental quality from the benefit side (Chapter 6) and from the cost side (Chapter 7), as well as the use of multiactivity economic-environmental quality models (Chapter 8).

As outlined here the approach presented in the *Guide* and illustrated in Figure 1.1 explicitly recognizes the multidisciplinary dimension of economic-environmental analysis. Few economists possess the necessary background or experience to perform the activity analysis capably and to trace all of the activity effects on the environment and on receptors. Thus the economist must rely on the specialized knowledge of other professionals, usually natural scientists and engineers, for this information. Economists (or planners) bring their training and skills to bear by

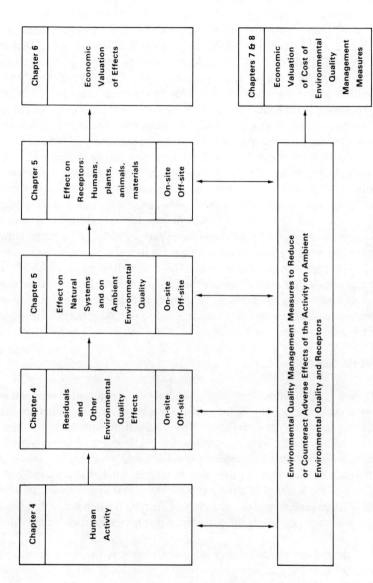

Figure 1.1 Valuation of natural systems and environmental quality effects and of environmental quality management measures (*Source*: Hufschmidt et al. 1983).

formulating a model that allows inclusion of these various dimensions and presents them in a framework usable for budgetary or policy decisions.

In fact, the idea of opportunity costs, or trade-offs, is key to this entire approach. If money, skilled manpower, or a natural resource were not in short supply (a constraint), one could undertake all of the projects that were feasible; and if problems are met, one could fix up, redo, or make payments later to rectify mistakes or undesirable side effects. Since we operate in a world with constraints—with *scarce* resources—the allocation of these resources should be as efficient as possible. In the belief that the environment should serve as a continuing supplier of goods and services to society, development should proceed in as environmentally sound a manner as possible given the constraints. This last point is crucial. We are not advocating "no development" or "only development that is 100 percent environmentally safe." Neither of these options is realistic. Only if the set of major realistic options is known and if the economic and environmental benefits and costs are made explicit for each option can better decision making take place. It is in this spirit that the *Guide* was prepared as an aid to the decision-making process. And yet, even within this broad perspective, some aspects, such as the income distribution effects of environmental externalities, are not explicitly considered. The approach presented in the *Guide* therefore can lead to better economic analysis, but it does not provide the final answer; the final decision on a project will depend on a combination of factors, including economic, social, and political. Economic analysis therefore can be seen as a necessary but not sufficient condition for informed decision making.

The Real World Context

Writing a *Guide* is one matter; applying it is another. This application problem is particularly acute because many of the environmental quality effects that are the focus of this approach are not easily quantified or valued. It is precisely for these reasons that they frequently have been ignored in traditional project evaluation. For example, an agricultural development project would normally be evaluated based on the costs of various inputs used and the benefits from products produced. The *boundary* of the analysis is quite narrow—the actual agricultural site. If a broader perspective is taken and the boundary of analysis is extended, it may well be that there are other, previously off-site, effects that have important benefits and costs.

If land is cleared for agricultural development, the result may be increased erosion from the land and sedimentation downstream on lands and in streams and reservoirs. These off-site effects might include some benefits, as well as costs. The land clearing also may destroy the natural habitat of a harmful insect or animal; this would be a benefit. Including these on-site and off-site environmental aspects in the project evaluation would result in a fuller accounting of the benefits and costs to society. Following this, the various development or management options can then be illustrated and the trade-offs involved can be made more explicit. (For some projects environmental effects may be small or nonexistent and can be ignored. In other cases, environmental quality effects may have already been internalized by existing laws or rules.)

As identified in the *Guide*, this assessment and valuation process can be seen as a four-step exercise. First, the important environmental effects have to be *identified*. Next, the effects have to be *quantified;* that is, how great are the increases in erosion rates and what are the associated reductions in physical outputs of crops or electric energy; or what is the decrease in insect-borne diseases after the project? These quantified changes must then be *valued* and monetary values placed on them, which is a difficult task. Monetary valuation is the focus of the methodological chapters in the *Guide:* What techniques can be used to place monetary values on such effects? The actual *economic analysis* is the last step. In most cases, some form of benefit-cost analysis is used.

Another way to express this approach is by using this simple equation:

$$NPV = B_d + B_e - C_d - C_p - C_e \qquad (1\text{-}1)$$

where NPV = net present value
   B_d = direct project benefits
   B_e = external (and/or environmental) benefits
   C_d = direct project costs
   C_p = environmental protection costs and
   C_e = external (and/or environmental) costs

All items on the right-hand side are discounted to present values.

Traditional project evaluation looks only at the direct project benefits and direct project costs; the expanded approach includes the external and environmental improvement benefits (plus the benefits from environmental protection), as well as the costs of external and/or environmental damages and of environmental control measures (being careful not to double count the latter). The first three steps mentioned previously (identifying, quantifying, and valuing) are aimed at deriving the values used in the equation.

As mentioned earlier, this workbook illustrates how this approach can be used and has been used in evaluating various development projects in the Asia-Pacific region. All of the Asian case studies presented in this workbook are based on actual projects but, in some cases, the data have been modified to simplify the presentation.

The workbook is divided into two parts. The first part contains three chapters including this introduction. Chapter 2 presents a hypothetical case study that illustrates many of the errors commonly made in project evaluation. Since the approach outlined in the *Guide* is largely concerned with *economic* rather than *financial* analysis, these differences are stressed in Chapter 2 of this workbook.

Financial analysis is carried out from an individual or corporate/private perspective and is more concerned with narrowly defined profits or losses. It is concerned primarily with the B_d and C_d of the equation mentioned earlier. *Economic* analysis is conducted from the standpoint of society's welfare and reflects the social opportunity costs and benefits of various actions. It includes B_e, C_p, and C_e, as well as the direct project components of B_d and C_d. Both approaches are valid, given the different perspectives involved. That is, a government may want to do both a financial and economic analysis to determine both the narrow "profitability" of a project, as well as its wider social costs and benefits. For example, an upland rehabilitation project could be evaluated from a narrow financial perspective with regard to project costs and direct project benefits in the project area. These benefits could include such things as increased crop or tree production. A broader economic analysis would also include the off-site benefits of reduced soil erosion and sediment deposition in downstream areas. An individual or private firm will quite properly only consider a financial analysis of the on-site effects of the proposed project.

There is another important reason to do a financial as well as an economic analysis of a project. It has been observed that the behavior of farmers or any other "private" decision-making unit based solely on the financial incentives they face creates problems for society at large. Soil erosion is one example: it is well known that the private sector's rate of investment in conservation practices (such as for soil) is much lower than would be optimal from society's viewpoint. This is due to nonrecognition of off-site effects, incorrect price signals, and institutional and social factors.

The financial analysis, done from the farmer's perspective, is extremely useful in determining how to design and implement "incentive schemes" such as those involving compensation or subsidies. In the final analysis the farmers will be the ones who will have to adopt the recommended conservation practices. Thus, even if a conservation project is perceived to be attractive from the country's viewpoint, if farmers do not have the necessary financial incentives to adopt such practices, the project is bound to fail. The financial analysis will then help identify the key constraints and indicate the type and size of subsidy required. Both financial and economic analysis, therefore, play an important role in project design and evaluation.

The main technical differences between economic and financial analyses can be addressed in two ways: (1) What should a set of economic prices include in comparison with financial prices, and (2) What should the type of project benefits (or costs) include in each analysis? The answers are similar. Traditional financial analysis only includes those benefits and costs faced by the production and decision-making unit (e.g., the farm, an industry). These benefits and costs are evaluated in monetary terms using existing market prices and taking into account taxes, subsidies, and other transfer payments.

Economic analysis, on the other hand, uses economic efficiency prices that remove the distortions introduced by regulations or transfer payments. "Traditional" economic analysis includes the same benefits and costs of the financial analysis, merely valuing them in efficiency prices. The "extended" social-welfare analysis advocated in the *Guide* and in this workbook includes a wider range of benefits and costs. In theory both forms of economic analysis (traditional and extended) should include the same benefits and costs and use the same prices. In practice this has not been true and hence the development of these materials.

Chapter 3 presents information on time horizons, discounting, and computational aids. Although details of the valuation techniques are presented in the *Guide* and traditional project evaluation is well handled by standard references (Gittinger 1982; Roemer and Stern 1975; Thompson 1980; Gramlich 1981), this chapter discusses points that have frequently been raised in initial dissemination workshops based on the *Guide* and various case studies. As with most questions in an actual analysis, there is no single correct answer to such frequently raised queries as to what is the appropriate time horizon or discount rate. Rather, information is presented that will assist the analyst in choosing a reasonable value given the facts of each case. Standard formulas used in project evaluation are also presented and discussed, and the use of discounting tables is covered.

The second part of the workbook consists of a brief introduction and seven case studies based on actual projects in five Asia-Pacific countries. Each case study is presented as a self-contained teaching unit in a standard format. The problem to be studied is explained and data are presented. The appropriate valuation technique is introduced, and the steps in the analysis are outlined for the reader. Finally, a separate sample solution is also presented for each case study. These case studies originally were developed for use in dissemination workshops in the Asia-Pacific region; workshops have been held in the Philippines (1982), Thailand and Korea (1983), China (1984), and Sri Lanka (1985). Because of the short time available for each workshop (one to two weeks), these case studies are condensed and only highlight the economic valuation of environmental quality effects of the development projects. A complete economic analysis of all dimensions of each project is usually not presented; the introduction to each case study briefly mentions aspects that are not covered in the case. A final point should be made about data requirements for project analysis, especially in developing countries. Although there is no doubt that data are usually incomplete or of mixed quality, there is also no doubt that a great deal can be done with existing data. The focus here is on conceptualizing problems in such a way that available data can be used for the analysis.

This case study workbook is designed for use in conjunction with the *Guide* to illustrate how environmental dimensions can be explicitly incorporated into project design and evaluation. As analysts gain experience with the approach and techniques illustrated, new approaches will be developed. In this regard the search for suitable methods to ensure sustainable development will continue to evolve as our understanding of the interdependence of economic development and the natural resource base grows.

References

Gittinger, J. P. *Economic Analysis of Agricultural Projects*. Baltimore: Johns Hopkins University Press, 1982.

Gramlich, E. M. *Benefit-Cost Analysis of Government Programs*. Englewood Cliffs, N.J.: Prentice-Hall, 1981.

Hufschmidt, M. M., D. E. James, A. D. Meister, B. T. Bower, and J. A. Dixon. *Environment, Natural Systems, and Development: An Economic Valuation Guide*. Baltimore: Johns Hopkins University Press, 1983.

Roemer, M., and J. J. Stern. *The Appraisal of Development Projects: A Practical Guide to Project Analysis with Case Studies and Solutions*. New York: Praeger, 1975.

Thompson, M. S. *Benefit-Cost Analysis for Program Evaluation*. Beverly Hills, Calif.: Sage Publications, 1980.

2
A Hypothetical Case Study: The Lake Burley Fishery Project

David E. James

The previous chapter introduced a broad approach to project evaluation—an approach that explicitly incorporates environmental quality effects into an economic analysis. Much of the focus in the *Guide* and in this workbook is on the quantification and valuation of these environmental quality effects. The actual mechanics of project evaluation have been largely glossed over. Many of the elements of project evaluation are well known and many benefit-cost analyses can be done with the use of inexpensive hand calculators. Discounting and other calculations simply become tedious chores. A more fundamental difficulty, however, is knowing what to include in the analysis and how to avoid problem areas such as double counting, confusing financial and economic analysis, and handling inflation.

Introduction

The case study presented here is completely fictitious. Lake Burley exists only in the imagination of the author, and none of the events described has ever occurred in reality. What occurs regularly in the real world, however, is decision making by governments on new development proposals that have significant economic and environmental implications. In making assessments and in ultimately determining whether a project should proceed and if so under what conditions, methods are required that permit comparisons of the project's direct project inputs and outputs and environmental effects.

Traditionally, project appraisal has consisted of an economic evaluation accompanied by an environmental impact statement. More recently, as described in the first chapter, new economic approaches have been devised that place monetary values on some environmental effects and include them in the overall balance of costs and benefits.

Decisions on projects rarely can be made solely on the basis of economic assessment, however widely that may be defined. Other noneconomic factors (e.g., social, cultural, political) invariably need to be considered. It is nevertheless important, when decisions are ultimately made, that the economic input be properly understood and seen as an aid and as a necessary but not sufficient requirement for decision making.

Many project appraisals submitted to governments under the guise of economic analysis leave much to be desired. There is frequently poor comprehension of what constitutes a proper economic evaluation, and the true economic benefits and costs of a project are often distorted through conceptual and measurement errors. Popular misconceptions are that *economic* evaluations are the same as *financial* studies prepared by accountants and that economic returns are synonymous with private profitability. In fact, economists are concerned with social economic welfare, which is not always reflected in the financial aspects of business activity. Under the *Pareto Welfare Criterion,* the allocation of resources will be economically efficient when it is impossible to make one individual better off without making some other individual worse off. (This Pareto improvement may involve a possible transfer of resources but not an actual one.)

Limited understanding of economic analysis is commonly encountered in training programs for environmental planners and managers. It is essential that those responsible for a country's environmental policies and regulations have a basic knowledge of economic principles applicable to a meaningful assessment of gains and losses. This does not mean that they need to become seasoned practitioners in economics, but they should know when to call for expert economic advice, how to establish the guidelines for an economic study, and how to interpret the results. In the same way, economists need to call on the advice of natural and environmental scientists to understand the natural system and environmental dimensions of projects.

The hypothetical case study described here illustrates some of the more important misconceptions that commonly arise in actual application of benefit-cost analysis. A scenario is constructed that characterizes many actual situations. A new project is proposed that, in the eyes of a private corporation wishing to undertake the development, will create substantial economic benefits for the community. The case is put to government and permission to proceed with the project is sought. Unfortunately, the project will exploit a large man-made lake, and the proposed development leads to protests by environmental groups and local citizens. The government must decide whether to approve the project and whether to impose any special conditions. (Although in this case the proponent of the project is a private corporation, many government-supported or public corporation projects are also subject to the same errors of analysis. Merely because the government proposes a project does not ensure correct economic analysis.)

The Setting

Lake Burley is a large man-made lake in the southeast part of Gondwanaland. Its shores are inhabited by a sedentary population engaged in agriculture, livestock grazing, and service industries. The lake is extensively used for recreational activities—swimming, boating, and fishing—by the local residents and by visitors from far-off urban centers. The lake supports a sizable stock of rainbow trout.

A consortium of business interests sees good commercial potential in developing a fishery operation on the lake. A preliminary feasibility study is carried out, and its findings are sufficiently encouraging to set up a new company: Lake Burley Fishing Corporation (LBFC). More detailed investigations are made, and an application is submitted to the government for permission to embark on the project.

Nature of the Fishery Project

The project involves the use of fishing vessels and nets to catch trout and process them in a factory with freezer facilities. After processing and packing, the trout are to be sold on domestic markets, but some can be exported overseas. To prevent depletion of fish stocks, a constant annual allowable quantity of fish will be caught.[1]

Before fishery operations can begin, a loading wharf and a processing factory must be built. The construction period is estimated to be three years (years 0, 1, and 2). The vessels, nets, and other equipment will be bought from domestic sources starting in year 1 and will be depreciated over a 15-year period covering the expected life of the project. Local workers will be employed on the boats and in the factory. A temporary work force will be brought in during the construction phase. The planning horizon for the project is 16 years—the project begins with year 0, and the first fish are caught and sold in year 3. The project ends in year 15 after 13 years of catching and selling fish (years 3 to 15).

Commercial aspects of the scheme are considerably enhanced by a special industrial assistance scheme established by the government. Under this scheme development loans are available at a very low rate of interest, and a generous annual subsidy is promised for the first four years of operation.

A few problems are anticipated with regard to siting the wharf and factory. The only suitable terrain is already occupied by local residents, and these would need to be moved to an alternative location. No other adverse impacts are foreseen.

Community Reaction

When LBFC's proposal becomes known to the general public, controversy immediately begins. Residents who would be forced to move because of the project are incensed, and they protest strongly to the government. There are also heated reactions from other local citizens and recreational groups who feel that the project

---

1. This is a simplifying assumption, adopted for ease of analysis. In actuality a sustained-yield management plan in which annual allowable catch would be allowed to vary, depending on the current and projected state of the ecosystem, would be adopted.

will adversely affect their leisure-time activities by introducing commercial operations to the area and by harvesting fish that would otherwise be caught by amateur anglers. People are angry that Lake Burley fish will be exported to other countries for foreigners to consume. Objections are widely aired in the press and on television. Calls are made for the project to be stopped.

Corporate Response

LBFC is understandably shaken by the community's reaction. The intensity of public opposition was never expected. Nevertheless, LBFC considers the proposition well worth pursuing and decides to convince the government and citizenry that substantial economic benefits will accrue (at both the local and national level), despite the few adverse environmental impacts. To begin with, it offers $20 million in compensation to the residents who must relocate their homes. LBFC also compiles an extensive list of what it terms economic benefits, which includes the following:

- Corporate profits over the life of the project totaling $1,429 million, much of which will be spent in the community, generating further income and jobs;
- Corporate income tax payments to the government;
- Direct employment of 6,000 workers who will be paid yearly wages of approximately $120 million once the project is under way;
- Stimulus to local service industries and indirect creation of another 4,000 jobs in the area;
- Resource rent payments to the government for fishing rights; and
- Generation of foreign currency earnings of $1,376 million that will have a favorable effect on Gondwanaland's balance of payments.

To support its claims, LBFC submits a detailed confidential report to the government containing a market study, details of costs, and estimates of corporate profits. The contents of the report are presented here.

LBFC's Market Study

Two outlets are available for fish harvested from Lake Burley: a new domestic market in the urban centers where retail outlets are strongly promoting trout as a specialty dish, and overseas export markets where prices are rising because of growing populations, higher incomes, and a relative shortage of trout on world markets.

From an in-depth market research survey, LBFC gets a fairly clear picture of the projected domestic market for trout. For the commencement year of the project (year 0), a linear demand function is estimated for the domestic market. Domestic demand patterns are expected to remain static over the life of the project, although all fish prices are predicted to rise by 6 percent per year because of inflation.

An unlimited quantity of trout can be sold on the export market at prevailing world prices. In the initial year, the forecast export price of trout is $10 per kg, but this is expected to rise by 2 percent per annum as world markets expand. The countries with which Gondwanaland trades, incidentally, are managed very effectively in macroeconomic terms and have a zero rate of inflation. The 2 percent annual price rise is therefore a real price increase, not a result of inflation.

LBFC has an anticipated constant annual trout catch of 25 million kg, which has to be split between the domestic and export markets. Fishing effort and total costs each year are fixed and independent of marketing decisions so LBFC, in maximizing its profits, only needs to determine how to divide its output between the two markets so that total revenue is maximized. Furthermore, LBFC is the only supplier of trout in the domestic market.

The condition for revenue maximization is that marginal revenue must be the same in both the domestic and export markets. The market demand (or average revenue) curve in the export market is a horizontal line as shown in Figure 2.1 for year 3. Under these circumstances, the demand curve also constitutes the marginal revenue curve, as each extra unit is sold at the prevailing world price. For the

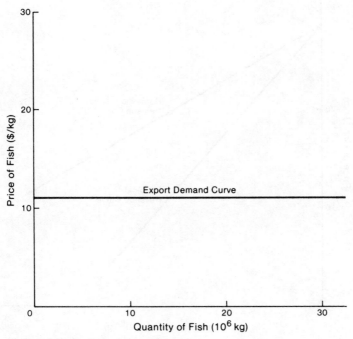

Figure 2.1 Export demand curve for trout.

domestic market, the demand curve has a negative slope, and the corresponding marginal revenue curve lies beneath it, as shown in Figure 2.2. Combining the two diagrams leads to Figure 2.3. In any given year, LBFC's average revenue curve is ABC, and its marginal revenue curve is ADC. The total quantity of fish supplied to the two markets is OQ_2. At Point D, marginal revenue is the same in both markets. LBFC will thus supply OQ_1 to the domestic market at a price of OP_1. The remainder, Q_1Q_2, can be sold on the export market at a price of OP_2. The mathematical analysis used to derive these results is presented in Appendix A2.1.

LBFC's marketing strategy is revealed in Table 2.1. As the domestic price of trout rises relative to the export price, an increasing proportion of total output is sold on the domestic market. In any one period, the domestic price of trout is affected by the quantity LBFC supplies to the market, but LBFC knows what the price-quantity relationships are and can choose a domestic sales volume that maximizes its total sales revenue. Inflation causes the rapidly increasing domestic price and planned expansion of domestic sales. Table 2.1 shows the resulting equilibrium prices and projected sales volumes in both markets, and the total revenue earned.

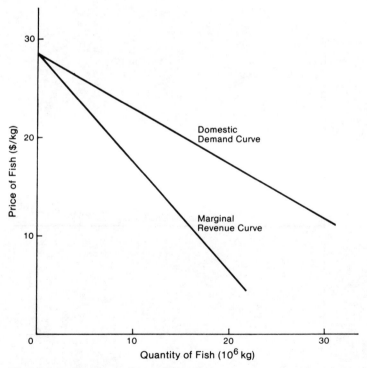

Figure 2.2 Domestic demand curve for trout.

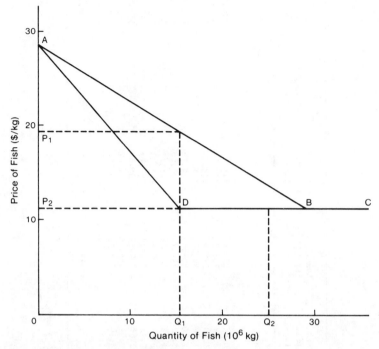

Figure 2.3 Total demand curve for trout.

Government Subsidy

The subsidy offered by the government as part of its industrial assistance scheme is an annual lump sum of $50 million for the first four operating years of the project (years 3 through 6). The subsidy is added to the income stream of LBFC's revenue calculations, as shown in Table 2.1.

LBFC's Cost Estimates

In constant prices, capital outlays of $450 million per year for the first three years are needed to purchase fishing boats and other gear from domestic suppliers and to construct the wharf and factory. However, price inflation for capital items of 4 percent per annum is expected, so in the second and third years of the project, outlays of $468 million and $487 million, respectively, must be incurred. Investment funds are to be borrowed from the government at a flat rate of interest of 3 percent.

Depreciation is calculated using the historic cost method (i.e., no allowance for capital appreciation due to inflation) and with a depreciation rate of 12.5 percent,

Table 2.1 Lake Burley Fishing Corporation: Estimated Returns

Year	Domestic sales (10^6 kg)	Export sales (10^6 kg)	Domestic price ($/kg)	Export price ($/kg)	Domestic revenue ($m)	Export revenue ($m)	Subsidy ($m)	Total revenue ($m)
0								
1								
2								
3	13.861	11.139	17.22	10.61	238.68	118.18	50	406.87
4	14.287	10.713	18.04	10.82	257.73	115.91	50	423.65
5	14.678	10.322	18.90	11.04	277.41	113.95	50	441.36
6	15.075	9.925	19.82	11.26	298.78	111.75	50	460.54
7	15.448	9.552	20.78	11.49	321.00	109.75		430.76
8	15.812	9.188	21.80	11.72	344.70	107.68		452.38
9	16.154	8.846	22.87	11.95	369.44	105.71		475.15
10	16.490	8.510	24.01	12.19	395.92	103.73		499.66
11	16.814	8.186	25.20	12.43	423.71	101.75		525.46
12	17.118	7.882	26.46	12.68	452.94	99.94		552.88
13	17.421	7.579	27.80	12.94	484.30	98.07		582.37
14	17.706	7.294	29.21	13.19	517.19	96.20		613.40
15	17.986	7.014	30.69	13.45	551.99	94.33		864.99[a]
Total					4,933.79	1,376.95	200	6,729.47

[a]Includes sale of capital assets ($218.67 m).

as allowed by the taxation department. At 'the end of the project, LBFC intends selling its depreciated capital items at book value, adding $218 million to its revenue stream in the final year. LBFC's capital cost components—interest payments and depreciation allowances—are presented in Table 2.2. Annual operating costs are estimated to be $225 million in base-year (year 0) prices. These include wage payments, fuels, materials, and maintenance costs. Because of inflation, operating costs are assumed to rise at a rate of 2 percent per annum, as in Table 2.3. In the first year of operation (year 3), operating costs are $238.71 million.

Total costs of the project appear in Table 2.3, consisting of capital costs, operating costs, and the $20 million offer of compensation to local residents.

LBFC's Profit Calculations

Net returns of the project are found by subtracting total costs from total revenues in each period, as indicated in Table 2.4. Initially, negative net returns are made, but these become positive as operations get under way. The break-even point occurs in year 4. Overall, a pretax profit of $1,429 million is estimated to accrue. Even if a 12 percent discount rate is applied, the present value of net returns is $233 million, indicating a highly profitable operation. A proportion of the profits would be handed to the government as corporate taxation and resource rent payments.

Objections to LBFC's Assessment

Although LBFC's case looks very convincing, it is a financial analysis and does not constitute an appropriate analysis of the project in terms of its effects on social economic welfare. This is quickly pointed out to the government by an independent environmental economist who is invited to comment on the proposal. To carry out a proper economic analysis of the project, several points require clarification. The most important ones comprise the following:

• *Financial versus economic analysis.* What LBFC has compiled is a financial appraisal, prepared by its accountants, concentrating on the profitability of the operation measured in terms of its cash flows. An economic analysis deals with the use of real resources to generate social economic welfare measured, in a benefit-cost analysis, by the willingness of the community to pay for the desired outputs of the project and willingness to accept compensation for its detrimental effects. Ownership of property rights (to the fish caught or land used for the factory) will determine whether willingness to pay or willingness to accept compensation is the appropriate concept. Market transactions and the cash flows of corporations do not necessarily reflect social economic welfare. Thus, the total corporate pretax profits of $1,429 million over the 15-year period, or even the present value of the profits of $233 million when discounted at a rate of 12 percent provide no measure of the net *economic* benefits of the project to the community as a whole.

As will be illustrated later, an economic analysis examines the real resource

Table 2.2 Lake Burley Fishing Corporation: Estimated Capital Costs ($m)

Year	Capital expenditure	Cumulated borrowed funds	Interest payments	Annual depreciation	Value of capital stock
0	450.00	450.00			450.00
1	468.00	918.00	13.50		861.75
2	486.72	1,404.72	27.54	56.25	1,240.75
3			42.14	107.72	1,085.66
4			42.14	155.09	949.95
5			42.14	135.70	831.21
6			42.14	188.74	727.30
7			42.14	103.90	636.39
8			42.14	90.91	556.84
9			42.14	79.55	487.23
10			42.14	69.60	426.33
11			42.14	60.90	373.04
12			42.14	53.29	326.41
13			42.14	46.63	285.61
14			42.14	40.80	249.91
15			42.14	35.70	218.67
				31.24	
Total	1,404.72	1,404.72	588.86	1,186.02	

Table 2.3   Lake Burley Fishing Corporation: Total Costs ($m)

Year	Operating costs	Interest	Depreciation	Total costs
0				20.00[a]
1		13.50	56.25	69.75
2		27.54	107.72	135.26
3	238.71	42.14	155.09	436.00
4	243.54	42.14	135.70	421.38
5	248.41	42.14	118.74	409.29
6	253.38	42.14	103.90	399.42
7	258.45	42.14	90.91	391.50
8	263.62	42.14	79.55	385.31
9	268.89	42.14	69.60	380.63
10	274.27	42.14	60.90	377.31
11	279.75	42.14	53.29	375.18
12	285.35	42.14	46.63	374.12
13	291.06	42.14	40.80	374.00
14	296.88	42.14	35.70	374.72
15	302.82	42.14	31.24	376.20
Total	3,505.13	588.86	1,186.02	5,300.07

[a]Payment of compensation.

Table 2.4   Lake Burley Fishing Corporation: Net Returns

Year	Net returns ($m)	Discount factor 12%	Discounted net returns ($m)
0	-20.00		-20.00
1	-69.75	.89286	-62.24
2	-135.26	.79719	-107.82
3	-29.13	.71178	-20.73
4	2.27	.63552	1.44
5	32.07	.56743	18.19
6	61.12	.50663	30.96
7	39.26	.45235	17.75
8	67.07	.40388	27.08
9	94.52	.36061	34.08
10	122.35	.32197	39.39
11	150.28	.28748	43.20
12	178.76	.25668	45.80
13	208.37	.22917	47.75
14	238.68	.20462	48.83
15	488.79	.18270	89.30
Total	1,429.40		232.96

costs and benefits of a proposed activity. Since a national, economy-wide perspective is taken, the alternate use of any resource must always be considered. That is, if funds are not invested in one place they could be used elsewhere to generate economic benefits (such as output, employment, or exports). Prices should be inflation free and should reflect real scarcity in the economy and, when appropriate, should take into account relative price changes.

  • *Double counting.* LBFC's purported economic benefits listed under "Corporate Response" earlier in this chapter include company profits, tax and resource rent payments, export revenue and wage payments—all to be added together to arrive at a total estimate. In fact, the list contains a mixture of transfer payments, secondary benefits, cost items (e.g., wages), and some double counting involving foreign exchange earnings and corporate profits.

  True economic benefits should be measured only once in terms of society's willingness to pay for output produced.

  • *Transfer payments.* Taxes paid to the government represent transfer payments. They are not community benefits, nor are they a legitimate component of economic cost as they do not reflect the use of real resources. For similar reasons, the subsidy paid to LBFC is also a transfer payment. It cannot be counted as an economic benefit because it does not measure any change in the utility derived by consumers of marketed fish, and it is not an economic cost because it bears no relation to the inputs that are actually used in the project.

  • *Real versus current price estimates.* LBFC has presented all of its calculations in terms of projected current prices including inflationary trends in the economy. It has even projected different inflation rates for different benefit and cost components—fish, 6 percent per year; capital, 4 percent per year; and operation and maintenance, 2 percent per year. Indeed, its marketing decisions are based on the maximization of current cash flows. Proper economic analysis relies on real price (inflation free) estimates of benefits and costs. Future prices should be converted, by means of price index numbers, to equivalent prices in a given base year, usually the starting year of the project. This does not imply that *constant* base-year prices should be applied to all successive years. Real *relative* prices may change over time and can affect both benefits and costs. This is in fact the implicit assumption behind the LBFC analysis. Relative prices change when a good or service becomes cheaper or more expensive than the general bundle of goods used to determine a price index. For example, the price of hand calculators has fallen both absolutely and relatively over the past decade while gasoline prices have been constant the last few years but, since the prices of other goods and services have risen, gasoline's *relative price* has fallen.

  • *Total revenue versus total willingness to pay.* Revenue from sales to domestic markets, even when measured in real prices, still does not accurately quantify the associated economic benefits. The total willingness to pay should include the value of domestic fish sales as well as the associated consumer's surplus calculated from the domestic demand curve for fish (see the *Guide,* Chapter 3). This assumes that Lake Burley is the only lake in the country supplying fresh trout. If other lakes are producing trout, then there are substitutes and only the value of fish sales, not consumer's surplus, should be counted. Therefore, if there are no substitute sources of fish, taking a figure for sales revenue only will clearly understate the total benefits. However, consumer's surplus does not enter the calculations for export sales. Benefit-cost analysis deals with economic welfare at the national level. Consumer's surplus arising in other countries has no beneficial effect in Gondwanaland and is therefore irrelevant in an economic assessment of LBFC's operations. As measured in Gondwanaland, the demand curve for exports is, in any case, a horizontal line so that no consumer's surplus would appear, even if an attempt were made to measure it.

• *Interest payments.* Interest payments, although representing a direct financial cost to a corporation, are not true economic costs. They do not measure real resource commitments. In fact, they constitute a transfer payment from borrower to lender—in this case, from LBFC to the government.

• *Depreciation.* Economists measure capital costs quite differently from accountants. The depreciation estimates used by accountants represent subtractions from current cash flows to provide for the replacement of capital when it eventually wears out.[2] To the economist, capital costs are incurred as resources are actually committed (e.g., the construction of a wharf and factory, and the acquisition of vessels and equipment in the first three years). The full cost of capital (in real prices) is debited as it arises. After the first three years, no further capital costs are incurred. "Cost" in this sense represents opportunity cost; that is, the value of resources is diverted to capital formation for this project instead of being used for some other economic purpose. Accordingly, depreciation estimates should not enter a benefit-cost analysis.

• *Compensation payments.* The offer of $20 million to displaced residents is regarded as a cost by LBFC. It is certainly true that resource costs will be involved if residents abandon their houses and have to build new ones, and compensation may also be needed to offset the psychological and social costs of dislocation. Economic measurement of such costs may yield a figure that is higher or lower than $20 million. Residents, for example, may secretly be quite prepared to accept

2. It can be shown that

$$K = dK\,[1 + (1 - d)^1 + (1 - d)^2 + (1 - d)^3 \ldots] \tag{2-1}$$

where K is an initial capital outlay, d is the annual depreciation rate, and the exponents 1, 2, 3, . . . represent future time periods. As the number of years approaches infinity, the right-hand side of the equation (sum of all the future depreciation allowances) approaches the initial capital cost.

much lower compensation payments, in which case the $20 million would contain an element of transfer payments. The opposite could also apply, whereby the residents might not be properly compensated, even though they are forced to leave. In such a case, compensation payments would constitute an underestimate of the resource costs and loss of utility involved.

• *The discount rate.* LBFC's submission uses a 12 percent discount rate (sometimes referred to as an "interest rate" in financial analysis) to obtain an estimate of the present value of the cash flow of the project. The high discount rate reflects the market rate of interest, which is a nominal rate including an inflationary component. High discount rates are often used by financial analysts to impute simultaneously the investment opportunity costs of using project funds and compensating for future inflation. Economists take quite a different approach. In a benefit-cost analysis the discount rate is always *a real rate applied to cost-and-benefit time streams measured in real prices.* There are several views on how the economic discount rate is chosen and what it measures. Burkhead and Miner (1971) provide a useful overview of this question and list four approaches to selecting a discount rate: private or social time preference and private or social productivity of capital. Chapter 3 of this workbook describes the social time preferences and social productivity approaches. Therefore, the discount rate used here reflects the community's real rate of time preference or the real productivity of capital. Inflation is handled by means of price index corrections, never by fiddling with the discount rate. This also helps to explain why the discount rate used in a benefit-cost analysis is frequently lower than prevailing market interest rates. Because annual inflation rates from 2 to 6 percent are projected for various project components over the 15 years of project life, the correct economic discount rate would be less than the 12 percent rate used by LBFC.

• *Generation of secondary benefits.* Other expenditures and income are naturally created when a project is undertaken. However, only in rare situations can secondary effects be counted as economic benefits. Two scenarios are compared: one with the project, the other without the project. Secondary economic benefits (additional employment or income generated) depend on the *net* outcome of the project. Under ordinary circumstances, if funds were not invested in LBFC's project, they would be invested elsewhere in the economy, and similar secondary income effects might be expected to occur. Thus the Lake Burley project in itself cannot be said to contribute significant net secondary benefits to the Gondwanaland economy. The distribution of benefits may be quite different from a regional viewpoint. LBFC's operation would bring economic gains to the Lake Burley region, whereas in its absence they would accrue elsewhere.

• *Wages as economic benefits.* As in the case of secondary economic benefits, claims that the wages paid to employees are benefits of the project are usually spurious from an economic viewpoint. In fact, wages represent an economic cost, not a benefit, and ideally indicate the value of a scarce resource—labor—used within a new project or other production activities. However, market wage rates are not always an accurate measure of the opportunity cost of labor. Where continued regional unemployment occurs, alternative uses of labor may not exist, so the real marginal opportunity cost (or *shadow price*) of labor may be quite low, despite high money wage rates. Difficulties arise in establishing the proper economic cost of labor in such circumstances, as once again the "with project" and "without project" situations must be forecast. In the Lake Burley region, many jobs are available, so LBFC's estimates of "wage benefits" are quite misleading. Even if it can be demonstrated in the "without project" situation that serious regional unemployment would prevail, such conditions must apply for the entire life of the project to justify use of a low shadow price for labor in all subsequent cost calculations. Just as with prices, the shadow wage rate may change over the life of the project as the opportunity cost of labor changes.

Other Economic Fallacies

LBFC is not the only interest group with misconceptions about economic aspects of the fishery project. Citizens complaining about the export of trout to other countries as a "loss" to the community fail to perceive that foreign currency is earned from export sales. This in turn can be used by Gondwanaland to pay for the imports of goods and services that will generate economic welfare. So export revenues do constitute an economic benefit. In the case study examined here, the predicted increase in the export price for trout is a real price increase. Gondwanaland's trading partners have a zero rate of inflation, and the export price of trout rises because of an expanding market. The terms of trade, therefore, are expected to move in Gondwanaland's favor so that, over time, more foreign currency will be earned from a given volume of exports of trout, and more imported goods and services can be purchased. Price index corrections for the export market are accordingly not required.

The main differences between financial and economic analysis are highlighted in Table 2.5. The criteria used by private enterprise to evaluate an investment project may be quite different from those required for an evaluation based on social economic welfare. Costs and returns are viewed from different perspectives. Governments clearly should not use private financial criteria to evaluate development projects that have wide effects on society.

Setting Up the Benefit-Cost Analysis Framework

After all the preceding discussion, how should an economic appraisal of the Lake Burley fishing project be carried out? The government's economic adviser argues that, in economic terms, the recommended decision is that which maximizes the

Table 2.5   A Comparison of Financial and Economic Efficiency Analysis

	Financial	Economic
Focus	Net returns to equity capital or to private group or individual	Net returns to society
Purpose	Indication of incentive to adopt or implement	Determine if government investment is justified on economic efficiency basis
Prices	Market or administered (may assume that markets are perfect or that administered prices have compensated for imperfections)	May require "shadow prices" (e.g., monopoly in markets, external effects, unemployed or underemployed factors, overvalued currency)
Taxes	Cost of production	Part of total societal benefits
Subsidies	Source of revenue	Part of total societal cost
Loans	Increase capital resources available	A transfer payment; transfers a claim to resource flow
Interest or loan repayment	A financial cost; decreases capital resources available	A transfer payment
Discount rate	Marginal cost of money; market borrowing rate	Opportunity cost of capital; social time preference rate
Income distribution	Can be measured re net returns to individual factors of production such as land, labor, and capital	Is not considered in economic efficiency analysis. Can be done as separate analysis or as weighted efficiency analysis

<u>Source:</u> Hitzhusen (1982). Reproduced by permission of the author.

present value of net benefits. He offers a simple identity (also shown in Chapter 1) that incorporates all benefits and costs of the project:

$$NPV = B_d + B_e - C_d - C_p - C_e \qquad (2\text{-}2)$$

where NPV = net present value
B_d = direct project benefits
B_e = external (and/or environmental) benefits
C_d = direct project costs
C_p = environmental protection costs and
C_e = external (and/or environmental) costs

All items on the right-hand side are discounted to present values.

For the Lake Burley project, direct project benefits comprise domestic sales revenues of fish plus consumer's surplus (domestic total willingness to pay) and export sales revenue. External benefits comprise the economic value of any improvements occurring as spillover effects, such as better environmental amenities, and any *true* secondary benefits. In this case, there appear to be no such benefits. The costs of the project consist of the value of resources directly used in the project, any resources committed to the prevention of environmental damage, and other external and/or environmental costs, such as dislocation costs faced by residents and a monetary estimate of the disutility incurred by recreationists deprived of their leisure pursuits. In some projects, resources are specifically allocated to environmental protection, as occurs in pollution control activities. Given the technology employed, pollution (air or water) is not a problem; thus, this component of costs can be ignored.

With these qualifications, the economic objective in the Lake Burley situation is

$$\text{maximize } NPV = B_d - C_d - C_e \qquad (2\text{-}3)$$

All items on the right-hand side are discounted to present values.

An important assumption about prices is made by the government's economic adviser. The LBFC financial analysis included inflation and assumed that domestic fish, capital, and operation and maintenance prices would inflate at different rates. This could be expected for several reasons such as uneven growth in money wages or changes in profit markups in different sectors of the economy. The economist is interested only in relative real prices. Therefore, the economic analysis will require that each set of financial benefit or cost streams (Tables 2.1, 2.2, 2.3) be discounted (or deflated) to bring the stream back to base-year relative prices by removing inflationary trends. For example, the series of fish prices is deflated by 6 percent whereas capital costs are deflated at a 4 percent rate and operation and maintenance costs are deflated at a 2 percent rate.

Estimation of Direct Economic Benefits

The projected sales volumes of fish on domestic and export markets in the benefit-cost analysis are the same as in LBFC's market study, as this is the marketing pattern that will maximize LBFC's revenue and the one that can be expected to prevail in practice (see Table 2.6). The same prices for exports should also be used, since they are free of an inflationary component.

Changes in the export market are shown in Figure 2.4. The export demand curve moves upward over time as foreign demand increases (D_3, D_6, D_9, . . . corresponding to years 3, 6, 9, . . .) and the supply curve moves to the left (S_3, S_6, S_9, . . .) as domestic sales increase leaving less trout available for export. Economic benefits correspond to export revenue, or quantity sold × export price.

As previously mentioned, price corrections, removing inflationary trends, are

Table 2.6 Lake Burley Fishery Project: Direct Economic Benefits (base-year prices)

Year	Domestic sales (10^6 kg)	Export sales (10^6 kg)	Domestic price ($/kg)	Export price ($/kg)	Domestic revenue ($m)	Export revenue ($m)	Consumer's surplus ($m)	Total benefits ($m)
0								
1								
2								
3	13.861	11.139	14.46	10.61	200.43	118.18	38.40	357.01
4	14.287	10.713	14.29	10.82	204.16	115.91	40.79	360.86
5	14.678	10.322	14.12	11.04	207.25	113.95	43.15	364.35
6	15.075	9.925	13.97	11.26	210.60	111.75	45.45	367.80
7	15.448	9.552	13.82	11.49	213.49	109.75	47.74	370.98
8	15.812	9.188	13.68	11.72	216.31	107.68	49.97	373.96
9	16.154	8.846	13.54	11.95	218.73	105.71	52.18	376.62
10	16.490	8.510	13.41	12.19	221.13	103.73	54.34	379.20
11	16.814	8.186	13.28	12.43	223.29	101.75	56.50	381.54
12	17.118	7.882	13.15	12.68	225.10	99.94	58.63	383.67
13	17.421	7.579	13.03	12.94	227.00	98.07	60.71	385.78
14	17.706	7.294	12.92	13.19	228.76	96.20	62.68	387.64
15	17.986	7.014	12.81	13.45	230.40	94.23	64.66	608.06[a]
Total					2,826.65	1,376.85	675.20	5,097.47

[a]Includes terminal capital stock ($218.67 m).

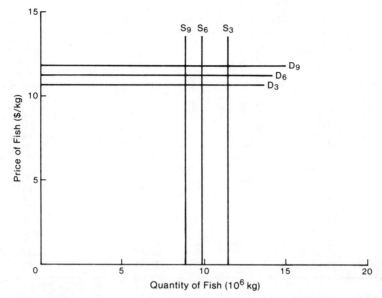

Figure 2.4 Supply and demand curve shifts for trout in the foreign market.

required for domestic sales. The necessary calculations appear in Table 2.7. For the base year, the index value is 100, but it rises at a rate of 6 percent per year in all subsequent years. Real prices (constant prices) are found by means of price deflators. Taking year 6 as an example:

Nominal price = $ 19.82
Price index   =   141.85
$$\text{Price deflator} = \frac{100.00}{141.85} = 0.705$$

Real price   = $ 19.82 × 0.705
              = $ 13.97

Similar calculations apply to other years. In real terms, a static domestic demand curve is used for the entire life of the project, as shown in Figure 2.5. The supply curve shifts outward over time as revenue maximization by LBFC leads to increasing domestic sales (as indicated for years 3, 6, and 9), thereby lowering the real equilibrium price. Under different circumstances—for example, with an expanding domestic market for fish—the demand curve would move outward over time, even when measured in real prices.

In each year, benefits from domestic sales consist of sales revenue plus consumer's surplus (assuming that there are no substitute trout sources). The measure-

Table 2.7   Domestic Market for Fish: Projected Prices

Year (1)	Fish price index (2)	Price deflator (3)	Projected nominal price ($/kg) (4)	Projected real price ($/kg)[a] (5)
0	100.00	1.000		
1	106.00	0.943		
2	112.36	0.890		
3	119.10	0.839	17.22	14.46
4	126.24	0.792	18.04	14.29
5	133.82	0.747	18.90	14.12
6	141.85	0.704	19.82	13.97
7	150.36	0.665	20.78	13.82
8	159.38	0.627	21.80	13.68
9	168.94	0.591	22.87	13.54
10	179.08	0.558	24.01	13.41
11	189.82	0.526	25.20	13.28
12	201.21	0.496	26.46	13.15
13	213.29	0.468	27.80	13.03
14	226.09	0.442	29.21	12.92
15	239.65	0.417	30.69	12.81

[a]Column 4 x column 3.

ment of benefits for year 6 is illustrated in Figure 2.6. Sales revenue is equal to the area OBCD, and consumer's surplus is the shaded area ABC. The total willingness to pay is the area OACD. Consumer's surplus is estimated from the demand curve which, in the initial year, is derived from the domestic demand equation

$$x_1 = 50 - 2.5p_1 \qquad (2\text{-}4)$$

where x_1 = quantity of trout demanded per year in 10^6 kg and
    p_1 = price per kg of trout, measured in $

This equation can be expressed as

$$p_1 = 20 - 0.4x_1 \qquad (2\text{-}5)$$

or as the general linear function

$$p_1 = a - bx_1 \qquad (2\text{-}6)$$

where a = intercept term (20) and
    b = slope of the demand curve (0.4)

Consumer's surplus is calculated as

$$\tfrac{1}{2} (ax_1 - p_1x_1)$$

Using year 6 again as an example, consumer's surplus is

$$\tfrac{1}{2} (20 \times 15.075 - 13.97 \times 15.075) = 45.4 \qquad\qquad (2\text{-}7)$$

Estimation of Direct Resource Costs

Capital costs of the project appear in Table 2.8. A 4 percent inflation rate was assumed, requiring a set of price deflators to estimate the real resource costs of capital. These are $450 million per year for the first three years of the project. Physical capital existing at the end of the project is assumed to be worth $218.67

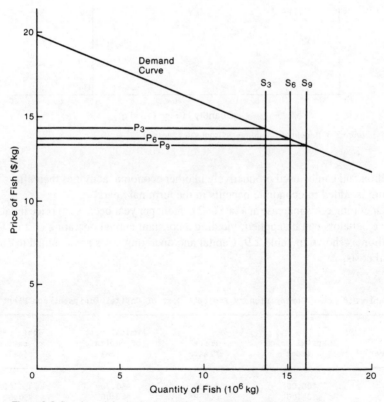

Figure 2.5 Supply and demand curve shifts for trout in the domestic market.

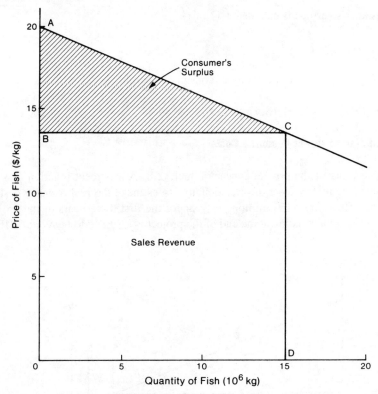

Figure 2.6 Benefits from domestic trout sales (year 6).

million and can be used productively in other economic activities thereafter. This figure is added to economic benefits in the terminal year.

Operating costs increase at a rate of 2 percent per year because of price inflation. Price deflators can be applied, yielding a constant annual operating cost of $225 million as shown in Table 2.9. Capital and operating costs are summed to obtain total costs.

Table 2.8 Lake Burley Fishery Project: Cost of Capital Equipment and Plant

Year	Capital price index	Price deflator	Nominal cost of capital ($m)	Real cost of capital ($m)
0	100.00	1.000	450.00	450.00
1	104.00	0.962	468.00	450.00
2	108.16	0.925	486.72	450.00

Table 2.9 Lake Burley Fishery Project: Real
Economic Costs (base-year prices, $m)

Year	Capital costs	Operating costs	Total costs
0	450		450
1	450		450
2	450		450
3		225	225
4		225	225
5		225	225
6		225	225
7		225	225
8		225	225
9		225	225
10		225	225
11		225	225
12		225	225
13		225	225
14		225	225
15		225	225
Total	1,350	2,925	4,275

Net Benefits and Net Present Value

The net benefit time stream for direct benefits and costs appears in Table 2.10. It is found by subtracting total direct costs from total direct benefits in each time period. Net benefits are initially negative because resources are used heavily in the capital construction phase and because no fish can be caught until capital works have been completed. The formula for obtaining net present value is

$$NPV = \frac{(B_0 - C_0)}{1} + \frac{(B_1 - C_1)}{(1 + r)} + \frac{(B_2 - C_2)}{(1 + r)^2}$$

$$+ \frac{(B_3 - C_3)}{(1 + r)^3} + \cdots \frac{(B_{15} - C_{15})}{(1 + r)^{15}} \tag{2-8}$$

where B_t = benefits in time period t
C_t = costs in time period t
r = social rate of discount

Each expression $1/(1 + r)^t$ can be converted to a discount factor. Tables of discount factors are available; thus, there is no need to actually carry out the calculation. Discount factors for years 1 to 15, for discount rates of 5 percent and 10 percent, are reproduced in Table 2.10. To illustrate their use: if a 10 percent

Table 2.10 Lake Burley Fishery Project: Net Economic Benefits (base-year prices)

Year	Net benefits ($m)	Discount factor 5%	NPV at 5% ($m)	Discount factor 10%	NPV at 10% ($m)
0	-450.00		-450.00	.9091	-450.00
1	-450.00	.9524	-428.58	.8265	-409.09
2	-450.00	.9070	-408.15	.7513	-371.92
3	132.01	.8638	114.03	.6830	99.17
4	135.86	.8227	111.77	.6209	92.79
5	139.35	.7835	109.18	.5645	86.52
6	142.80	.7462	106.55	.5132	80.61
7	145.98	.7107	103.74	.4665	74.91
8	148.96	.6768	100.81	.4241	69.48
9	151.62	.6446	97.46	.3855	64.30
10	154.20	.6139	94.66	.3505	59.44
11	156.54	.5847	91.52	.3186	54.86
12	158.67	.5568	88.34	.2897	50.55
13	160.78	.5303	85.26	.2633	46.57
14	162.64	.5051	82.14	.2394	42.82
15	383.06	.4810	184.25		91.70
Total	822.47		82.98		-317.29

discount rate is chosen, $1 of benefits in year 6 is worth only $0.5645 at the present time, and $1 of benefits in year 15 is worth only $0.2394 at the present time.

By applying discount factors to the net benefit time stream, the present value of the net direct benefits can be found. With a 5 percent discount rate, the net present value is $82.98 million; with a 10 percent rate, it is −$317.29 million.

Interpretation of the Results

The analysis shows that choice of the discount rate is quite important. If the government insists on a 10 percent rate, the outcome is very clear: the project is not desirable on economic grounds. Furthermore, with a 10 percent discount rate there would be no need to evaluate environmental effects, since these are all adverse and can only add to the negative result.

If a 5 percent (or lower) discount rate is chosen, the results are somewhat ambiguous. The project yields positive direct economic benefits, but these must be compared with the external costs of the project, which are mainly environmental. Suppose the total dislocation costs of residents (appropriately measured as compensation demanded) do amount to $20 million. What needs to be decided is whether the loss of recreational amenity (sport fishing, boating, swimming) caused by the project exceeds $82.98 million minus $20 million, i.e., $62.98 million; if it does, then once again the project is not desirable in terms of social economic welfare.

To put the figure of $62.98 million into perspective, it is worth consulting a set of annuity tables. An annuity is an annually recurring fixed sum such as recreational benefits that could be obtained from the lake in perpetuity if there were no development. For a 5 percent discount rate and a 15-year period, the annuity factor is 10.3797. The present value of any annuity (A) is thus $10.3797 \times A$. Consider now the relation

$$62.98 = 10.3797 \times A \tag{2-9}$$

The solution to this equation is

$$A = 6.06 \tag{2-10}$$

Annual recreational benefits destroyed by the project (external environmental costs) must exceed $6.06 million for the project to be judged undesirable on economic grounds. One of the indirect economic valuation techniques, such as the travel cost method or a structured questionnaire, could be used to determine whether this is the case for Lake Burley.

The results of the benefit-cost analysis—the calculations, assumptions adopted, and policy interpretations—are then handed to the government for due consideration.

Epilogue

How does the government use this information? Life was never meant to be easy. Before a decision is reached, a general election is held and a new political party gains office. The new government is not convinced that the previous government properly investigated the Lake Burley situation. Other alternatives were not considered. The new government is very enthusiastic about constructing a large reservoir and hydroelectric scheme not far from Lake Burley that will supply electricity to the national grid and provide one of the finest aquatic recreation areas in Gondwanaland, including trout populations. LBFC sees good commercial fishing prospects here as well and begins working on a second proposal involving Lake Burley and the new hydro scheme. With careful zoning policies for recreation and commercial fishing, LBFC argues, it should be possible to accommodate both types of activity. The government agrees to undertake a new assessment. Submissions from LBFC, the general public, and environmental groups are requested. A great deal of economic advice will be needed. The environmental economist heaves a sigh of relief. At least he will still have an income. . . .

Appendix A2.1: Lake Burley Fishing Corporation's Revenue-Maximizing Exercise

In the commencement year of the project, the domestic demand function, specified in terms of price, is

$$p_1 = a - bx_1 \tag{A2-1}$$

where

p_1 = domestic price
x_1 = quantity sold domestically
a = intercept term
b = slope of demand curve

Initially $a = 20$ and $b = 0.4$. The export price p_2 is exogenously determined, and initially is \$10.

Over time, the domestic price is expected to rise by 6 percent per year. LBFC has to deal with a projected domestic demand function of the form

$$\phi p_1 = \phi(a - bx_1) \tag{A2-2}$$

where ϕ is an inflationary markup factor. In successive years, ϕ takes the values 1, 1.06, 1.12, 1.19. . . . The export price (p_2) is initially \$10 and grows at a rate n of 2 percent per annum. In successive years n takes the value 1, 1.02, 1.04, 1.06, 1.08, 1.10, 1.13. . . .

LBFC's problem is thus:

maximize $\phi p_1 x_1 + np_2 x_2$ (A2-3)

subject to $x_1 + x_2 = C$ (A2-4)

where p_2 = export price
x_2 = quantity exported
C = total output

To solve the problem, substitute equation (A2-2) into (A2-3) and form a Lagrangian incorporating the constraint described by equation (A2-4). It then becomes necessary to

maximize $L = \phi(a - bx_1)x_1 + np_2 x_2 + \lambda(x_1 + x_2 - C)$ (A2-5)

Taking partial derivatives of L and equating them to zero gives

$$\frac{\partial L}{\partial x_1} = \phi a - 2\phi b x_1 + \lambda = 0 \qquad\qquad\qquad\text{(A2-6)}$$

$$\frac{\partial L}{\partial x_2} = np_2 + \lambda \qquad\qquad = 0 \qquad\qquad\qquad\text{(A2-7)}$$

$$\frac{\partial L}{\partial \lambda} = x_1 + x_2 - C \qquad = 0 \qquad\qquad\qquad\text{(A2-8)}$$

Equations (A2-6) and (A2-7) provide the condition that marginal revenue should be the same in the domestic and export market.

$$-\lambda = \phi a - 2\phi b x_1 = np_2 \qquad\qquad\qquad\text{(A2-9)}$$

Equation (A2-9) yields a solution for the quantity supplied to the domestic market (x_1^*).

$$x_1^* = \frac{\phi a - np_2}{2\phi b} \qquad\qquad\qquad\text{(A2-10)}$$

Substitution in equation (A2-8) leads to

$$x_2^* = C - x_1^* \qquad\qquad\qquad\text{(A2-11)}$$

The equilibrium domestic price is found from equation (A2-2).

$$p_1{}^* = \phi(a - bx_1{}^*) \tag{A2-12}$$

$$= \frac{\phi a + np_2}{2} \tag{A2-13}$$

Note that $x_1{}^*$, $x_2{}^*$, and $p_1{}^*$ are the required values to maximize sales revenue.

Taking year 6 as an example:

$a = 20 \qquad b = 0.4 \qquad C = 25$
$\phi = 1.4185$
$n = 1.1262$

The solution values for $x_1{}^*$, $x_2{}^*$, and $p_1{}^*$ are calculated as

$$x_1{}^* = \frac{1.4185 \times 20 - 1.1262 \times 10}{2 \times 1.4185 \times 0.4}$$

$$= 15.075$$

$$x_2{}^* = 25 - 15.075$$

$$= 9.925$$

$$p_1{}^* = \frac{1.4185 \times 20 + 1.1262 \times 10}{2}$$

$$= 19.82$$

References

Burkhead, J., and J. Miner. *Public Expenditure*. Chicago: Aldine and Atherton, 1971.

Hitzhusen, F. J. "The 'Economics' of Biomass for Energy: Towards Clarification for Non-Economists." Ohio State University, 1982. Mimeo.

Hufschmidt, M. M., D. E. James, A. D. Meister, B. T. Bower, and J. A. Dixon. *Environment, Natural Systems and Development: An Economic Valuation Guide*. Baltimore: Johns Hopkins University Press, 1983.

3
Time Horizons, Discounting, and Computational Aids

John A. Dixon and Anton D. Meister

The steps in project evaluation were mentioned briefly in the first chapter. After a project has been specified, the various inputs and outputs, both direct products and external effects, are identified. These inputs and outputs are then measured and quantified, and monetary values are placed on them. This information is then used for project analysis. All these steps are essential to an economic analysis of a project, and most of the steps have been illustrated in the hypothetical case study in the second chapter.

This workbook, however, does not present detailed discussions of what should or should not be included in an economic analysis and how such variables should be valued. Some of these topics are covered in the *Guide* but fuller explanations are found in standard project appraisal texts. For example, see Gittinger (1982) for a comprehensive discussion of the various steps involved in an economic analysis of agricultural projects. He discusses in detail what to include and exclude in actual project evaluation; some of these points were mentioned in the preceding chapter. Other concepts, especially on the use of shadow prices and questions on equity/income distribution, are covered more completely in other references (Squire and van der Tak 1975; Helmers 1979). The reader is directed to these references for coverage of these topics.

The analyst also must make decisions about the inclusion and weighting of benefits and costs that occur at different points of time. Because of the importance of economic time horizons and discount rates in project analysis, and the confusion frequently found over these concepts, this chapter briefly discusses the problems of selecting an appropriate time horizon and discount rate for an economic analysis. These two concepts are not independent and, as will be shown, have major implications for the results of the analysis performed. The uses of standard computational formulas and tables are also discussed.

The Appropriate Time Horizon

In theory, an economic analysis should extend long enough to include *all* benefits and costs of a project. In practice, two factors are important in selecting an appropriate time horizon for an investment project: (1) the expected useful life of the project in terms of yielding the outputs and associated economic benefits for which it was designed, and (2) the level of the discount rate used in the economic analysis of the project. Concerning the first factor, when beneficial project outputs become very small or cease altogether, the effective project life can be considered as terminated. As for the discount rate factor (which is selected exogenously), the higher the rate, the shorter the appropriate economic time horizon. This is because discount rates act progressively to reduce the present value of outputs and benefits obtained in future years. For any given discount rate and nominal value of annual benefit, the more distant the year in the future, the smaller the present value of the benefit for that future year. Accordingly, for a project with a long useful life in terms of beneficial outputs (say, 100 years) but with a high discount rate (say, 10 percent), the time horizon used would be much shorter than the expected useful life of the project because net benefits in later years would have negligible effect on net present value. This fact leads to the general rule that the appropriate time horizon for a project is the *shorter* of (1) the expected useful life of the project or (2) the effective economic life of the project when discounting is taken into account.

In theory, with proper maintenance and capital replacements, some investment projects could continue to be useful in perpetuity. In fact, many projects have very long, useful lives. An example of this type of project is the development of an outdoor recreational area or an agricultural development project for rice or wheat production. In each case, the expected outputs (recreation or grain production) and associated benefits could continue indefinitely if resources are provided for systems maintenance and capital replacements. With care, production of the service or good for which the project was designed would continue far into the future.

Other projects have shorter natural time boundaries based upon the nature of the resource used. In the agricultural area, many perennial crops have a finite expected life after which the entire cropped area has to be renewed or replanted. For rubber, the expected productive life is from 20 to 30 years. After this period, rubber yields fall off rapidly and the area should be cleared and replanted. This forms a natural economic time horizon for consideration. Similarly, projects based on the extraction of minerals or fossil fuels (such as coal or oil) have useful lives dependent on the volume or extent and value of the deposit, trend of extraction costs, and the extraction rate.

Other projects involve capital equipment or machinery that has a finite expected life, either because the equipment wears out or becomes technologically obsolete. In some cases, however, capital equipment is expected to have a very long, useful life. A dam may be designed to last several hundred years before its reservoir silts up and further production becomes uneconomic; a properly maintained road or railbed may be expected to serve for 50 or more years. These longer periods are usually not used in economic analysis when benefits and costs are discounted. Discounting at any discount rate above 5 percent reduces the present value of any cost or benefit that is incurred 40 or more years in the future to a very small amount. As the discount rate increases, the meaningful time horizon for project evaluation contracts.

The relationship of the discount rate to the choice of the appropriate time horizon is shown in Table 3.1. Assume that the project under consideration is a dam with a long, useful physical life; at a 2 percent discount rate $100 in net benefits received 100 years in the future still has a sizable present value ($13.80). The comparable time horizon drops to 40 years at a 5 percent discount rate, 25 years at 8 percent, and only 20 years at 10 percent, which leads to the problem of selecting the appropriate discount rate.

Discounting

Discounting is the glue of project analysis. It is the mechanism whereby benefits and costs that occur at different points of time can be compared and weighted. It is also one of the most misunderstood concepts in economic analysis.

In order to use discounting, two preconditions are required. The first is that all of the variables to be included in the discounting (e.g., resource costs, benefits from project outputs) have to be put into common units. For ease we usually use a monetary unit (e.g., dollars, yen, rupiah, marks, SDR). Nonmonetary units (such

Table 3.1   Present Value of $100 in Future Years at Various Discount Rates

Time (year)	Discount rate (%)			
	2	5	8	10
0	$100.00	$100.00	$100.00	$100.00
10	82.03	61.39	46.32	38.55
20	67.30	37.69	21.45	14.86
25	60.95	29.53	14.60	9.23
40	45.29	14.20	4.60	2.21
60	30.48	5.35	0.99	0.33
100	13.80	0.76	0.05	0.01

Note: Different combinations of discount rates and time will yield the same present value of the same amount of money received in the future. For example, a present value of $14-15 is yielded by a $100 benefit received 100 years in the future if the discount rate is 2 percent; at a 5 percent discount rate the present value of $100 declines to $14 in 40 years' time; for an 8 percent discount rate the decline to $14 occurs in only 25 years in the future, and with a 10 percent discount rate it takes only 20 years (see the dotted line in the table).

as utiles) as the numeraire could also be used, but this is of limited use and is rarely done. The second precondition is the acceptance of the assumption that we value a unit of present cost or benefit more highly than a unit of cost or benefit in the future. That is, if we had a choice of receiving one dollar (or one apple) today or one dollar (or one apple) next year, we would place a greater value on the dollar or apple received today. This is referred to as time preference of consumption.

When environmental factors are included in the analysis, these two preconditions may become more difficult to meet. However, the *Guide* was written on the premise that there are many environmental quality dimensions of development projects that can be quantified and monetized; that is, monetary values can be placed on these aspects and they can then be explicitly included in project analysis and appraisal. The *Guide* presents many techniques for this valuation process; some approaches are more widely accepted than others, while some are more useful in one socioeconomic setting than in another. Nevertheless, some environmental goods or services cannot be easily quantified or priced. Some examples are collective or public goods such as unobstructed views or the existence of certain animals. Other environmental goods and services are very difficult to identify and measure; the worth of a tropical forest gene pool or value of maintenance of the CO_2 concentrations in the global atmosphere may be unquantifiable and best left unpriced.

The second precondition, time preference of consumption, also presents philosophical problems. Many people believe that the goods and services produced by natural systems will increase in value over time as demand and their relative scarcity increases. For many goods and services this is probably true, and this characteristic can be handled in an economic analysis by changing *relative prices* for the good or service in question. As explained in the preceding chapter, all ex ante economic analyses of projects deal with the inflation issue by using real, constant dollar prices rather than current or nominal inflation-affected prices. Since discounting is not a device to adjust for price inflation (price deflators can be used to do that), the only price changes over time that should be introduced in ex ante analysis are those that are due to changes in relative prices. For example, a project is proposed to produce tropical hardwoods. Increasing world demand for these woods indicates that their price will increase faster than general price levels. Therefore economic analysis of the project could include an adjustment factor for an increase in real prices for the wood produced (say, 2 percent per year) while all other prices (for both benefits and costs) remain constant. Because of this the price of the wood would increase by almost 50 percent over 20 years, thereby improving the economic attractiveness of the proposed project.

The issue of intergenerational equity still remains. If any positive discount rate is used, benefits or costs that occur many years or generations in the future will be largely ignored. This does not mean that there should be no concern in public policy for the welfare of future generations, but merely that this problem is one that is inappropriately handled by straight economic analysis. Intergenerational equity is a policy area where government as a representative of society at large has to make certain decisions. The economist can help in making such decisions by calculating the opportunity costs of these decisions; that is, what benefits will have to be foregone now in order to preserve the option of reaping benefits in the future.

Using a low or zero discount rate for environmental costs or benefits is not the answer; a zero discount rate is still a discount rate—it implies indifference between present and future consumption or costs. In fact, use of low or zero discount rates in this way can lead to serious misallocation of resources even in terms of achieving environmental objectives. For example, use of such rates favors capital-intensive developments with long pay-back periods.

In most economic analyses the question of intergenerational equity is not crucial. Most projects use renewable resources or have project time horizons that are sufficiently short (15, 20, 25 years) so that most benefits and costs of a project, both direct and indirect, occur within the span of the current generation. The intergenerational equity concerns are most pronounced when unique or exhaustible resources are involved. In these cases present consumption may eliminate future options. This is especially true of actions with irreversible results whereby unique natural environments are destroyed with little or no possibility of replacement (e.g., a scenic canyon flooded by a dam, a unique rain forest leveled, an estuary filled in).

The Appropriate Discount Rate

What then is the appropriate discount rate to be used in an economic analysis? This is not an easy question to answer. Several conditions will be taken as given in this workbook:

- Only one discount rate will be used in any single economic analysis, although the analysis may be repeated several times using different discount rates (sensitivity analysis); separate discount rates will not be used for the cost and the benefit streams in the analysis or for different categories of benefits (environmental or developmental).
- The discount rate used does not reflect inflation; all prices used in the analysis are real or constant dollar prices.
- In theory, the discount rate can be positive, zero, or negative; ignoring the concept of discounting (in effect, adapting a zero discount rate) does not do away with the problem of trade-offs between present and future consumption (time preference).

Whereas in financial analysis an interest rate is usually used that reflects market rates for investment and working capital, and hence is sensitive to current or expected inflation rates, the discount rate used in economic analysis is usually not readily observable in the economy. In fact, the discount rate is consciously decided upon. Economists have developed a number of approaches for determining and justifying a discount rate.

In the *Guide* and other references (Gittinger 1982; Baumol 1968) several explanations are given of possible choices of a discount rate for use in economic analysis. They are all based on economic or social phenomena:

Opportunity Cost of Capital

This approach is based on the foregone production that results when capital is invested in one project rather than another, or invested by government in a particular project rather than by the private sector. In this sense the opportunity cost of capital is directly related to the theory of capital productivity. Invested in plant or equipment, a dollar's worth of investment should yield net benefits over time. The discount rate is this rate of return.

This approach is also closely related to the financial (or nominal) interest rate, although the latter may include an upward adjustment for inflation. The real (inflation adjusted) opportunity cost rate is affected by changes in real income, the distribution of wealth, taste, and technology (Hyman and Hufschmidt 1983).

The opportunity cost approach appears to be used (implicitly) by the World Bank in requiring that, to be eligible for loans, proposed projects promise an annual rate of return at least equal to a specified rate—which appears to be based on the opportunity cost of capital.

The Cost of Borrowing Money

Governments frequently have to borrow money, either domestically or internationally, to finance development projects. The financing mechanisms used include government debt from borrowing, inflation, or taxation of private consumption (Haveman 1969). Especially when a country expects to borrow abroad, this approach may be used to set the discount rate.

A danger in this cost of borrowing money criterion is that extremely favorable loans (at very low, subsidized interest rates) will favor projects with long-term net benefits and vice versa, a high discount rate will favor short-term payoff projects. To the extent that these extremes represent distortions of true scarcity in the economy, they will lead to misallocation of scarce resources.

The Social Rate of Time Preference

A third school of thought relies on the ability of society to reflect more accurately than the private market the trade-offs between present and future consumption. If from society's viewpoint individuals overconsume in the present rather than save for investment and future production, the social rate of time preference will lead to a lower discount rate than that exhibited by individuals in private markets (the lifetime of an individual is much shorter than the relevant time horizon of society). How this rate is actually set depends upon the circumstances in the particular country involved. (If the social rate is determined by the political process, this in turn is influenced by elected officials who may have a very short time horizon—namely, until the next election.)

In summary, the actual rate to be used in economic analysis will be country-specific and will probably be established as a matter of government policy. Important factors governing the choice of rate will be the opportunity cost of capital, donor or lending agency requirements, cost of money to the government, and government's current views of the private-sector consumption-investment mix in relation to its concerns for future generations.

Our position in this workbook is that project analysts should seek guidance from responsible government policymaking agencies on the discount rate to be used. In the absence of such guidance, analysts should undertake project economic analyses using a range of rates reflecting those recently or currently in use in the country for public and private investment projects. It is important to reemphasize that these rates should be on a *real* cost, *inflation-adjusted basis*.

Computational Aids

Once the appropriate time horizon and discount rate have been chosen, the actual calculations can take many forms. This section discusses the various formulas in common use, as well as the use of compounding and discounting tables. Numerical examples are provided to illustrate the use of these techniques.

Calculation of Present Value

Most analyses examine a proposed project by comparing the streams over time of benefits (returns) and costs (expenditures). In the preceding chapter the differences between financial and economic analysis were discussed. It is assumed that all examples presented in this workbook are based on economic analysis of projects.

A few assumptions regarding the timing of cash flows are needed. The initial year of any project can be designated as year 0 or year 1. The Lake Burley example began with year 0; most of the other case studies presented here began with year 1. It does not matter which convention is chosen just so long as the base year is clearly stated. Additional assumptions concerning the timing of cash flows include the following:

- All cash flows (costs or benefits) are assumed to take place at the *end* of the year. Hence a flow in year 2 occurs at the end of year 2. This means that any cost or benefit occurring during a year is discounted for the entire year. For example, a cost incurred any time in year 5 is discounted for the entire five years. This assumption introduces a small error since actual expenditures or receipts should be discounted from when they occur. These errors are usually overlooked in the interest of simplicity but, if desired, all cash flows can be discounted from the exact time they occur.

- All costs (capital and operating) and benefits are treated the same way as cash flows.

A number of symbols are commonly used in the valuation formulas and include the following:

r = the discount or interest rate expressed as a decimal (also known as i)
n = the number of years involved in the economic time horizon
t = the relevant year, usually expressed as a running subscript $1, 2, \ldots, n$
B_t = benefit in year t
C_t = cost in year t (these may be capital, operations, maintenance, or replacement costs)
Σ = sigma, the summation sign that indicates the sum of some function, in this case over some period of time

Perhaps the single most widely used formula in project analysis is that which calculates the *net present value* (*NPV*) of a project. Also known as net present worth, the *NPV* determines the present value of net benefits by discounting the streams of benefits and costs back to the beginning of the base year (year 1). Two formulas can be used; both yield identical results:

$$NPV = \sum_{t=1}^{n} \frac{B_t - C_t}{(1 + r)^t} \tag{3-1}$$

or

$$NPV = \sum_{t=1}^{n} \frac{B_t}{(1 + r)^t} - \sum_{t=1}^{n} \frac{C_t}{(1 + r)^t} \tag{3-2}$$

The *internal rate of return* (IRR) is defined as the rate of return on the investment that equates the present value of benefits and costs. It is found by an iterative process and is equivalent to the discount rate (r) that satisfies the following relationship:

$$\sum_{t=1}^{n} \frac{B_t - C_t}{(1 + r)^t} = 0 \tag{3-3}$$

or

$$\sum_{t=1}^{n} \frac{B_t}{(1 + r)^t} = \sum_{t=1}^{n} \frac{C_t}{(1 + r)^t} \tag{3-4}$$

The *IRR* is widely used by financial institutions, but there are some theoretical and practical problems associated with its usage. These are discussed in the *Guide* in Chapter 3 (pages 41–43).

The *IRR* is the discount rate that would result in a zero net present value for a project. If the *IRR* calculated is 15 percent and the cost of project funds is 10 percent, the project would be financially attractive. If project funds "cost" 18 percent, however, the project would be financially unattractive. The IRR does not give one the discount rate; it merely finds the value of *r* that meets the set condition of a zero net present value. The calculated *IRR* then must be compared to some other financial interest rate or discount rate to determine whether the project is financially or economically attractive.

The *benefit-cost ratio* (*B/C* ratio) is a simple derivative of the net present value criterion:

$$B/C \text{ ratio} = \frac{\displaystyle\sum_{t=1}^{n} \frac{B_t}{(1+r)^t}}{\displaystyle\sum_{t=1}^{n} \frac{C_t}{(1+r)^t}} \tag{3-5}$$

This ratio compares the discounted benefits to discounted costs. (In this case, benefits are assumed to be in *gross* terms, while costs include capital plus operation, maintenance, and replacement (OMR) costs. An alternative form of the *B/C* ratio defines benefits as net of operating costs and limits *costs* to capital costs. This assumes that annual operating costs are met by user charges or other revenues and, in effect, measure net benefits against a capital constraint.) If the *B/C* ratio is exactly equal to 1, the project will produce zero net benefits over its lifetime—the discounted benefits just equal discounted costs. A *B/C* ratio of less than 1 means that the project generates losses from an economic perspective.

Comparing the Three Measures of Present Value

All three measures presented here rely on the concept of present value of a stream of benefits and costs. In fact, a verbal explanation of the three measures points out this similarity (Gittinger 1973):

$$\text{Net present value} = \left[\begin{array}{c} \text{Present value} \\ \text{of benefits} \end{array} - \begin{array}{c} \text{Present value} \\ \text{of costs} \end{array} \right]$$

That discount rate which results in:

$$\text{Internal rate of return} = \left[\begin{array}{c} \text{Present value} \\ \text{of benefits} \end{array} = \begin{array}{c} \text{Present value} \\ \text{of costs} \end{array} \right]$$

$$\text{Benefit-cost ratio} = \frac{\text{Present value of benefits}}{\text{Present value of costs}}$$

Not surprisingly, there are also parallels between the values for these measures. The following comparison points out these relationships:

NPV	B/C ratio	IRR
If > 0 then	> 1	and IRR > r
If < 0 then	< 1	and IRR < r
If = 0 then	1	and IRR = r

It might appear that it does not matter which of the three measures are used in formulating or selecting projects since they all share a common origin in discounted benefits and costs. We do not agree; it is net present value that is the economic objective (the "objective function") that we seek to maximize. In contrast, it is *incorrect* to seek to maximize the internal rate of return or the benefit-cost ratio (whatever its form) while it is *always correct* to seek to maximize net present value. Accordingly, net present value must always be a part of any choice criterion or ranking scheme for accepting or rejecting projects or project increments.

In cases where projects or project increments are not mutually exclusive, and there are no constraints on costs, all projects (or increments) that yield positive net present values can be accepted. In cases where not all projects or increments can be selected because of a cost constraint, the goal is to select those projects or increments that yield the greatest *total* net present value. To achieve this the projects or increments should be ranked in terms of the *contribution to net present value* of each project *per unit of constrained cost*. For this purpose a special form of the B/C ratio, in which the present value of the constrained cost (whether capital, OMR, or a combination) is placed in the denominator and gross benefits net of remaining costs are placed in the numerator, can be used.

Gittinger (1982) undertakes a comparative analysis of these three measures of present value and presents the results in tabular form. In Table 3.2, which is an adaptation of the Gittinger table, we distinguish between project selection or ranking under three conditions: independent projects with no constraints on costs; independent projects with an overall constraint on costs; and mutually exclusive projects. For independent projects in the absence of cost constraints, each of the three measures can be used to select or reject projects (Table 3.2). However, when there is a constraint on costs for independent projects, such that not all economically justifiable projects can be selected, only the B/C ratio measure can give correct rankings for project selection. For the B/C ratio ranking to be correct, it must be formulated so that the costs constrained appear in the denominator of the ratio. For mutually exclusive projects (such as two or more projects using the same site) the NPV measure is the only one that will always lead to the correct selection. In all of the above cases, "correct" selection or ranking is defined as the one that yields the largest net present value.

Table 3.2 Comparison of the Three Measures of Present Value

Selection or ranking rule for:	Net present value	Internal rate of return	Benefit-cost ratio
Independent projects:			
No constraint on costs	Select all projects with NPV > 0; project ranking not required	Select all projects with IRR greater than cut-off rate of return; project ranking not required	Select all projects with B/C > 1; project ranking not required
Constraint on costs	Not suitable for ranking projects	Ranking all projects by IRR may give incorrect ranking	Ranking all projects by B/C where C is defined as constrained cost will always give correct ranking
Mutually exclusive projects (no constraint on costs)	Select alternative with largest NPV	Selection of alternative with highest IRR may give incorrect result	Selection of alternative with highest B/C may give incorrect result
Discount rate	Appropriate discount rate must be adopted	No discount rate required, but cut-off rate of return must be adopted	Appropriate discount rate must be adopted

Source: Adapted from Gittinger (1982).

More complex rules than the above will be required for special situations, such as the scheduling of projects over time, but they will not be discussed here. A good reference for these purposes is Helmers (1979), Chapter 5.

Manipulating Data

Understanding the underlying concepts is essential to good economic analysis; being able to manipulate data and perform calculations swiftly makes project evaluation much easier. This section discusses the key procedures used in the formulas already presented, as well as the use of prepared compounding and discounting tables.

As in the previous section, the work of J. Price Gittinger of the Economic Development Institute of the World Bank is very useful. A page from his 1973 publication, *Compounding and Discounting Tables for Project Evaluation,* is given as Table 3.3. Similar tables are available in many standard accounting and statistical texts.

Compounding is the process of finding the future value of a present sum.

$$FV_n = P(1 + r)^n \qquad (3\text{-}6)$$

where FV_n = the future value in year n
P = the principal (present amount)
r = interest rate

This formula is commonly used when funds are deposited in a savings account. The future value in five years of $5,000 invested today at a 10 percent interest rate with interest compounded yearly is

$$
\begin{aligned}
FV_5 &= \$5{,}000\ (1 + 0.10)^5 \\
&= \$5{,}000\ (1.6105) \\
&= \$8{,}052.50 \qquad (3\text{-}7)
\end{aligned}
$$

The compounding factor is found in the first column at year 5 (1.610510) in Table 3.3.

Discounting is the reverse of compounding. It tells us how much some future sum is worth today. To find the present value of a future sum, the same elements in the compounding formula are used, but they are rearranged:

$$PV = \frac{P_n}{(1 + r)^n} \qquad (3\text{-}8)$$

where PV = the present value
P_n = the principal received or to be paid in year n
r = discount rate

RATE 10%

Year	COMPOUNDING FACTOR FOR 1 — What an initial amount becomes when growing at compound interest	COMPOUNDING FACTOR FOR 1 PER ANNUM — Growth of equal year-end deposits all growing at compound interest	SINKING FUND FACTOR — Level deposit required to reach 1 by a given year	DISCOUNT FACTOR — How much 1 at a future date is worth today	PRESENT WORTH OF AN ANNUITY FACTOR — How much 1 received or paid annually for X years is worth today	CAPITAL RECOVERY FACTOR — Annual payment that will repay a $1 loan in X years with compound interest on the unpaid balance	Year
1	1.100 000	1.000 000	1.000 000	909 091	909 091	1.100 000	1
2	1.210 000	2.100 000	476 190	826 446	1.735 537	576 190	2
3	1.331 000	3.310 000	302 115	751 315	2.486 852	402 115	3
4	1.464 100	4.641 000	215 471	683 013	3.169 865	315 471	4
5	1.610 510	6.105 100	163 797	620 921	3.790 787	263 797	5
6	1.771 561	7.715 610	129 607	564 474	4.355 261	229 607	6
7	1.948 717	9.487 171	105 405	513 158	4.868 419	205 405	7
8	2.143 589	11.435 888	087 444	466 507	5.334 926	187 444	8
9	2.357 948	13.579 477	073 641	424 098	5.759 024	173 641	9
10	2.593 742	15.937 425	062 745	385 543	6.144 567	162 745	10
11	2.853 117	18.531 167	053 963	350 494	6.495 061	153 963	11
12	3.138 428	21.384 284	046 763	318 631	6.813 692	146 763	12
13	3.452 271	24.522 712	040 779	289 664	7.103 356	140 779	13
14	3.797 498	27.974 983	035 746	263 331	7.366 687	135 746	14
15	4.177 248	31.772 482	031 474	239 392	7.606 080	131 474	15
16	4.594 973	35.949 730	027 817	217 629	7.823 709	127 817	16
17	5.054 470	40.544 703	024 664	197 845	8.021 553	124 664	17
18	5.559 917	45.599 173	021 930	179 859	8.201 412	121 930	18
19	6.115 909	51.159 090	019 547	163 508	8.364 920	119 547	19
20	6.727 500	57.274 999	017 460	148 644	8.513 564	117 460	20
21	7.400 250	64.002 499	015 624	135 131	8.648 694	115 624	21
22	8.140 275	71.402 749	014 005	122 846	8.771 540	114 005	22
23	8.954 302	79.543 024	012 572	111 678	8.883 218	112 572	23
24	9.849 733	88.497 327	011 300	101 526	8.984 744	111 300	24
25	10.834 706	98.347 059	010 168	092 296	9.077 040	110 168	25
26	11.918 177	109.181 765	009 159	083 905	9.160 945	109 159	26
27	13.109 994	121.099 942	008 258	076 278	9.237 223	108 258	27
28	14.420 994	134.209 936	007 451	069 343	9.306 567	107 451	28
29	15.863 093	148.630 930	006 728	063 039	9.369 606	106 728	29
30	17.449 402	164.494 023	006 079	057 309	9.426 914	106 079	30
31	19.194 342	181.943 425	005 496	052 099	9.479 013	105 496	31
32	21.113 777	201.137 767	004 972	047 362	9.526 376	104 972	32
33	23.225 154	222.251 544	004 499	043 057	9.569 432	104 499	33
34	25.547 670	245.476 699	004 074	039 143	9.608 575	104 074	34
35	28.102 437	271.024 368	003 690	035 584	9.644 159	103 690	35
36	30.912 681	299.126 805	003 343	032 349	9.676 508	103 343	36
37	34.003 949	330.039 486	003 030	029 408	9.705 917	103 030	37
38	37.404 343	364.043 434	002 747	026 735	9.732 651	102 747	38
39	41.144 778	401.447 778	002 491	024 304	9.756 956	102 491	39
40	45.259 256	442.592 556	002 259	022 095	9.779 051	102 259	40
41	49.785 181	487.851 811	002 050	020 086	9.799 137	102 050	41
42	54.763 699	537.636 992	001 860	018 260	9.817 397	101 860	42
43	60.240 069	592.400 692	001 688	016 600	9.833 998	101 688	43
44	66.264 076	652.640 761	001 532	015 091	9.849 089	101 532	44
45	72.890 484	718.904 837	001 391	013 719	9.862 808	101 391	45
46	80.179 532	791.795 321	001 263	012 472	9.875 280	101 263	46
47	88.197 485	871.974 853	001 147	011 338	9.886 618	101 147	47
48	97.017 234	960.172 338	001 041	010 307	9.896 926	101 041	48
49	106.718 957	1.057 189 572	000 946	009 370	9.906 296	100 946	49
50	117.390 853	1.163 908 529	000 859	008 519	9.914 814	100 859	50

RATE 10%

Source: Gittinger (1973:20-21). Reprinted by permission of The World Bank and The Johns Hopkins University Press.

What is the present value of $12,000 receivable in two years' time if the discount rate is 10 percent?

$$PV = \$12,000 \times \frac{1}{(1 + 0.10)^2} \tag{3-9}$$

$$= \$12,000(.826446)$$

$$= \$9,917.35$$

What if the same sum was receivable in 50 years' time?

$$PV = \$12,000 \times \frac{1}{(1 + 0.10)^{50}} \tag{3-10}$$

$$= \$12,000(.008519)$$

$$= \$102.23$$

In project evaluation we usually discount the net benefits (benefits − costs) for each year by the appropriate discount factor. In this way each year's net benefits are discounted separately.

For example, a project gives the following cash flows (the discount rate is 10 percent):

Year	0	1	2	3	4	(3-11)
Costs	−$1,000	0	0	0	0	
Benefits	0	$500	$600	$700	$800	
Net benefits	−$1,000	$500	$600	$700	$800	

$$PV = -\$1,000 + \$500(0.9091) + \$600(0.8264) + \$700(0.7513)$$

$$+ \$800(0.6830)$$

$$PV = \$1,022.74$$

If the net benefits are the same each year, or over some period of time, another factor may be used that discounts the stream of equal amounts back to the present (labeled *Present Worth of an Annuity Factor* in Table 3.3). The formula for this factor is as follows:

$$\frac{(1 + r)^n - 1}{(r[1 + r]^n)} \tag{3-12}$$

For a five-year period, at a 10% discount rate, the annuity factor is

$$= \frac{(1 + 0.10)^5 - 1}{[0.1(1 + 0.10)^5]} \qquad (3\text{-}13)$$

$$= 3.790787$$

Thus, if a project produced net benefits of $5,000 per year for the first five years, the present value of that sum would be

$$PV = \$5,000 \ (3.790787)$$
$$= \$18,953.94 \qquad (3\text{-}14)$$

This is the same result as obtained by discounting $5,000 separately for each of the five years.

For example, an investment gives a guaranteed income of $5,000 per year for seven years. How much can we afford to pay for that investment given that the current interest (discount) rate is 10 percent per annum?

$$PV = \$5,000 \ [(1 + 0.10)^7 - 1] \ / \ [0.10(1 + 0.10)^7]$$
$$= \$5,000 \times 4.8684$$
$$= \$24,342 \qquad (3\text{-}15)$$

If in the foregoing example there is a further income of $10,000 per year for years 8 to 10, by how much would the present value increase?

PV $10,000 years 1 → 10

$$PV = \$10,000 \times 6.1446 \text{ (using the preceding formula, or}$$
$$\text{Table 3.3)}$$
$$PV = \$61,446 \qquad (3\text{-}16)$$

PV $10,000 years 1 → 7

$$PV = \$10,000 \times 4.8684$$
$$PV = \$48,684 \qquad (3\text{-}17)$$

PV $10,000 years 8 → 10

$$PV = \$61,446 - \$48,684 = \$12,762 \qquad (3\text{-}18)$$

This is the same as taking the difference between the values of the discount factors

$$6.1446 - 4.8684 = 1.2762$$
then $\quad PV = \$10,000 \times 1.2762 = \$12,762 \qquad (3\text{-}19)$

The same result is obtained by summing the discount factors for years 8, 9, and 10:

$$.4665 + .4241 + .3856 = 1.2762 \tag{3-20}$$

When the number of periods involved gets very high, or can be assumed to be infinite, the present value of an annuity formula simplifies to

$$PV = \frac{P}{r} \tag{3-21}$$

This is often referred to as the *capitalization formula*.

For example, a project produces a stream of equal annual benefits of $24,000 forever. The discount rate is 15 percent.

The present value of this stream is

$$PV = \$24,000/0.15 = \$160,000 \tag{3-22}$$

Another project has the following cash flows:

Years	0	1	2	3	4	. . .	∞	(3-23)
Net benefits	−$10,000	0	$1,000	$3,000	$8,000	. . .	$8,000	

With a 15 percent discount rate, the present value of this project equals

$$PV = -\$10,000 + \frac{\$1,000}{(1.15)^2} + \frac{\$3,000}{(1.15)^3} + \frac{(\$8,000/0.15)}{(1.15)^4} \tag{3-24}$$

$$PV = -\$10,000 + \$756 + \$1,972 + \$30,493$$

$$PV = \$23,221$$

A final formula is that used to find the *amortization rate* or *capital recovery factor*. Under this formula a present sum is converted into a number of equal payments (or annuities) that will be made in the future. In this way, a loan can be retired over *n* years at a given discount rate with compound interest paid on the remaining balance.

This formula is usually not used in economic benefit-cost analysis because interest repayments are treated as financial transactions or transfer payments and are left out. However, in financial analysis this formula is of great importance and is therefore included here.

$$A = P\,[r(1 + r)^n]\, /\, [(1 + r)^n - 1] \tag{3-25}$$

where A = annuity value

P = principal to be repaid over n years at r discount rate

For example, to finance a project $95,000 has been borrowed for ten years at 15 percent per annum rate of interest. How much will the periodic payments be if the installments of interest plus principal are to be equal?

$$
\begin{aligned}
A &= \$95{,}000\,[0.15(1 + 0.15)^{10}]\, /\, [(1 + 0.15)^{10} - 1] \\
&= \$95{,}000 \times 0.1993 \\
&= \$18{,}933.50 \text{ per annum}
\end{aligned}
\tag{3-26}
$$

The same formula can be used to calculate monthly payments on a large loan (e.g., a home), if n is set equal to the number of months of the loan and r is set equal to the *monthly* interest rate.

References

Baumol, W. J. "On the Social Rate of Discount." *American Economic Review* 58 (1968):788–802.

Gittinger, J. P. *Economic Analysis of Agricultural Projects.* Baltimore: Johns Hopkins University Press, 1982.

————, ed. *Compounding and Discounting Tables for Project Evaluation.* Baltimore: Johns Hopkins University Press, 1973.

Haveman, R. "The Opportunity Cost of Displaced Private Spending and the Social Discount Rate." *Water Resources Research* 5 (1969):947–57.

Helmers, F. L. C. H. *Project Planning and Income Distribution.* The Hague: Martinus Nijhoff, 1979.

Hufschmidt, M. M., D. E. James, A. D. Meister, B. T. Bower, and J. A. Dixon. *Environment, Natural Systems, and Development: An Economic Valuation Guide.* Baltimore: Johns Hopkins University Press, 1983.

Hyman, E. L., and M. M. Hufschmidt. "The Relevance of Natural Resource Economics in Environmental Planning." Honolulu: East-West Center, Environment and Policy Institute Working Paper, April 1983.

Squire, L., and H. G. van der Tak. *Economic Analysis of Projects.* Baltimore: Johns Hopkins University Press, 1975.

II
Case Studies from Asia: Organization and Use

The case studies presented here illustrate various techniques discussed in the *Guide*. Each case study is based on an actual development project or natural resource/environmental problem; examples are cited from five different countries in the Asia-Pacific region. These case studies are designed to be worked out; thus the problem, the data, and the required analysis are presented as an exercise. A sample solution is provided separately at the end of each case study. Not all of the techniques discussed in the *Guide* are illustrated because of the large number of approaches covered in the *Guide* and the specialized data or computational assistance needed for some of the valuation techniques.

The selection of case studies in this workbook is designed to show how different economic valuation techniques have been applied. The emphasis is always on what is practical and feasible, given limitations of data, manpower, time, and other factors. Simplifying assumptions are frequently made and are identified as such. In most cases the required calculations are easily done using a hand calculator and discounting tables. The examples are designed to illustrate basic economic principles as well as valuation techniques. As such, these approaches can be applied to many other cases.

The actual cases vary in complexity, type, and length. Five different countries, seven different types of projects, and eight different valuation techniques used are shown in Table I.1. These cases have all been used in dissemination and training workshops held in the Asia-Pacific region from 1982 to 1985. The format of each case study is similar and consists of seven parts:

- A *summary* identifies the type of case presented and the valuation techniques used, and discusses aspects of the valuation that are not covered in the case.
- *Background information* is presented, which describes the project or question under consideration and places it within the country setting.
- *Environmental dimensions* are described in the next section. This part explicitly relates the project to the environmental effects caused by or addressed by the project.

59

- *The approach or technique used* is briefly discussed with reference to the appropriate section in the *Guide*.
- *The data* are then presented in tabular, graphical, or verbal form. These are realistic data based on actual projects.
- *The economic analysis* to be performed is described. This section explains what calculations are required and offers hints for possible approaches.
- *The results* present one set of solutions to the problems posed in the previous section. In actual practice the solution obtained may vary depending on the assumptions made by the analyst. There is not always one correct answer; sensitivity analysis is used to test the sensitivity of results to changes in key variables. A concluding part discusses the case and some of the alternative solutions possible.

Although each case study was prepared by a researcher from or resident in the country where the project is located, all case studies have been edited to conform to the common format and to resolve ambiguities or supply missing data. In some cases, data have been fabricated to complete a time series or to simplify an analysis; these data could be called "synthetic but realistic" and are identified as such. These caveats are meant as a caution—the case studies are based on real projects but should not be taken as actual results from these projects. Likewise, the original authors should not be held responsible for the data presented here.

Taking these liberties with the case studies does not make them less worthwhile or less realistic as examples of economic valuation techniques that are useful in valuing environmental quality dimensions of development projects. Since each project has to be approached individually and adjustments made for the particular

Table I.1   Case Study Classification

Country	Project	Valuation technique(s) used
China	Beijing water quality	Resources saved or alternative costs avoided
Japan	Tokyo Bay fishery	Compensation paid and market value of lost productivity
Korea	Upland agriculture soil management	Productivity and replacement-cost approach
Philippines	Tongonan geothermal wastewater disposal	Cost effectiveness
Philippines	Rural fuelwood development	Productivity
Thailand	Nam Pong reservoir watershed management and sedimentation	Market valuation
Thailand	Recreational use of Lumpinee Park	Travel cost and hypothetical valuation

circumstances involved, the case studies are designed to illustrate how some of the techniques presented in the *Guide* can be used, rather than to present the definitive economic analysis for particular projects.

Coverage of Techniques

Table 3.2 in the *Guide* (reproduced here as Table I.2) presents a classification of benefit and cost valuation techniques. The various techniques are divided between those that are market oriented and those that are survey oriented. Market-oriented techniques are usually preferred because they use information on observed behavior to directly value benefits or costs, or both, due to changes in productivity, provision of goods and services, environmental protection inputs, and other environmental quality dimensions. Some of these techniques rely on actual market prices for valuation of the good or service in question while others rely on surrogate markets to determine values.

The second set of techniques relies on surveys of attitudes and preferences to determine the values of environmental goods or services. These are also known as hypothetical valuation techniques that rely on statements of willingness to pay and willingness to accept compensation as a measure of worth. Since these values are hypothetical and are not based on observed market prices, more caution must be taken in interpreting these results.

Most of the case studies in this workbook rely on market-oriented techniques. Although not every case study falls neatly into one of the classifications in Table I.2, a rough allocation is possible. The Korean upland agriculture case is an example of both the change in productivity technique (on the benefit side) and the replacement cost approach (on the cost side). The Tokyo Bay fishery case combines acceptance of compensation (surrogate market) with a productivity (actual market) approach. The Philippine geothermal wastewater disposal case uses a cost-effectiveness approach, which is a technique commonly used in environmental mitigation actions. The Chinese case, Beijing water quality, is based on resources saved or preventive expenditures avoided. Market valuation of changes in output is also used to assess the Thai reservoir sedimentation and watershed management case. Rural fuelwood development in the Philippines combines standard productivity approaches with surrogate market valuation of environmental goods. The urban park case in Thailand is the only one to use a survey-based technique, which is used to measure user willingness to pay and, hence, value of the park. In addition, the park case also calculates a value using the surrogate market-based travel cost approach.

Classes of techniques not represented here are largely those that require large data sets. Among these are loss-of-earnings approaches that require large-scale morbidity and mortality studies and property value and other land-value approaches. Such techniques require detailed data usually available only in devel-

Table I.2 Classification of Cost and Benefit Valuation Techniques for
Assessing Effects on Environmental Quality

	Examples of application	
Valuation technique	Producer goods and services	Consumer goods and services
Market oriented		
1. Benefit valuation using actual market prices of productive goods and services		
(a) Changes in value of output	Loss of value of agricultural crops caused by seepage of toxic chemicals	
(b) Loss of earnings	Value of productive services lost through increased illness and death caused by air pollution	
2. Cost valuation using actual market prices of environmental protection inputs		
(a) Preventive expenditures	Cost of environmental safeguards in project design	Cost of noise insulation; cost of intake water treatment
(b) Replacement cost	Cost of replacing structures damaged by acid rain	Cost of additional painting of houses damaged air pollution
(c) Shadow project	Cost of restoring commercial fresh-water fisheries damaged by discharges	Costs of supplying alternative sport fishing and recreational facilities destroyed by developm project
(d) Cost-effectiveness analysis	Costs of alternative means of disposing of waste-water from a geothermal energy project	
3. Benefit valuation using surrogate markets		
(a) Marketed goods as environmental surrogates	Cost of sewage treatment processes as proxy for water purification by ecosystems	Price paid for visits to private parks and enterta ment as proxy for value of visits to wilderne area
(b) Property value approach	Changes in commercial property value as a result of water pollution	Changes in residential property value from air pollution
(c) Other land value approaches		Prices paid by government for land reserved fo national parks
(d) Travel cost		Valuation of recreational benefits of a public pa
(e) Wage differential approach		Estimation of willingness of workers to trade of wages for improved environmental quality
(f) Acceptance of compensation	Compensation for damage to crops	Compensation for adverse health effects, e.g., Minamata disease
Survey Oriented (hypothetical valuation)		
1. Direct questioning of willingness to pay		
(a) Bidding games		Estimate of willingness to pay for access to an urban park
2. Direct questioning of choices of quantities		
(a) Costless choice method		Hypothetical applications to air pollution

Source: Hufschmidt et al. (1983).

oped, highly modernized economies. These techniques are covered in the *Guide* and can be applied where data are available.

JOHN A. DIXON

Reference

Hufschmidt, M. M., D. E. James, A. D. Meister, B. T. Bower, and J. A. Dixon. *Environment, Natural Systems, and Development: An Economic Valuation Guide*. Baltimore: Johns Hopkins University Press, 1983.

4
Economic Valuation of Environmental Quality Aspects of Upland Agricultural Projects in Korea

Sung-Hoon Kim and John A. Dixon

Summary

This case study examines two alternative soil management approaches designed to stabilize upland soils and enhance agricultural production in Korea. In comparing these techniques the *replacement-cost approach* is used; this approach is discussed in Chapter 7 of the *Guide* (pp. 266–67). In this case study the costs of physically replacing lost soil and nutrients are taken as a measure of the minimum benefits from preventing erosion and soil and nutrient losses from occurring by means of a new soil management technique. This approach assumes that erosion is worth preventing, and an analysis of the without-management scenario indicates that the value of lost agricultural production would be very high. Soil management would thus appear to be economically attractive. This case does not examine the social and cultural factors of the region, but their importance in explaining adoption (or lack of adoption) of the new techniques is discussed briefly. In addition the case does not consider alternative cropping patterns; such patterns could be evaluated easily using the same approach.

Background Information

Korea is a rapidly urbanizing country with a growing population and increasing needs for food and fiber. As relatively flat farmland is lost to urban growth and industrial development, the development of hilly upland areas is seen as a major option for future expansion of agricultural production. In the past improper management techniques for upland areas have led to decreased productivity in upland fields and negative on-site and off-site environmental effects. This case examines new soil management options and explicitly incorporates the benefits and costs due to changed environmental and other factors resulting from these new soil management techniques.

In this case study, "uplands" refer to all cultivated uplands other than terraced rice paddy fields; most of these uplands are located on hillsides. Uncultivated uplands are classified as "forest" lands (even though some of these lands are only marginally forested). About 67 percent of the total land area in Korea is classified as forest lands, 13 percent as paddy fields, and the remaining 20 percent split between cultivated uplands and "others."

Total cultivated area in Korea is about 2.2 million hectares and the nonpaddy field uplands account for about 40 percent of this total. Average farm size is small; there are about 2.1 million farm families in Korea and each farm is therefore slightly larger than 1 hectare on average. The government has embarked on an ambitious program of upland agricultural development to expand food production. The ultimate potential for further upland development of land with a slope of less than 30° has been estimated by the Agricultural Development Corporation as 516,000 hectares, divided among 2,400 parcels.

Environmental Dimensions

In the past the agricultural performance of upland development areas has not been entirely satisfactory, in part due to errors in field layout and construction, coupled with inadequate soil management techniques used in cultivation. This resulted in heavy soil erosion and deterioration of the existing natural systems. Soil erosion and the subsequent downstream deposition of silt have resulted in serious damage in the environment, both upstream and downstream, as well as losses to downstream paddy growers. Some upland areas developed for agricultural production by private initiative were later abandoned as productivity fell. The low level of both fertility and moisture-retaining capacity of the upland fields helped cause the reduced productivity.

Although it is true that upland soil erosion and downstream sedimentation can have positive effects by creating fertile valleys (e.g., the Nile, the Ganges, the Yellow River), in Korea soil erosion has had largely negative impacts on existing cultivated fields. Potential "benefits" of erosion also depend on what types of soils are being eroded. For example, silt is frequently beneficial while sand or gravel is not.

As a result of both upland and downstream effects, Korean policymakers and farmers have had increasing doubts about the feasibility of continuing upland development. Despite the need to expand the agricultural production base of Korea, the government seems ready to reduce its strong commitment to upland development.

In the past, little emphasis was given to environmental aspects in planning for and evaluating upland development projects. Conventional benefit-cost analysis techniques were used, and only such positive products as increased production of food grains and fresh produce were included as benefits. Environmental factors such as soil erosion, water runoff, and siltation effects on streams, rivers, and paddy lands were ignored (off-site effects). To the extent that these negative environmental factors also lead to decreased productivity of the uplands themselves (on-site effects), they were included in conventional benefit-cost analysis. Therefore, a comprehensive reevaluation of upland agricultural projects is required to properly include both on-site and off-site environmental consequences.

In this context, economic valuations of the environmental effects of various proposed soil management techniques are presented in this case study. The case compares costs and benefits of one proposed new technique with an alternative approach of maintaining upland productivity. Both on-site and off-site effects are included in the analysis.

The Test Sites

These analyses are based on physical data obtained by the Office of Rural Development Soil Science Research Team in Icheon and Gochang where net areas of 272 and 325 hectares, respectively, of hillside lands were initially developed in 1974 (Appendix Figure A4.1). These areas are hilly uplands with an average slope of 15 percent and red-yellow sandy loam soils. The fields were planted twice a year with a soybean crop followed by a barley crop. Using a lysimeter, soil and nutrient loss rates were measured on test plots with the soybean-barley cropping system under nine different types of soil management.

Because the main environmental problems were rapid water runoff (causing soil erosion) and lack of deep percolation of rainwater into the fields, the soil management techniques were designed to slow runoff and increase water infiltration. The soil management techniques (treatments) used included various forms of trenching, chiseling, mulching, and vertical mulching. These techniques are illustrated in Figure 4.1. Effects on soil moisture of two mulching techniques are shown in Figure A4.2. The reduction in soil erosion between the control (check) plot and the other treatments is presented in Table 4.1. Annual soil losses were reduced by up to 90 percent in some cases. The different soil treatments used are defined in Table 4.2, and their annual costs are presented in Table 4.3.

These conservation practices are derived from experimental results and experiences from comparable watersheds. Field trials allow the selection of a set of "better conservation practices" suitable for the given location. In this case study, field trials in the two regions had already identified that a combination of conservation practices (mulch plus vertical mulch) was *most* efficient in reducing erosion. A more complete analysis would evaluate the benefits and costs of all feasible alternatives.

The Approach Used

In order to evaluate the trade-offs between the various improved agricultural practices, a replacement-cost approach analysis will be used. This technique is briefly mentioned in Chapter 7 of the *Guide*.

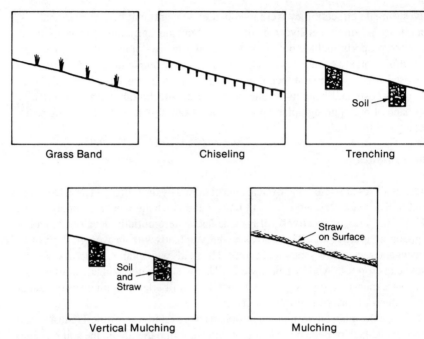

Figure 4.1 Soil management techniques.

The *replacement-cost approach* is based on the premise that the costs of replacing productive assets that have been damaged because of pollution or improper on-site management can be measured. These costs are taken as a minimum estimate of the value of measures that will reduce pollution or improve on-site management practices and thereby prevent damages. This minimum value is then compared to the costs of the new measures.

In this case study the productive asset that has been damaged is the soil in the upland areas. Leaching of nutrients and soil erosion have both occurred and have reduced the value of the land by reducing its productivity. The cost of physically replacing lost soil, restoring lost nutrients, and compensating for downstream losses is measured. This is the replacement cost that will maintain the productivity of the system and compensate for off-site damages. The same level of field productivity and off-site damage mitigation can be obtained by using appropriate preventive steps. When the proposed preventive steps (the new soil management techniques) cost less than the replacement costs, the preventive measures are economically justified. It is assumed that these replacement costs are not greater than the value of the productive resources destroyed, that is, the replacement is worth doing. If the replacement or preventive costs are greater than the value of the goods produced, it would usually be a misallocation of resources to undertake these steps.

Table 4.1 Soil Loss in Upland Areas: A Comparison of Existing Practices and Alternative Management Techniques, 1976-77 Test Plot Data (kg/0.1 ha/yr)

Year	Crop	Existing practices (control plot)	Alternative management techniques							
			Grass band	Chisel-ing	Trench-ing	Vertical mulching	Mulch-ing	Mulch + chisel	Mulch + trench	Mulch + vertical mulch
1976	Soybean	4,275	1,802	2,217	2,092	1,269	940	707	542	512
	Barley	432	52	188	212	100	70	70	58	52
	Annual total	4,707	1,854	2,405	2,304	1,369	1,010	777	600	564
1977	Soybean	3,116	689	1,276	2,062	1,961	227	235	310	149
	Barley	246	20	184	211	221	3	3	0.3	1
	Annual total	3,362	709	1,460	2,273	2,182	230	238	310.3	150
	Annual average	4,035	1,282	1,933	2,289	1,776	620	508	455	357
	Index	100	31.8	47.9	56.7	44.0	15.4	12.6	11.3	8.8

Note: These results are from trial plots measured in 1976 and 1977. The data are given as presented in the test results; the level of accuracy for annual soil loss is probably at best two significant figures (i.e., 4,000 kg/0.1 ha rather than 4,035 kg/0.1 ha).

Table 4.2 Definitions of Soil Management Techniques

1. Control plots of conventional soil management practice--Topsoil is plowed to a depth of 20 centimeters for the first crop of the year; it is also limed and fused phosphate is applied.

2. Grass band--Weeping love grass is planted in bands 20 centimeters wide at 2-meter intervals.

3. Chiseling[a]--The soil surface is broken to a depth of 60 centimeters and a width of one meter by using tractor-attached bullet-headed driller. The bands are 2 meters apart.

4. Trenching[a]--A line of trenches is dug, 80 centimeters deep with a width of 20 centimeters, at 2-meter intervals. The trenches are filled with loose soil.

5. Vertical mulching[a]--Trenches are dug as above but filled in part with rice straw. The topsoil is treated as in the control plot.

6. Mulching--The surface is covered with rice straws at a rate of 300 kg/10 Are[b] (0.1 ha) after every seed sowing.

[a]The so-called "subsoiling techniques" include chiseling, trenching, and vertical mulching.

[b]1 ha = 100 Are.

Table 4.3 Estimated Costs of the Various Upland Soil Management Techniques (won/ha)

1. Control plot of conventional practices (annual cost) (tiller plowing + lime and phosphorus application)	35,000
2. Establishing grass bands (once every 3 years) (weeping love grass + 5 man-days labor)	125,000
3. Chiseling (once every 2 years) (tractor hire + 2 man-days labor)	110,000
4. Trenching (once every 2 years) (tractor hire + 4 man-days labor)	120,000
5. Vertical mulching (once every 4 years) (tractor hire + rice straw + 2 man-days labor + lime and phosphorus application)	185,000 (1st yr) 85,000 (years 5, 9, 13, ...)
6. Mulching (annual cost) (rice straw + 2 man-days labor)	90,000

Note: The farm wage for one man-day is W5,000. The exchange rate is US$1 = W690.

The Data

In the case study three types of physical losses are considered—soil, nutrients, and water. Although these losses frequently occurred simultaneously (heavy rains leading to soil erosion and water runoff), they are considered as separate elements in this analysis.

Soil Loss

The two sample survey areas (Icheon and Gochang) were measured for soil loss by the Research Bureau of the Office of Rural Development. They found average, annual soil losses of 40.35 tons per hectare, close to the theoretical loss of 39.9 tons per hectare estimated from the Universal Soil Loss Equation. (See Appendix A4.1 for details on the USLE. The values in the USLE can be used in a sensitivity analysis of factors affecting soil erosion. The environmental effects of this erosion are considered later.)

Nutrient Loss

Average annual nutrient loss per hectare was calculated by using a lysimeter on trial plots. The losses were as follows:

Nutrient	Kg lost per ha
N	15.7
P	3.6
K	14.6
Ca	10.6
Mg	1.6
Organic matter	75.4

Water Runoff

During the two-year observation period, average annual runoff per hectare was 1,380 tons, or equivalent to roughly 1,380 millimeters of rainfall. Although average rainfall in Korea is about 1,200 millimeters per year (see Appendix Figure A4.1), the sample areas had heavier rainfall than the average. A very high percentage of total rainfall was lost in runoff, causing the observed soil erosion and nutrient leaching.

The Economic Analysis

The economic analysis evaluates the environmental costs associated with present upland management practices and the benefits and costs of alternative soil management techniques. Soil erosion has resulted in siltation of downstream paddy fields, especially in the first two years after establishing the upland area. To counteract this erosion, a number of soil management techniques have been devised to stabilize the upland soil; however, each technique has associated costs (Tables 4.2, 4.3).

Table 4.1 shows the soil loss associated with soybean and barley production in upland areas under conventional and various proposed management practices as measured in trial plots. The type of crop grown, as well as rainfall quantity and timing, obviously affects the soil loss rates. With conventional practices, soil losses are high: more than 40 tons per hectare. New management techniques cause a dramatic drop in erosion rates, especially when combined with the mulch application.

Tables 4.4 and 4.5 show nutrient loss levels and water runoffs associated with the proposed new management practices. Two options are considered in this case:

1. The costs of replacing lost nutrients and soil in upland areas, cleaning up silted paddy fields downstream, and thereby maintaining crop productivity (replacement cost).

2. The costs associated with various new management practices. The use of these practices will reduce soil erosion and nutrient loss; the costs of implementing these practices and thereby reducing erosion need to be compared to the benefits of these actions, namely, the replacement costs saved.

The analysis will use a 10 percent discount rate and will include a 15-year period. This period was arbitrarily chosen to simplify calculations. In fact, however, benefits or costs occurring after 15 years become rather small when a 10 percent discount rate is applied. All prices and quantities used are as shown in the tables. *It is assumed that crop production, labor inputs, and crop yields are the same under both options; that is, the on-site benefits, the value of agricultural production, are constant.*

Replacement-Cost Approach

Calculate the net present value (*NPV*) of the annual replacement of soil and nutrients over a 15-year period under existing cultivation practices.

In order to evaluate this approach, additional information is needed. Soil lost from the upland fields is in part deposited in streams, rivers, and fields in lower areas. This soil can then be dug up and returned. The cost to recover and replace eroded soil in the upland fields is composed of truck rental and spreading costs. These charges are divisible and average *won* (W)2,000 per ton of soil. In addition, lost nutrients have to be replaced. The 1980 market values of nutrients (on an elemental basis) are W480/kg for N, W345/kg for P, W105/kg for K, W60/kg for Ca, W1,400/kg for Mg, and W175/kg for organic matter. Labor costs for spreading nutrients and other materials average W40/kg spread. If the replacement approach is taken, soil and nutrient replacements are yearly phenomena.

The conventional system also requires a recurring annual per hectare expendi-

Table 4.4 Estimated Losses of Nutrients from Test Plot Results (kg/0.1 ha/yr)

Components	Existing practices (control plot)	Alternative management techniques							
		Grass band	Chisel-ing	Trench-ing	Vertical mulching	Mulch-ing	Mulch + chisel	Mulch + trench	Mulch + vertical mulch
N	1.572	0.643	1.132	1.141	0.869	0.634	0.485	0.404	0.494
P	0.358	0.041	0.187	0.121	0.080	0.033	0.014	0.010	0.013
K	1.459	0.700	1.120	1.193	0.922	0.689	0.544	0.454	0.556
Ca	1.061	0.296	0.670	0.587	0.432	0.283	0.201	0.165	0.203
Mg	0.162	0.039	0.105	0.096	0.072	0.049	0.036	0.029	0.036
Organic matter	7.535	0.874	3.931	2.512	1.638	0.655	0.328	0.218	0.223

Table 4.5 Estimated Amount of Water Runoff from Test Plot Results (ton/0.1 ha/yr)

Year	Existing practices (control plot)	Alternative management techniques							
		Grass band	Chisel-ing	Trench-ing	Vertical mulching	Mulch-ing	Mulch + chisel	Mulch + trench	Mulch + vertical mulch
1976	121.90	42.40	60.90	73.60	26.90	34.60	7.80	9.30	7.60
1977	153.92	67.76	87.78	102.31	66.22	26.31	28.92	19.22	19.91
Average	137.91	55.08	74.34	87.96	46.56	30.46	18.36	14.26	13.76
Index	100.00	39.90	53.90	63.80	33.80	22.10	13.30	10.30	10.00

ture of W35,000 for field maintenance and repair. This is in addition to soil and nutrient replacement costs. However, the continuing erosion leads to downstream siltation of paddy fields, creating damage and leading to decreased productivity. The analyst examined the damage to lowland fields and the resultant decrease in rice production. The total loss of rice production was valued at the local market price (W500 per liter), and this amount was then prorated among the upland fields that created the siltation. The value of the *lowland* loss is estimated at W30,000 per year per upland hectare (equivalent to the value of 60 liters of rice). A compensation payment of W30,000 per year per upland hectare is made from the upland to the lowland farmers to cover these losses. We assume that market prices reflect economic scarcity and, therefore, the compensation amount reflects both financial and economic costs.

A final cost under the conventional system is for supplemental irrigation. Assume that one-third of the annual runoff has to be replaced by commercial irrigation at an average cost of W200 per ton of water. No irrigation is required under improved soil management practices.

New Management Technique

In this example only one new management technique, that of combined straw mulching and vertical mulching, is considered. This combination gave the best experimental results in physically controlling soil erosion (see Tables 4.1, 4.4, and 4.5). The net present value calculation, again over 15 years with a 10 percent discount rate, will include the costs associated with the new techniques, as well as those for reduced soil and nutrient replacement and paddy farmer compensation payments. Calculate the latter costs based on the data presented in Tables 4.1, 4.4, and 4.5 and the other information given in the first technique. Assume that the irrigation and field maintenance and repair needs are eliminated because of the new management technique's soil- and water-conserving characteristics.

The new combined technique, mulching plus vertical mulching (items 5 and 6 in Table 4.2), requires that appropriate measures be taken every four years. In the first year (year 1), the cost of vertical mulching is high: W185,000 per hectare; in succeeding periods (years 5, 9, 13, etc.) the cost is reduced to W85,000 per hectare since less labor and materials are required. In addition, there is a yearly expense for straw mulch of W90,000 per hectare.

Additional Analysis

Recalculate the two net present values, assuming a 5 percent and a 20 percent discount rate. (Table 4.6 gives discount factors for 5 percent, 10 percent, and 20 percent.) Does this change the relative results? How realistic are the assumptions made in the case study, and which ones would be appropriate for further examina-

Table 4.6 Discount Factors

Year	Discount rate 5%	10%	20%
1	.952	.909	.833
2	.907	.826	.694
3	.864	.751	.579
4	.823	.683	.482
5	.784	.621	.402
6	.746	.564	.335
7	.711	.513	.279
8	.677	.467	.233
9	.645	.424	.194
10	.614	.386	.162
11	.585	.350	.135
12	.557	.319	.112
13	.530	.290	.093
14	.505	.263	.078
15	.481	.239	.065

tion? Have any important variables been omitted from the analysis? What are likely constraints to introducing the new management technique?

An additional factor that should be considered is what would happen if no actions were taken by the upland farmers, that is, if erosion was allowed to continue unchecked. No data are available, but one could hypothesize that yields would drop from the higher, with-management levels to the lower, control plot levels (1,810 kg of soybeans and 2,250 kg of barley per hectare). Using the soybean and barley yields for the mulch plus vertical mulch option as year 0 base (that is, with management yields of 2,350 kg of soybeans and 3,220 kg of barley per hectare), assume that yields dropped to the *control plot levels* in a linear fashion over five years (to year 5). Using 1980 prices (of W521/kg for soybeans and W301/kg for barley) and a 10 percent discount rate, calculate the net present value of this lost production. If, with continuing erosion, yields dropped to half of their control plot levels after five more years of no management and then stabilized, calculate the value of the lost production over the entire 15-year period. How do these figures compare with the two management options?

The Results

The net present value of the costs of both approaches can be calculated from the data given in the case study. The analysis covers a 15-year time period and uses a 10 percent discount rate. A useful aid in this analysis is a table of discount factors; that is, what multiplicative factor will reduce any benefit or cost received *x* years in the future into the present value at a given discount rate. Table 4.6 presents these factors for years 1 to 15 for three discount rates: 5 percent, 10 percent, and 20 percent.

Replacement-Cost Approach

The replacement-cost approach is evaluated first; the calculation details how much it costs to replace lost soil and nutrients and maintain a given level of crop production. It also includes compensation payments and mitigation measures for downstream losses. These costs occur annually and do not vary from year to year. Once the cost per year is known, the discount factors in Table 4.6 can be used to calculate the net present value of these costs over a 15-year period.

The five main components of the replacement cost are as follows:

1. *Field maintenance and repair.* This cost is W35,000 per hectare per year and does not vary over the 15-year period.

2. *Compensation payments.* These payments are made by upland farmers to lowland paddy farmers to compensate the latter group for decreased paddy production. The payments average W30,000 per year from every upland hectare.

3. *Irrigation costs.* Supplemental irrigation is required to replace water lost by runoff. The runoff from the control plot using existing practices averaged 1,379 tons per hectare (see Table 4.5). One-third of this amount is to be replaced at an average cost of W200 per ton:

$$1,379 \times 0.333 \times W200 = W91,841$$
$$= W92,000 \text{ per hectare}$$

4. *Soil replacement costs.* Eroded soil is recovered downstream and replaced in the upland fields. The cost to do this is W2,000 per ton (truck rental and labor for soil recovery and spreading). Soil loss rates can be calculated from Table 4.1; for the control plot using existing practices soil losses are about 40 tons per hectare. Therefore, $40 \times W2,000 = W80,000$ per hectare.

5. *Nutrient replacement costs.* Nutrients are also lost by water runoff and erosion. The assumption is made that lost nutrients are replaced by use of chemical fertilizers and organic matter although lost soil has also been replaced. The cost to replace nutrients includes materials and labor.

From Table 4.4, the amount of lost nutrients per hectare can be obtained and, when multiplied by the market value of these nutrients, their cost is derived:

Nutrient	Kg lost per ha	Cost per kg (won)	Cost per ha (won)
N	15.7	480	7,536
P	3.6	345	1,242
K	14.6	105	1,533
Ca	10.6	60	636
Mg	1.6	1,400	2,240
Organic matter	75.4	175	13,195
	121.5		26,382

The nutrients cost W26,382 per hectare; spreading or application costs are W40 per kg or W4,860 for 121.5 kg. Total cost is therefore W26,382 + W4,860 = W31,242 or W31,200 per hectare.

Cost per Hectare per Year

The yearly cost per hectare is therefore W268,200, the sum of these five components.

W35,000 (field maintenance and repair)

W30,000 (compensation)

W92,000 (irrigation)

W80,000 (soil replacement)

W31,200 (nutrient replacement)

This amount is the annual recurring cost to maintain agricultural production and repair damages caused by soil erosion. When this value is discounted over 15 years, the present value is obtained:

Year	Replacement cost	10% discount factor	Present value
1	268,200	.909	243,794
2	268,200	.826	221,533
3	268,200	.751	201,418
:			
5	268,200	.621	166,552
:			
10	268,200	.386	103,525
:			
15	268,200	.239	64,100
			2,039,662

The present value of the replacement costs over a 15-year period with a 10 percent discount rate is therefore about W2,040,000.

New Management Technique

The new soil management technique was also evaluated using the data presented in the case study. Because of the use of vertical mulching and mulch, the streams of costs are somewhat different. The assumption has been made that yields are the same as under the replacement-cost approach, and labor and inputs used for crop production are also the same.

The new management technique eliminates the need for supplemental irrigation and field maintenance or repair. There are still annual costs for compensation and soil replacement, but the values are less because of the decreased loss of soil and nutrients.

1. *Compensation payments.* Compensation payments are calculated as previously but adjusted for the decreased soil erosion under the new management technique. If erosion rates are compared (40 tons versus 3.6 tons) and this factor is used to adjust the previous compensation paid to lowland paddy farmers, the new compensation payments are

$$\frac{3.6}{40} \times W30,000 = W2,700 \text{ per hectare}$$

This assumes that there is a linear relationship between upland soil erosion and production losses in downstream paddy fields.

2. *Soil replacement costs.* Soil losses are much smaller under the new management system (see Table 4.1). At W2,000 per ton replaced, these costs are now as follows:

$$3.6 \text{ tons} \times W2,000 = W7,200 \text{ per hectare}$$

3. *Nutrient replacement costs.* Based on the data in Table 4.4, nutrient replacement costs can be calculated as in the previous example.

Nutrient	Kg lost per ha	Cost per kg (won)	Cost per ha (won)
N	4.9	480	2,352
P	0.1	345	35
K	5.6	105	588
Ca	2.0	60	120
Mg	0.4	1,400	560
Organic matter	2.2	175	385
	15.2		4,040

Materials cost W4,040 and application costs are 15.2 kg × W40 = W608. Total cost per hectare is therefore W4,040 + W608 = W4,648 or W4,650 per hectare.

4. *Mulching costs.* The new management technique requires the use of machinery, labor, and straw mulch. In the first year (year 1), the cost of vertical mulching is high: W185,000 per hectare for tractor hire, rice straw, labor, and fertilizer. In succeeding years the cost is lower (W85,000) and only occurs every four years, that is, in years 5, 9, and 13. In addition, there is a yearly cost for straw mulch placed on the fields, amounting to W90,000 per hectare per year.

Table 4.7   Cost Flows for New Management Technique (won/ha)

Year	Compensation	Soil replacement	Nutrient replacement	Mulching costs Vertical mulch	Straw	Total costs
1	2,700	7,200	4,650	185,000	90,000	289,550
2				-		104,550
3				-		104,550
4				-		104,550
5				85,000		189,550
6				-		104,550
7				-		104,550
8				-		104,550
9				85,000		189,550
10				-		104,550
11				-		104,550
12				-		104,550
13				85,000		189,550
14				-		104,550
15	↓	↓	↓	-	↓	104,550

Cost per Hectare per Year

Since the costs associated with the new management technique vary from year to year, it is useful to set up a table to keep track of these costs (Table 4.7). The total costs for each year are then multiplied by the appropriate discount factor to calculate the present value. The cost per hectare over a 15-year period with a 10 percent discount rate is W1,076,742, or slightly more than half of the replacement costs calculated earlier. This indicates that the new management technique is economically attractive based on the data presented and the assumptions made.

Additional Analysis

If the two approaches are reevaluated using a 5 percent and 20 percent discount rate, the relative results are unchanged.

	Present value at various discount rates		
	5%	10%	20%
Replacement-cost approach	2,780,000	2,040,000	1,250,000
New management technique	1,430,000	1,075,000	700,000

As the discount rate increases, the economic advantage of the new management technique decreases slightly because of the large initial cost for vertical mulching that is not discounted heavily since it occurs in year 1. Under all discount rates, however, the new management technique will be more attractive than the replacement approach since its yearly costs are lower for all years except for the first. The conclusion, therefore, is that the new soil management technique is an economically attractive alternative to replacing lost soil and nutrients each year. In addition, there are other negative effects associated with yearly erosion and soil replacement that are not included in this analysis. These costs are also avoided by using the new soil management technique. In general, prevention of erosion or negative environmental effects is preferred to mitigation measures after a negative effect has been felt.

The third alternative, the no-management/no-replacement approach, that leads to a "mining" of the soil and a rapid decrease in agricultural production was also evaluated. The value of agricultural products not produced (the value of the decrease in average yields) is the cost of not undertaking any soil management plan. For management plans to be attractive, their costs should be less than this lost revenue from decreased agricultural production.

As stated in the text, average yields declined from the high base-year yields of the managed soils to the control plot yields over a five-year period. These yields then declined by a further 50 percent of the control plot yields over the next five years and then stabilized. That is, soybean yields declined from 2,350 kg/ha in year 0 to 1,810 kg/ha in year 5, and to 905 kg/ha in year 10. Barley yields showed similar declines: 3,220 kg/ha (year 0) to 2,250 kg/ha (year 5), and to 1,125 kg/ha (year 10).

The value of lost production for each of the 15 years in the analysis is calculated by multiplying the decrease in each year's grain output by the appropriate grain price. The decrease is the difference between actual yield and the base-year yield. Table 4.8 shows the calculations for soybeans; a similar calculation has to be done for barley. After the value of lost production of both soybeans and barley has been found, the yearly values are discounted. Using a 10 percent discount rate, the

Table 4.8   Value of Lost Soybean Production with No Management

Year	Soybean yield (kg/ha)	Decrease in yield compared to base year (kg)	Soybean price (won/kg)	Value of lost production (won/ha)
0	2,350	0	520	0
1	2,242	108		56,160
2	2,134	216		112,320
3	2,026	324		168,480
4	1,918	432		224,640
5	1,810	540		280,800
6	1,629	721		374,920
7	1,448	902		469,040
8	1,267	1,083		563,160
9	1,086	1,264		657,280
10	905	1,445		751,400
11–15	905 (per yr)	1,445 (per yr)		751,400 (per yr)

value of lost production mounts rapidly. For example, the value of lost production per hectare is as follows:

For years 1–5:   W1,239,000
           1–10: W3,692,000
           1–15: W5,739,000

When compared to the discounted costs of either soil management alternative (soil replacement or mulch plus vertical mulch), these lost production values are very high and, as such, soil replacement and new soil management techniques would appear to be very attractive economic propositions.

Discussion

In this case both management techniques are clearly preferable from both an economic and ecological perspective to the no-management alternative if the assumptions made are correct. In practice, however, not all farmers have adopted the new management techniques. It is therefore necessary to ask why this is true and determine whether the assumptions made are correct and if there are other handicaps or constraints that have been ignored.

A number of factors may explain this difference between what is expected and what actually happens. These factors include the following:

1. Has the proper discount rate been used from the farmers' viewpoint? Sensitivity analysis will illustrate how the results will change with higher and lower discount rates.
2. The mulch plus vertical mulch technique may require large cash expenditures. Is credit a constraint to the farmers?
3. Is land ownership a problem? Do farmers own their land or lease it? If leased, what sort of security of lease is available; that is, what incentives are there to invest in land management?

Other questions can and should be asked to understand fully the implications and constraints of the proposed changes. This example has shown how on-site and off-site environmental aspects of an upland development program have been incorporated into an economic analysis. The replacement-cost approach was used to determine the costs involved with an existing management system and then these costs were compared to those of a proposed alternative soil management technique. The fact that both systems appear very attractive economically from the social view may not assure their acceptance by farmers, however. The farmers must see them as attractive in terms of their own perceptions of costs, that is, in a financial analysis. These costs include cash outlays, in-kind contributions, and the timing of costs and benefits. If the social and private (farmer) perspectives vary, appropriate incentives may be required to secure adoption of the new system.

Appendix A4.1: The Universal Soil Loss Equation

The Universal Soil Loss Equation (USLE) relates a number of variables in predicting annual soil loss from any given piece of land.

The generalized form of the equation is

$$A = R \times K \times LS \times C \times P \tag{A4-1}$$

where
A = annual soil loss in tons per hectare
R = rainfall factor
K = soil erodibility factor
LS = length and slope factor
C = cropping factor
P = erosion control practice factor

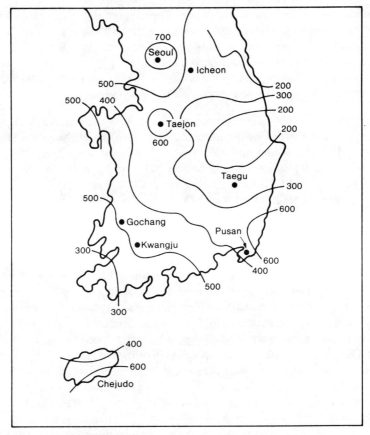

Figure A4.1   Rainfall factor (R) map of Korea.

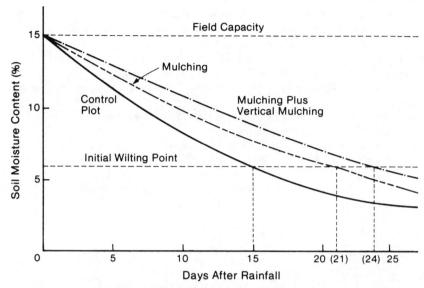

Figure A4.2 Soil moisture changes as a function of time after rainfall for different management techniques.

In Icheon, one of the two sample areas, the values of the variables were estimated to be

$R = 500$
$K = 0.25$ for the sandy loam of Icheon
$LS = 1.2$ (average slope of 15%)
$C = 0.35$ for soybean-barley mix
$P = 0.76$ for contoured terraces

Therefore, $A = 500 \times 0.25 \times 1.2 \times 0.35 \times 0.76 = 39.9$ tons/ha/yr.

Standard reference works on soils explain how the USLE was developed and the ranges of values for the different parameters. See also the discussion in Chapter 5 in the *Guide*.

Selected References Used in Preparation of the Case Study

Agricultural Development Corporation. "Economic Analysis of Large-Scale Upland Reclamation Projects." Seoul, Korea, 1979 and 1980.

Ahn, J. S., et al. "Engineering Aspect in Upland Reclamation." *Journal of Korean Society of Soil Science and Fertilizer* 2, 4 (1978).

Choi, Jae-Sun. "Evaluation Study on Upland Reclamation Project under IBRD Loan." Korean Rural Economics Research Institute, 1978.

Hufschmidt, M. M., D. E. James, A. D. Meister, B. T. Bower, and J. A. Dixon. *Environment, Natural Systems, and Development: An Economic Valuation Guide.* Baltimore: Johns Hopkins University Press, 1983.

Im, J. N., et al. "Studies on Soil Erosion Control in Newly Reclaimed Upland Soil." A series of studies, Office of Rural Development, Seoul, Korea, 1978–80.

Kim, Don-Min. "Case Studies of Hillside Farms." Korean Rural Economics Research Institute, 1978.

Kim, Sung-Hoon. "Economic Evaluation of Upland Reclamation Project." Korean Rural Economics Research Institute, 1977.

Park, Johng-Moon. "The Impact of the Reclamation and Utilization of Idle Hillside Lands on Future Food Production in Korea." *Journal of Korean Society of Soil Science and Fertilizer* 2, 4 (1978).

Um, Ki-Tae. "Area of Potential Arable Land Distributed on Hillside." *Journal of Korean Society of Soil Science and Fertilizer* 2, 4 (1978).

5
Tongonan Geothermal Power Plant Project in Leyte, Philippines

Adapted by Somluckrat Grandstaff
from materials prepared by Beta Balagot

Summary

This case study presents a *cost-effectiveness analysis* of various options for disposing of wastewater generated by a geothermal power plant built in the Philippines. The decision to build the power plant and tap the geothermal energy resource had already been made; the question under consideration here is limited to the selection of the wastewater disposal option that provides protection to the environment on the most cost-effective basis. This approach is discussed in Chapter 7 of the *Guide* (pp. 272–85).

Each of the seven wastewater disposal options considered has differing monetary costs for construction and operation, as well as different environmental effects associated with it. The analysis examines each option in turn and determines monetary values, where possible, for environmental quality effects.

Not all environmental quality effects can be quantified and monetized. These nonmonetizable effects are not ignored in the analysis; they are listed and considered in the final decision-making process. In this way the decision maker is presented with a range of information on the actual construction and operating costs of each wastewater disposal option, as well as the various types (monetized and nonmonetized) of environmental quality effects associated with each option.

Although the analysis of each option is a complete benefit-cost analysis of that option, a more complete presentation would include a benefit-cost analysis of the entire project with various power plant design and wastewater disposal options. In this way the true economic worth of the entire project (not just one component) could have been explored.

In the broader context of developing an optimal time sequence of energy sources—hydroelectric, fossil fuel, geothermal—for a given economy, a more complete analysis would be required. In this context a geothermal project would be adopted only if at that point in time the project was part of a least-cost sequence of energy sources to satisfy a given energy demand over time.

Background Information

The Philippines had been highly dependent on imported crude oil to meet its energy requirements. The ever-increasing trend in oil price has led the government to adopt an energy policy favoring the development of domestic energy resources, namely, nuclear energy, hydro-power, coal, petroleum and natural gas, and geothermal. Nonoil sources of energy are expected to meet 66 percent of the country's energy demand by 1989. Due to its location, the Philippines has a number of potentially commercial geothermal fields defined as localized geological deposits of heat concentrated at attainable depths, in confined volumes and at temperatures sufficient for electric or thermal energy utilization.

Several geothermal power plants are now in operation: a 165-megawatt (MW) power plant in Tiwi, Albay; 110 MW in Bay, Laguna; and 3-MW trial plant in Tongonan, Ormoc, Leyte. Eight geothermal fields are now in advanced stages of exploration or development. By 1982, geothermal power-generating capacity was expected to be 548 MW, second only to the United States.

Geothermal energy is derived from the natural heat of the earth. Under existing technology, only geothermal reservoirs associated with recent hot intrusive rocks and volcanism are harnessed for electrical power generation. High temperature geothermal energy is found in two forms—dry steam fields exemplified by the geysers of the United States and hot water (wet) fields exemplified by the Wairakei and Broadland fields in New Zealand. Only the wet fields yielding mixed water and steam are now being exploited in the Philippines. Priority areas for exploration and development are determined based on the strength of surface thermal manifestations. Tiwi in Albay was the first site selected, followed by Los Banos in Makiling-Banahaw, Tongonan Valley in Leyte, Palimpinon Dauin in Southern Negros, Mambucal in Northern Negros, Marat-Amacan in Davao Province, Daklan-Bokod in Benguet, and Manito in Albay.

Exploration at Tongonan started in 1973, and a potential productive capacity of 3,000 MW years of geothermal electricity was confirmed in 1978. In 1977 a small 3-MW turbine was installed to supply Ormoc City. Phase 1 of the Tongonan Geothermal Power Plant (TGPP) with a 112.5-MW capacity in Leyte is now being implemented (see Figure 5.1). The Tongonan power station relies on a wet steam geothermal resource and produces residual liquids and gases. These residuals have chemical and thermal characteristics that may have adverse effects on the environment, the degree of which depends on the rate and frequency of discharge and the method of disposal adopted.

Environmental Dimensions

An Environmental Impact Report prepared in 1979 by Kingston, Reynolds, Thom, and Allardice Limited (KRTA), consultants to the Ministry of Energy, Philippine National Oil Corporation, indicated that the major adverse effects on

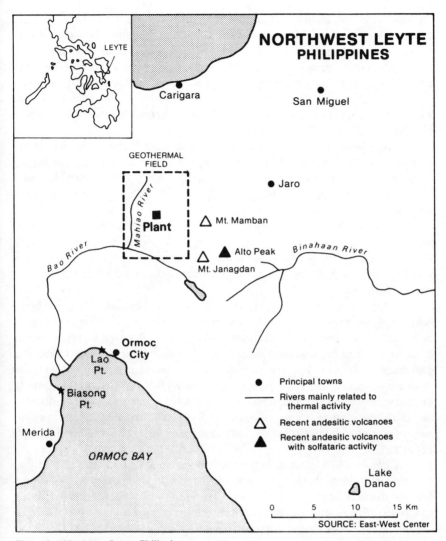

Figure 5.1 Northwest Leyte, Philippines.

the environment would be from the disposal of geothermal waste fluids. Fluids from the Tongonan wells have a higher dissolved solids content than those of most other geothermal fields. The fluids contain large quantities of chloride, silica, arsenic, boron, and lithium. Data on chemical effluents are based on medium-term discharge tests of the Tongonan wells from 1977–79. The concentrations of the various chemicals in the rivers following discharge can be determined through physical and chemical formulas by using various residual wastewater flow rates ranging up to full-loaded operation of the power station. Table 5.1 shows the expected levels of chemical pollutant concentrations from the alternative waste-water disposal schemes as compared with the limits recommended by the National Pollution Control Communication (NPCC). These limits are, of course, subject to considerable uncertainty and are subject to change as additional information on environmental and health effects becomes available. Also, these limits may be affected by the costs of achieving them. However, in this case the NPCC-recommended limits are used as the base.

Concentrations of arsenic, boron, and lithium were found to exceed recommended environmental limits. For example, at maximum operational load, the boron level would be 47 parts per million (ppm) at the Bao River, which is well above the recommended safe levels of 5–20 ppm. Potentially harmful chemical effluents from the TGPP project are as follows:

1.   *Arsenic:* The toxicity of arsenic for living organisms varies widely. Experiments dealing with the effects of arsenic concentration below the lethal dosage show its effect in a reduction of fish growth and crop yields, although it does not magnify along food chains. Rice is the major crop in Leyte being affected by river arsenic.

2.   *Boron:* Boron exists in geothermal fluids in the forms of borates and boric acid. These components are relatively inert in the environment and tend to remain in the water phase rather than accumulate in river or sea-floor sediments. Boron in drinking water is not generally considered a health hazard to people. Above a concentration of 30 milligrams per liter (mg/l), boron may interfere with the digestive processes due to its preservative action on food. Toxicity of boron is more severe in plants. Although boron is an essential trace element for nutrition of higher plants, concentrations exceeding 0.5 mg/l in irrigation waters may be harmful to certain crops. In Leyte, rice yields would be seriously affected by high boron levels.

3.   *Lithium.* High levels of lithium have been found in Tongonan Geothermal Power Plant fluid discharges. Since lithium cannot be precipitated by any known process, dilution is the only way to bring its concentration within accepted limits. Compared with other chemical pollutants, little is known about the effects of lithium on the environment. Although the KRTA report indicated that most crop plants except citrus can tolerate 5 ppm of lithium, the Australian Water Resources Council has also found a level of lithium above 1.2 ppm to be toxic to trout. Adverse effects on the delta and marine ecosystems in Leyte are thus expected.

4.   *Mercury.* All chemical forms of mercury are toxic to some extent, but the toxicity of methylmercury to many organisms is of special concern. In humans, ingested methylmercury is neurotoxic and is only slowly excreted from the system. A mercury concentration of less than 0.01 mg/l (less than 0.0025 mg/l for organic mercury) has caused sublethal effects such as growth retardation, inhibition of sexual development, reduction of egg production and hatchability, and embryo deformities in fish. In Leyte, although mercury levels in the aquatic

Table 5.1 Expected Levels of Chemical Pollutant Concentration from Alternative Disposal Schemes and Recommended Limits

Element	Alternative				Recommended limits with respect to environmental concern[a]
	2 Into Mahiao w/o treatment	4 Into Bao w/o treatment	6 Disposal at Lao Point	7 Disposal at Biasong Point	
Arsenic (As)	13 ppm	4.4 ppm	1.0 ppm	1.4 ppm	1 ppm—River water As levels during construction and commissioning 0.1 ppm—As levels after commissioning phase in river water, delta, bay
Boron (B)	140 ppm	47 ppm	n.a.	n.a.	5 ppm—River water B levels at irrigation diversion during construction 0.75 ppm—River water B levels at irrigation diversion after commissioning 20 ppm—B levels for drinking water
Lithium (Li)	16.4 ppm	n.a.	n.a.	n.a.	2.5 ppm—Li levels in waterways and only for brief periods
Mercury (Hg)	0.005 ppm	n.a.	0.002 ppm	0.00235 ppm	0.1 mg/1—Hg levels at waterways, delta, bay 0.5 mg/1—Hg levels in fish

[a] 0.01 or less can cause sublethal effects (e.g., growth retardation, reduced hatchability, and embryo deformities in fish).

n.a.—not available.

ecosystem will be below the toxic levels, fish and other aquatic animals may be affected via the food chain through the biomagnification process.

The Approach Used

The Tongonan Geothermal Power Plant project is an example of a situation where a development project has already been approved for implementation. The relevant decision, therefore, is no longer to examine the expected benefits and costs to see whether the project is economically justified and should be undertaken. The decision to develop geothermal power is based on the national policy to become less dependent on imported oil for energy; geothermal is one of several alternatives being pursued to reduce both the growth rate of imports and eventually the level of oil imports. Since the adverse effects on the environment from disposal of geothermal waste fluids are known, the relevant decision is to choose the least costly alternative among several wastewater disposal schemes taking into account both treatment costs and environmental damage costs. This evaluation technique is known as the "cost-effectiveness approach" and is discussed in Chapter 7 of the *Guide*.

The Data

Seven alternative wastewater disposal methods have been proposed. Each method has associated capital, operation, and maintenance costs as well as different effects on the environment. The seven methods are (1) reinjection, (2) discharge into the Mahiao River without treatment, (3) discharge into the Mahiao River with treatment for arsenic removal, (4) discharge into the Bao River without treatment, (5) discharge into the Bao River with treatment for arsenic removal, (6) disposal at sea without treatment with outfall at Lao Point, and (7) disposal at sea without treatment with outfall at Biasong Point.

In the first alternative, geothermal fluids from separator stations will be piped to reinjection wells within the field. At full capacity the 112.5-MW power plant in Tongonan will require seven reinjection wells. A standby disposal system consisting of thermal ponds and other contingency structures will also be constructed in conjunction with reinjection. This will be used under short-term shutdown of the reinjection system during maintenance or limited emergency situations. For longer shutdown periods of the reinjection system, the standby scheme will enable disposal of chemically treated waste fluids to the river.

The second and third alternatives involve direct discharge of waste fluids into the Mahiao River (see Figure 5.2). Before discharge into the river, the waste fluids are retained for a few days in a thermal pond. Waste fluids in the thermal pond may be treated with chemicals to remove arsenic.

In alternatives 4 and 5, waste fluids are discharged into the Bao River through a pipeline. A thermal pond is also required where waste fluids are cooled before

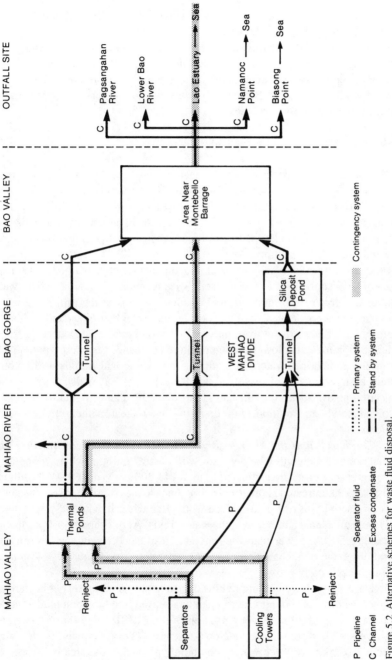

Figure 5.2 Alternative schemes for waste fluid disposal.

MAHIAO VALLEY · MAHIAO RIVER · BAO GORGE · BAO VALLEY · OUTFALL SITE

Separators

Cooling Towers

Reinject

Reinject

Thermal Ponds

Tunnel

WEST MAHIAO DIVIDE

Tunnel

Tunnel

Silica Deposit Pond

Area Near Montebello Barrage

Pagsangahan River

Lower Bao River

Lao Estuary → Sea

Namanoc Point → Sea

Biasong Point → Sea

P Pipeline
C Channel

—— Separator fluid
—— Excess condensate

········· Primary system
–··–··– Stand by system

Contingency system

transport into the Bao River. Alternative 5 entails treatment of waste fluids in the thermal pond to precipitate the arsenic.

Alternatives 6 and 7 involve selection of an outfall at sea to discharge the geothermal wastewater. Two possible outfall sites, Lao Point and Biasong Point, have been studied. An outfall at Lao Point involves construction of a 22-kilometer pipeline while an outfall at Biasong Point needs a 32-kilometer pipeline. Figure 5.2 illustrates alternative schemes.

Costs and Environmental Effects of Alternatives[1]

1. *Reinjection.* Construction of the reinjection wells, pipeline system, and stand-by waste disposal system will take two years. Construction of reinjection wells will cost ₱10 million per well. Construction of a pipeline system from separator stations to the reinjection wells will cost ₱20 million. The standby waste disposal system will entail an outlay of ₱17 million. Annual operation and maintenance costs will total ₱10.4 million.

Although reinjection is seen as the most ecologically sound method of disposal, it cannot be described yet as a well-established technology. In areas where water supplies are drawn from underground aquifers such as in the project site, it is important to be knowledgeable of the local groundwater hydrology and to monitor carefully any effects arising from the injected geothermal wastewater.

Reinjection may also lower the temperature and hence the energy potential of subsurface geothermal water. In addition, the geothermal liquids at Tongonan contain a large amount of dissolved solids such as silica, which may clog the reinjection pipes. Such problems could be solved by chemical additives to keep dissolved solids in solution, but their use may create other environmental problems.

2. *Discharge into the Mahiao River without treatment.* Construction of a thermal pond, which will take one year, will cost ₱7 million, whereas operation and maintenance costs are estimated to total ₱43,300 per year (₱0.0433 million).

Discharge of untreated geothermal waste fluids to the river system is expected to affect productivity of rice fields served by the Bao River Irrigation System due to high levels of arsenic and boron in the waste fluids. At full capacity of production for the 112.5-MW power plant in Tongonan, estimated arsenic and boron concentrations in the Bao River after receiving separator waste fluids are 4.4 ppm and 47 ppm, respectively.

Table 5.2 shows the costs and returns of rice (palay) production per hectare per crop by type of farm. For a two-crop planting season, the total potential area that can be served by the Bao River Irrigation System (BRIS) is 4,000 hectares per crop. Average yield per hectare per crop is 61 cavans (1 cavan equals 50 kilograms) or about 3,050 kg. The rice variety commonly planted in the area is IR 36.

---

1. Capital, operation, and maintenance costs are expressed in 1980 prices.

Table 5.2 Costs and Returns of Producing Palay per Hectare
per Crop by Type of Farm, Eastern Visayas (₱)

		Irrigated	Nonirrigated
Total costs	1975	1,441.4	703.8
	1976	1,567.6	831.4
	1977	1,509.9	766.9
	1978	1,451.4	731.2
	Average	1,492.6	758.3
Total returns	1975	1,752.1	947.3
	1976	1,769.5	1,132.6
	1977	1,925.4	1,076.7
	1978	1,904.8	1,171.4
	Average	1,838.0	1,082.0

In the event that irrigation waters become highly polluted, farmers have the option of not using the irrigation facilities. The average yield in rice fields without irrigation is 37.9 cavans per hectare. In addition, there will only be one rice crop per year. Since the rice produced in the area of the Bao River Irrigation System is only a small part of the regional total, it can be safely assumed that production changes will not affect local rice prices.

A brief survey was conducted by KRTA on water use other than for irrigation purposes. The survey covered upstream and downstream areas and revealed the following information. Among the total of 94 people interviewed, only 3 percent drank water from the Mahiao River. Springs are the more common sources of drinking water in the area. Slightly more than half of those interviewed (58 percent) use the river water for bathing and washing, although 68 percent use it for laundry purposes. More than a third (34 percent) of the livestock drink from the river.

Thus, an added environmental cost of discharging wastewater into the river system is the risk to human health and livestock. To evaluate this environmental effect, the cost of a water purification system that will render the river water safe for domestic and potable uses has been estimated. Construction of the purification system will cost ₱50 million and take two years to complete. Operation and maintenance costs are ₱15 million annually.

Estimation of the costs to the freshwater ecosystems is more difficult, since there are no data on the economic value of fishing activities along the river.

Direct discharge of untreated wastewater into the Mahiao River will result in the following concentrations of pollutants:

Arsenic	13	ppm
Boron	140	ppm
Lithium	16.4	ppm
Mercury	.0005	ppm

Therefore, another environmental cost arises from the pollution of the delta, which may adversely affect marine fisheries in the area. The delta or mangrove area in Ormoc Bay plays an important role in sustaining productivity in the adjoining fishing grounds, because it serves as the feeding and spawning ground of several species of fish.

Fishing is a major industry in the Ormoc area. Table 5.3 shows data on the value of fishery output from the Ormoc Bay and Camotes Sea fishing grounds during the period 1974–81. Table 5.4 presents a summary on costs and returns of an average fishing operator in Leyte.

3. *Discharge into the Mahiao River with treatment.* A thermal pond will be constructed at a cost of ₱7 million and completed in one year. Operation and maintenance costs will be incurred for treatment of arsenic in addition to regular operation and maintenance costs of the pond itself. Arsenic removal will entail an annual cost of ₱4 million per producing well. There will be 15 producing wells providing steam for the 112.5-MW power plant.

There are no scientific studies of the interactive effects of boron and arsenic on rice yield; hence, there is no basis at this point to determine whether the effects on rice productivity will be less severe in the absence of arsenic.

Capital costs for a water purification system are estimated at ₱25 million, with annual operation and maintenance costs of ₱7.5 million.

The information on fishery productivity in Tables 5.3 and 5.4 will be used to estimate costs to the marine environment.

4. *Discharge into the Bao River without treatment.* A thermal pond will cost ₱7 million. In addition a pipeline, 6 to 7 kilometers long, will be constructed at a cost of ₱13 million over a two-year period. Operation and maintenance costs will be ₱6.2 million per year. Since the discharge site in the Bao River will be beyond the irrigation diversion, the Bao River Irrigation System area will not be affected by the waste fluids.

Table 5.3 Fishery Productivity in the Camotes Sea and Ormoc Bay

Year	Municipal fishing[a] Output (kg)	Value (₱m)[b]	Commercial fishing Output (kg)	Value (₱m)[b]
1974			303,490	2.1
1975			499,126	3.7
1976			566,020	4.7
1977	644,910	5.7	645,210	5.7
1978	2,674,397	27.4	1,994,139	20.4
1979	955,000	11.5	2,022,000	24.3
1980	2,451,000	32.4	531,750	7.0
1981			616,200	9.2

[a]Municipal fishing includes fishing done in vessels 3 tons gross and below.

[b]All values in current price.

Table 5.4   Summary on Costs and Returns Profile
of an Average Fishing Operator in Leyte, 1978

Item	₱
Gross return	6,914
Total cost, of which	4,918
Cash cost	2,923
Noncash cost	1,995
Net return	1,996

Source: Laopao and Latorre (1980).

A water purification system will be needed to service residents living along the lower reaches of the Bao River beyond the point of discharge. Construction will take two years at a cost of ₱15 million. Annual operation and maintenance costs are estimated at ₱4.5 million.

The information on fishery productivity in Tables 5.3 and 5.4 will also be used to estimate costs to the marine environment.

5.   *Discharge into the Bao River with treatment.* The same capital costs will be incurred as in alternative 4. However, operation and maintenance costs will be higher. The treatment cost for arsenic in the waste fluids is estimated at ₱4 million per producing well.

With the arsenic treatment, the cost for establishing a water purification system will be lower in this case than alternative 4. The capital cost is estimated at ₱7.5 million, although the time needed for construction remains the same. Operation and maintenance costs of ₱2 million per year are expected.

Environmental costs to the marine ecosystem will be estimated using information on marine productivity in Tables 5.3 and 5.4

6.   *Disposal at sea with an outfall at Lao Point.* This scheme will involve the construction of a 22-kilometer long pipeline over a period of two years at a cost of ₱45 million and an operation and maintenance cost of ₱41.8 million per year.

Disposal of wastewater at sea may affect productivity of coastal fishing as well as commercial fishing in the Ormoc Bay and Camotes Sea areas.

Concentration of arsenic at the outfall site will be 1.0 ppm while mercury levels will be 0.002 ppm.

7.   *Disposal at sea with an outfall at Biasong Point.* Under this alternative, a 32-kilometer pipeline will be constructed over a two-year period costing ₱65 million. Operation and maintenance costs are ₱60.8 million per year.

Marine fishing productivity may be affected. Concentrations of pollutants at the outfall site are 1.4 ppm of arsenic and 0.00235 ppm of mercury.

In estimating the effects of alternatives 6 and 7 on marine productivity, hydrology and dispersion patterns in Ormoc Bay and Camotes Sea should be taken into account.

The Economic Analysis

In order to maximize the return from the use of limited resources, only projects that are economically justifiable should be considered for implementation. That is, the values of incremental outputs of goods and services, including environmental services received from the project, must be at least equal to or greater than the values of incremental real resources used by the project. In the case of the Tongonan Geothermal Power Plant project, however, the decision has already been made to undertake the project. The relevant task is to implement the wastewater treatment part of the project at the lowest cost possible. Seven methods of waste disposal have been proposed. Only the disposal scheme with the lowest total cost (i.e., the most cost-effective method) should be adopted.

The required analysis here is to calculate the present value of the total cost under each alternative disposal scheme. To the extent possible, adverse effects on the environment must be quantified, valued, and counted as part of the cost. There are certain environmental effects that cannot be quantified, either because of lack of knowledge given the current level of technology or lack of complete information at the time the analysis is performed. However, even in the case when nonquantifiable effects exist, they cannot be ignored and left out in making the final decision. It is possible that under such a situation the decision is not to risk the unknown but potentially significant adverse consequences.

For possible loss of agricultural production, the data in Table 5.2 can be used to estimate the loss arising from harvesting only one nonirrigated crop (if no irrigation water is used). Possible ocean fishery losses can be estimated from the data in Tables 5.3 and 5.4. Table 5.4 can be used to calculate the net return (or profit) from fishing. This value in turn can be used to determine the net economic loss if ocean fishing is stopped. Based on data in Table 5.3, an assumption must be made about what is the *average* annual value of fishery products (based on one year? based on several years?); this value is then adjusted by the net return figure and the present value over the project life time calculated.

The assumption is made that market prices can be used to place values on agricultural and fishery production; that is, there are no major distortions requiring the use of shadow prices. This may or may not be correct for the Philippines but, in this example, no price adjustments are made. A similar assumption is made for imported capital equipment used in disposal systems and for petroleum products. Again, if major distortions exist (e.g., subsidies, foreign exchange controls, capital rationing), shadow prices would be needed.

The task is to calculate the present values of the direct costs and the associated environmental costs for each proposed wastewater disposal scheme. In the calculations use a discount rate of 15 percent (which is the rate used in benefit-cost evaluation of government-funded projects in the Philippines) and an estimated project life of 30 years for the geothermal power plant. Compare the costs, both measurable and nonquantifiable, for the alternative schemes and discuss the results. State your assumptions clearly. How do you account for nonquantifiable variables, and how can they best be brought into the analysis?

The Results

The results of the cost valuation for all seven alternatives of waste disposal are summarized in Table 5.5. The summary, in turn, is based on calculations of direct and indirect costs as shown in Appendix A5.1. Obviously from the analysis, not all relevant costs and benefits can be quantified and monetized. To the extent that certain environmental effects of a project can be evaluated, however, more options are available to decision makers. Excluding the values of environmental costs, alternative 4 under which waste fluids from the geothermal power plant are discharged to the Bao River without any treatment would have been chosen for its lowest direct cost. After the environmental effects are valued and added to the direct cost, the total direct and indirect measurable costs are obtained.

Table 5.5. Costs of Waste Disposal under Alternative Schemes (₱m)

Alternative	Direct cost	Environmental cost	Total measureable cost	Nonquantifiable
1. Reinjection	138.3	Unknown	138.3	Energy loss
2. Untreated Mahiao discharge	120.2	Rice 7.3 Fishery 56.3	183.8	Freshwater fishery, stock health, laundry, bathing use, human health, marine ecosystems
3. Treated Maniao discharge	359.3		359.3	Rice production; a lower loss on items in alternative 2 with the exception of marine ecosystems
4. Untreated Bao discharge	81.1	Fishery 56.3	137.4	Freshwater fishery, stock health, domestic use, human health, marine ecosystems
5. Treated Bao discharge	359.1		359.1	Less than alternative 4
6. Untreated Lao Point disposal	243.1	Unknown	243.1	Nonquantifiable but high
7. Untreated Biasong Point disposal	353.2	Unknown	353.2	Nonquantifiable but high

Alternatives 3, 5, 6, and 7 can be rejected as they are relatively more costly alternatives compared to alternatives 1, 2, and 4. The choice appears now to be among alternatives 1, 2, and 4. If the decision is based strictly on measurable costs, then alternative 4 is still the cheapest scheme. However, since alternatives 2 and 4 are expected to generate unknown, nonquantifiable effects, particularly on the marine ecosystem, the risk of losing the whole marine ecosystem is possible if alternative 2 or 4 is adopted. Since alternative 2, untreated discharge into the Mahiao River, has the potential for the same type of nonquantifiable negative effects as alternative 4 but is also relatively more expensive, it is rejected in comparison to alternative 4. In contrast, the known environmental effects from alternative 1 are the possible loss of energy (due to lower steam temperature) and the possible contamination of local groundwater supplies. Alternative 1, reinjection, is therefore adopted as the most desirable method although the total measurable costs are slightly higher for alternative 1 than for alternative 4.

Discussion

The main shortcomings in this case study are the limited data and associated uncertainties, which can lead to serious problems if the choice of reinjection proves to be more costly, especially environmentally, than other methods in the future. For example, chemical additives needed to keep the reinjection pipes from being clogged by the high level of dissolved solids may result in health hazards not now known. Also, during the longer periods of shutdown of the reinjection system, the standby disposal scheme would be used to dispose of chemically treated waste fluids into the river. Information is not provided, however, on the types and concentration levels of the chemical effluents that will eventually be carried along in the river. Data on the freshwater fishery were not available during the initial evaluation; this may also significantly affect the calculation of costs resulting from discharge of treated or untreated wastewater into the river. The calculated fish losses, both marine and fresh water, are only a *minimum* valuation of this resource. The possibility of a future expansion of the fishery or an increase in the relative price of fish has not been considered.

Another unanswered question is the extent to which adverse effects on the freshwater or ocean fishery would cause the dislocation of fishing families. If a fishery is destroyed and the families dependent on it have to move to seek new employment, this would be an additional quantifiable cost. This is a particularly important concern for options 2, 4, 6, and 7. Option 1, reinjection, should present no problem and the treated river discharge options (3 and 5) should eliminate much of the potential problem.

Since the decision was largely based on two types of quantifiable costs—direct costs and measurable environmental costs—it is important to consider how non-quantifiable environmental costs could be included more explicitly. For example, the implicit assumption is that these latter costs are not as large as the quantifiable ones. This may be true but care is needed to ensure that a major nonquantifiable cost is not overlooked.

Even with these caveats, however, this case study presents an example of how benefit-cost analysis can be used as an aid to project design. By clearly identifying the range of possible impacts of the alternative geothermal fluid disposal systems available, and by placing monetary values, where possible, on those impacts, a more informed and environmentally sensitive project design is possible.

Appendix A5.1: Calculations of Direct and Indirect Costs of Seven Waste Disposal Alternatives

Direct cost

1. *Reinjection*
   1. Construction (2 years)   Million ₱
      a. Reinjection wells   70
      b. Pipelines   20
      c. Standby systems $\underline{17}$
                                                           107
         Construction costs per year   =   107/2
                                                  =   53.50
   2. Operation and maintenance per year   10.4
      Cash flow:
Year	1	2	3 . . .	
Million ₱	53.5	53.5	10.4	30
				10.4

      Present value at 15% discount rate
      Year 1   = 53.5 × 0.8696 =   46.5
      Year 2   = 53.5 × 0.7561 =   40.4
      Year 3–30 = 10.4 × 4.9405 = $\underline{51.4}$
      Present value of total direct cost   138.3
2. *Discharge into the Mahiao River without treatment*
   1. Construction   Million ₱
      a. Thermal pond (1 year)   7
      b. Water supply system (2 years)   50
   2. Operation and maintenance per year
      a. Thermal pond   0.0433
      b. Water supply system   15.0
      Cash flow

Year	1	2	3 . . .	
Million ₱	25	25	15	30
		7	0.0433	15.0
Cost/year	25	32	15.0433	0.0433
				15.0433

Present value at 15% discount rate
Year 1   = 25   × 0.8696 = 21.74
Year 2   = 32   × 0.7561 = 24.20
Year 3–30 = 15.0433 × 4.9405 = 74.32
Present value of total direct cost   120.26

3. *Discharge into the Mahiao River with treatment*
    1. Construction   Million P
        a. Thermal pond (1 year)   7
        b. Water supply system (2 years)   25
    2. Operation and maintenance per year
        a. Thermal pond   0.0433
        b. Arsenic removal for 15 steam-producing wells
            (at P4 million each)   60
        c. Water supply system   7.5
        Cash flow

Year	1	2	3 . . .		30
Million P	12.5	12.5	0.0433		0.0433
		7	60		60
			7.5		7.5
Cost/year	12.5	19.5	67.5433		67.5433

        Present value at 15% discount rate
                    10.87   14.74   (------------ 333.7 -------------)
        Present value of total direct cost   10.87
                                                   14.74
                                                  333.70
                                                  359.31

4. *Discharge into the Bao River without treatment*
    1. Construction   Million P
        a. Thermal pond (1 year)   7
        b. Pipeline (2 years)   13
        c. Water supply system (2 years)   15
    2. Operation and maintenance per year
        a. Thermal pond   0.0433
        b. Pipeline   6.2
        c. Water supply system   4.5
        Cash flow

Year	1	2	3 . . .		30
Million P	6.5	6.5	0.0433		0.0433
	7.5	7.5	6.2		6.2
		7.0	4.5		4.5
Cost/year	14.0	21.0	10.7433		10.7433

Present value at 15% discount rate

Year 1 = 12.17

Year 2 = 15.88

Year 3–30 = 53.08

Present value of total direct cost   81.13

5. *Discharge into the Bao River with treatment*

1. Construction   Million ₱
   a. Thermal pond (1 year)   7
   b. Pipeline (2 years)   13
   c. Water supply system (2 years)   7.5
2. Operation and maintenance per year
   a. Thermal pond   0.0433
   b. Pipeline   6.2
   c. Water supply system   2.0
   d. Arsenic treatment at 15 steam-producing wells
      (at ₱4 million each)   60
   Cash flow

Year	1	2	3 . . .	30
Million ₱	6.5	6.5	6.2	6.2
	3.75	3.75	2.0	2.0
		7.0	0.0433	0.0433
			60.0	60.0
Cost/year	10.25	17.25	68.2433	68.2433
Present value	8.91	13.04	(----------- 337.16 -----------)	

Present value of total direct cost   359.11

6. *Disposal at sea with an outfall at Lao Point*

1. Construction   Million ₱
   a. Pipeline (2 years)   45
2. Operation and maintenance per year   41.8
   Cash flow

Year	1	2	3 . . .	30
Million ₱	22.5	22.5	41.8	41.8
Present value	19.57	17.01	(----------- 206.51 -----------)	

Present value of total direct cost   243.09

7. *Disposal at sea with an outfall at Biasong Point*

1. Construction   Million ₱
   a. Pipeline (2 years)   65
2. Operation and maintenance per year   60.8
   Cash flow

Year	1	2	3 . . .	30
Million ₱	32.5	32.5	60.8	60.8
Present value	28.26	24.57	(----------- 300.38 -----------)	

Present value of total direct cost   353.21

Indirect (environmental) cost
1. *Reinjection.* The environmental cost cannot be estimated although it involves (1) possible loss of potential energy, (2) treatment cost for dissolved solids in reinjection pipes, and (3) additional environmental problems from chemicals used to keep the reinjection pipe from being clogged.
2. *Discharge into the Mahiao River without treatment.* The environmental effects in this case include both the quantifiable and the nonquantifiable consequences, namely,
   a. Rice productivity: 4,000 hectares per season serviced by the Bao River Irrigation System
   b. River fishery: no data
   c. Stock health
   d. Laundry, bathing, and human health
   e. Marine ecosystems

Quantifiable effects:
a. Value of rice production loss
   Total rice area = 4,000 hectares
   Return/ha for irrigated rice
     (average 1975–78)   = 1,838 − 1,492 = ₱346
   Return/ha for nonirrigated
   rice   = 1,082 −   758 = ₱324
   Annual loss if irrigation water cannot be used due to heavy contamination   = 4,000 × 346 × 2 − 4,000 × 324
                               = 2,768,000 − 1,296,000
                               = 1.47 million ₱
   Present value of rice loss at 15% discount rate (yrs 3–30)
     1.47 × 4.9405   = 7.26 million ₱
b. Value of fishery product loss
   Assuming total loss of product currently obtained:
   From Table 5.4 on average costs and returns profile of a fishing operator in Leyte, the net return
                               = 6,914 − 4,918
                               = 1,996
                   or = 29% of gross return
   Total value of fishery product in the Camotes Sea and Ormoc Bay in 1980   = 32.4 + 7.0
                               = 39.4 million ₱
   Annual loss of fishery product = 39.4 × 0.29
                               = 11.4 million ₱
   Present value of fishery loss at 15% discount rate (yrs 3–30)
     11.4 × 4.9405   = 56.3 million ₱

Nonquantifiable effects:
River fishery, stock health, human health, loss of water use for laundry
and bathing, effects on marine ecosystems, plus possible family dislocation

3. *Discharge into the Mahiao River with treatment*
   Environmental effects:
   a. Rice productivity: unknown
   b. River fishery: no data
   c. Stock health, laundry, bathing, and human health: nonquantifiable
      but less than alternative 2.
   d. Marine ecosystems: unknown

4. *Discharge into the Bao River without treatment*
   Environmental effects:
   a. Rice production: not affected
   b. River fishery: no data
   c. Stock health, laundry, bathing, and human health: nonquantifiable
   d. Marine ecosystems: same estimate as in alternative 2

5. *Discharge into the Bao River with treatment*
   Same types of effect with unknown magnitude, as in alternative 3

6. *and 7.   Disposal at sea*
   Environmental effects: unknown effects on marine ecosystems

References

Hufschmidt, M. M., D. E. James, A. D. Meister, B. T. Bower, and J. A. Dixon. *Environment, Natural Systems, and Development: An Economic Valuation Guide.* Baltimore:
Johns Hopkins University Press, 1983.

Kingston, Reynolds, Thom, and Allardice Limited. Environmental Impact Report.
Auckland, N.Z., 1979.

Laopao, M. L., and E. M. Latorre. "Small-Scale Fishing in Leyte Province: A Socio-
Economic Survey." *Economic Research Report No. 8,* Bureau of Agricultural Economics, Philippines, 1980.

6
Valuation of Losses of Marine Product Resources Caused by Coastal Development of Tokyo Bay

Adapted by Maynard M. Hufschmidt and John A. Dixon from materials prepared by Yuzuru Hanayama and Ikuo Sano

Summary

This chapter seeks to evaluate the losses of marine product resources in Tokyo Bay associated with coastal development of the bay during the past decades. This study is not a complete benefit-cost analysis of the development or preservation of the bay. Such a complete study would have to examine the benefits of industrial development on the reclaimed lands. These developments include many heavy industries and transportation facilities and, in terms of their contribution to gross domestic product, employment, and exports, would have a very large value. The appropriate measure of their value at this location, of course, is the opportunity cost of not using Tokyo Bay for these facilities and siting them elsewhere.

The case study focuses on the valuation of marine production lost when fishermen sold their fishing rights to the government so that the land could be reclaimed. Two valuation techniques are examined and their results are compared. First, *changes in productivity* are used to estimate a value for the lost marine product resources from the areas developed. This approach uses data on changes in catch, average marine product prices, and gross profit margins to place a value on lost production. The second technique uses information on *compensation paid* to the fishermen's unions in exchange for their fishing rights to estimate the value of the lost resources. This approach is based on the willingness-to-accept compensation principle that can be used when the owners of a resource are asked to give up their rights to that resource.

In general, the issue of compensation addresses four questions: What to compensate for; how to compensate; when to compensate; and how much to compensate. In this case, fishermen were compensated for the economic value of their rights to access to fishery resources; their compensation was in a lump sum of money; time of compensation was at the time of transfer of fishing right; and amount of compensation was as shown in the data for the case study (Table 6.4). The case study is explicitly concerned with only this last question—the amount of compensation.

Background Information

Sometimes a natural resource such as a fishery becomes subject to personal property rights often authorized by statute. In such cases owners of the right should be compensated if the natural resource is destroyed. To evaluate the economic worth of the resource is equivalent to assessing the economic value of the right. Such rights may not necessarily be priced, for often the rights are authorized for local collectives such as groups of fishermen and are seldom exchanged in markets.

The original study analyzed two types of natural resource values of Tokyo Bay: marine product values and recreational values. In this study the fishermen had an "environmental right" to the marine resource authorized by statute while recreational rights were not recognized by law. In this abstract of the paper, only the marine product values are analyzed although the lost recreational use of Tokyo Bay also represented a welfare loss.

Natural Aspects of Tokyo Bay

Tokyo Bay, which is surrounded by highly industrialized and populated lands (Tokyo, Kanagawa, and Chiba prefectures [equivalent to a province]), now has the heaviest shipping traffic in Japan. Several decades ago Tokyo Bay was a very productive source of fish and seaweed and a popular recreational area.

Tokyo Bay has a surface area of 1,200 square kilometers (km^2), an average depth of 15 meters (m), and contains 18 cubic kilometers (km^3) of water. By tidal action the bay water is continuously mixed with fresh water from rivers. The beaches and the estuaries play a key role in the bay's ecological cycle. In the past the bay's high productivity was due to the rich nutrients and oxygen contained in the fresh water inflows and to the solar energy reaching the seabed through clear water. The wetland areas between high- and low-tide level and the contiguous areas of shallow water sustained thousands of marine species. The beaches also provided bathing opportunities for the public.

The recent urbanization of the surrounding land has resulted in polluted water; industrial development of the coastal area has destroyed the coastal ecosystem. During the past two decades 200 km^2 of new land were created by reclamation, that is, new land claimed from the sea by filling with earth, sand, and rubble (Figures 6.1 and 6.2). Many large industries are now established on the reclaimed lands including three iron works, thirteen oil refineries, six petrochemical plants (ethylene centers), twelve other chemical plants, ten shipyards, two automobile factories, and seventeen power stations.

At the same time the population of the bay catchment area has increased from 15 million to 27 million during the period 1955 to 1975. Water used by households and industries has increased from 23 billion to 77 billion cubic meters (m^3) a year during the same period. Since development of the sewerage system has lagged far

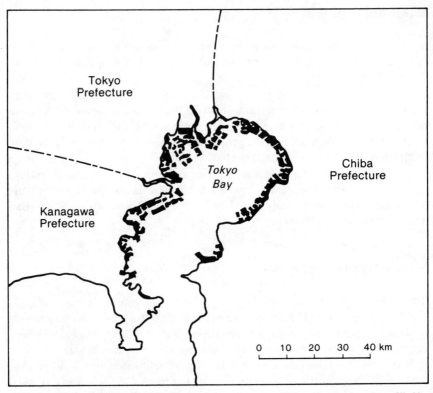

Figure 6.1 Reclamation in Tokyo Bay. The black areas are parts of Tokyo Bay that have been filled in and built upon.

behind water supply system development, wastewater disposal has contributed to the pollution of the bay.

Institutional Aspects of Bay Development

In Japan economic development has been closely involved with government policies, both at the national and at the prefectural (provincial) level. Given the special nature of Tokyo Bay—it is the industrial heartland of Japan and the location of the capital—these institutional aspects are important.

To understand the institutional aspects of industrial development in Tokyo Bay, at least three statutes must be mentioned. They are the Port Act (*Kowan-ho*), the Reclamation from Public Water Act (*Koyusuimen-Umetate-ho*) and the Fishery Act (*Gyogyo-ho*).

The *Port Act* is a law typical of those introduced by the occupation forces into Japan after the Second World War in order to democratize the feudalistic Japanese society. Before the war every port in Japan was managed directly by the central government. Neither the prefectural government nor the local communities could participate in developing port policy, although at that time the difference between the central and local government did not matter as much in decision making as today because all governors and mayors were appointed by the central government. Under the present Port Act either the governor or the mayor (of major cities limited by the act) is authorized to manage the port located in the prefecture or city. The act strongly recommends that local governments organize port authorities to

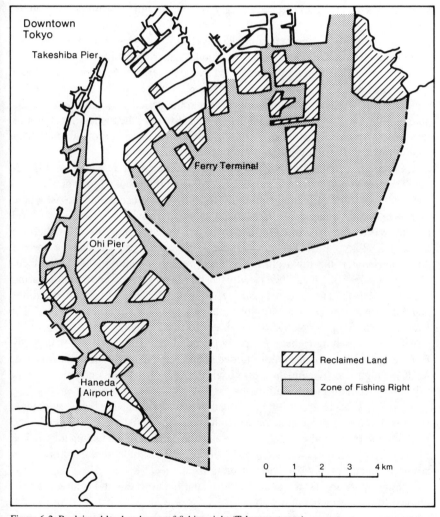

Figure 6.2 Reclaimed land and zone of fishing right (Tokyo port area).

manage the ports efficiently. However, in reality the central government retains strong influences over local governments. An amendment enacted in 1973 gave the central government the authority to select and control directly the important sea routes in any port area.

In contrast with port policy, the authority to issue licenses for reclamation from public waters was decentralized even before the Second World War. The governors are entitled to do it by the *Reclamation from Public Water Act*. They can do it independently, unless the site is within any port area defined by the port plan. In many cases, the governors establish a public corporation for reclamation and give it the licenses, although in some other cases private enterprises apply for licenses. In both cases the governors are required by the act to examine the proposed plan for reclaimed land.

The *Fishery Act* is another example of reforms introduced after the Second World War. Before the war a somewhat feudal pattern prevailed in which a few elite families had fishing rights authorized by the governors. In many cases, these families had boats and fishing gear and were responsible for the support of other families, who were required to work free for some period during the year for the elite families. To dissolve this feudalistic social structure, the Fishery Act requires fishermen to organize a fishermen's union and requires the governors to grant them fishing rights only if they succeed in organizing the union.

There are three categories of fishing rights: common, demarcated, and fixed-net. The *common fishing right* is the least regulated right, but a fishermen's union can claim this type of fishing right only for the water closest to the coast where members live. In many cases the wetland areas between high- and low-tide level are covered by this type of right, and these areas are generally used for shellfish farming in Tokyo Bay. The *demarcated fishing right* can be claimed for the contiguous water, but this right is regulated by season and type of fishing technology. In Tokyo Bay fishermen usually use this water for seaweed farming during the winter season. The *fixed-net fishing right* is rather special. Some elite families had the right to semipermanently install large fishing nets in order to gather fish; later, some of the fishermen's unions inherited these rights.

All of these fishing rights are strictly bounded and defined on the map. Only members of the fishermen's union entitled to the right can fish in the bounded zone, while the high seas (outside the authorized zone) are open to anyone who wants to fish, using technology allowed by the Fishery Act.

If anyone wants to apply for a reclamation license for an area that may include some part of the bounded zone on which fishing rights exist, he is required by the Reclamation from Public Water Act to obtain the consent of the fishing union. The Fishery Act also requires a resolution by the general assembly of the fishing union before forfeiture of any part of the fishing right.

Fishing rights are not the same as individual land ownership because they are granted to a fishermen's union collectively. Nevertheless, any fisherman can demand assurance of adequate compensation for a fishing right in the general assembly of the fishermen's union before the right is abandoned. However, local people other than members of a fishermen's union do not have any statutory basis for claiming an interest in the good environment which the sea gives them.

Moreover, in the acts cited above, local governments are frequently not allowed to participate in the decision-making process. This is particularly true when a governor wants to promote industrial development and reclamation. In this case it is very difficult, if not impossible, for local governments to participate in the decision-making process through the legal process offered by the various statutes.

In Chiba Prefecture, for example, the governor was very eager to attract heavy industry since Chiba was less developed than the two neighboring prefectures—Tokyo and Kanagawa. In 1961 the governor of Chiba Prefecture announced a very ambitious "industrialization plan" to promote development. This plan included several important policies: (1) The governor promoted land reclamation all along its seashore in Tokyo Bay to provide cheap land to heavy industries. (2) The governor established a public corporation for implementation of this plan, and reclamation licenses were exclusively given to this corporation. (3) This corporation compensated the fishermen's union.

The public corporation set up to implement the plan had to finance itself without government funds. As a result the corporation "sold the sea" to the industries, although the sea itself was not a commodity. As the first step the public corporation had to pay compensation for fishing rights in order to obtain the consent of the fishermen's union, because this is required by the Reclamation from Public Water Act. However, having no money for this, the public corporation had to ask the industries that it hoped to attract to provide the funds.

Because of pressure from the prefectural and central governments to promote industrial development, land reclamation proceeded with little regard for possible environmental effects other than lost fishing rights. Some local residents who were concerned about these other environmental effects tried to sue for an injunction to stop the reclamation, but the court rejected it, judging that the plaintiff was not eligible to sue because the reclamation did not impinge upon the plaintiff's right that was protected by law.

Environmental Dimensions

The main marine products of Tokyo Bay were seaweed and shellfish caught within the authorized zone; other fish products were also important but were mainly caught in high water (outside the authorized zone). When reclamation projects were proposed, many fishermen preferred to abandon their fishing rights totally. Even if some parts of the previously authorized zone were saved from reclamation, and high water areas were still open to their fishery, once the heart of the productive zone (the shallow water) was lost, it would be very difficult to maintain an economic fishery with the small amount of products from the remaining authorized zone or high water areas. During these years a number of fishermen's unions abandoned their fishing rights in the bay in exchange for pecuniary compensation. Between 1953 and 1973 the number of fishermen in Tokyo Bay declined from 15 thousand to 6 thousand.

This means that the principal cause of the decline of fishery output was the reclamation of wetland areas and contiguous shallow water along the shore, while the fishery catch in deep water was still not greatly affected by water pollution. Although progress in fishery technology has somewhat compensated for the loss of deep-water productivity due to polluted water, as industrial activity increases and population in the region grows, water pollution in Tokyo Bay is expected to increase and lead to further losses in marine production.

The Approach Used

This case study uses two approaches to place a value on the lost fishery resource. The first is based on the value of lost fish production; the second is based on the compensation paid to fishermen for their fishing rights.

Undoubtedly, wetland and shallow water reclamation has destroyed the important fisheries that previously existed in those areas. The total fishery catch in the bay declined from 155 thousand tons in 1956 to 50 thousand tons in 1972 based on statistics from the Ministry of Agriculture, Forestry and Fishery. The catch of seaweed, shrimp, and crab declined by 95 percent, and clams by 66 percent, although the catch of fish did not decline at all (Table 6.1).

Nevertheless, the value of the output in current prices increased from 8 billion yen in 1956 to 29 billion yen in 1977 because of price inflation. Using constant 1979 prices, however, the total value of the catch declined from 49 billion yen in 1960 to 27 billion yen in 1977.

Obviously, the productivity of the bay declined, but some portion of the lost productivity was also compensated for by payments made to the fishermen. Compensation was done from place to place (when fishermen's unions abandoned their fishing rights) by capitalizing the average annual return to fishermen (gross output value minus capital cost) of the past few years, using an interest rate of 8 percent and adding payments for depreciated value of unneeded capital equipment (e.g., boats, gear).

Each of the valuation methods used, lost productivity and compensation, requires making major assumptions as to the nature of the resource, the behavior of marine product markets, and capital and labor costs. Both methods are discussed in Chapter 6 of the *Guide*.

The theory behind the first approach is that the economic value of the lost production per year is the decline in physical productivity (in tons per year) multiplied by the net profit per unit caught (tons), which in turn is obtained by subtracting the capital and operating costs of production from the market price. A

Table 6.1   Marine Product Output, Tokyo Bay, 1956-77, by Type of
Product (10^3 tons)

	Type of marine product				
Year	Shrimp and crab	Seaweed	Fish	Clam	Total
1956	2	19	5	129	155
1957	3	25	6	116	150
1958	3	19	7	116	145
1959	4	24	8	109	145
1960	2	32	9	159	202
1961	2	33	9	150	194
1962	4	20	8	140	172
1963	1	10	7	95	113
1964	1	6	7	90	104
1965	1	3	7	84	95
1966	1	5	6	88	100
1967	1	5	7	60	73
1968	1	3	11	67	82
1969	1	0	8	71	80
1970	0	0	6	90	96
1971	0	0	6	75	81
1972	0	1	5	44	50
1973					53[a]
1974					55[a]
1975					44[a]
1976					53[a]
1977					97[a]

Source: Unpublished data provided by the Ministry of Agriculture, Forestry
and Fishery, Japan.

[a]Computed from data in this table and Table 6.2, as follows:

Total output
   in X year = Value of output in X year/price (1979 prices) in X year

where price
   in X year = Price in 1972 (1979 prices) x

         price index of X year/price index of 1972

where price
   in 1972   = Value in 1972 (1979 prices)/total output in 1972

   Total output is in 10^3 tons.

   Value of output is in 10^9 yen.

major issue is how to treat the value of fishermen's labor—at market prices or at a
shadow rate, which may be somewhat lower.

   The theory behind the compensation method is that if bargaining power is
roughly equal between the fishermen and the developers, the compensation price
will be reasonably related to the perceived economic value of the resource to the
fishermen. If proper account is taken of capital costs (including compensation for

unused capital facilities), the compensation figure should reflect the value of the resource per se, net of operating costs and the value of the fishermen's labor.

In reality both approaches are closely related. They both capitalize annual benefits that are lost because of development of Tokyo Bay. The main difference is that the lost productivity approach calculates a value based on physical yield changes, while the compensation-approach is the result of bargaining (the compensation demanded may well be larger than the value of lost fish catch). This larger value is in part due to other nonquantifiable environmental losses such as aesthetic factors and loss of a life-style.

The Data

Productivity Data

Table 6.1 shows the marine product output in Tokyo Bay for the years 1956–72 by type of product and total physical production. These were the years when fishery rights were bought out, and the long-term decline in output reflects the retirement of fishery rights. Although output data were not available for the years 1973–77, total output for those years was estimated by using available data on value of total output and adjusting for price changes, as shown in Table 6.1.

Table 6.2 shows the value of the marine product output both in current prices and in 1979 prices. Because of increases in marine product prices over the period, the decline in physical productivity as shown in Table 6.1 is not reflected fully in the value of output as measured in current prices. When values are converted to 1979 prices, however, the long-term decline in value becomes evident. The marine product price index is for total product output. Ideally, one would like separate price indices for each major type of marine product (shrimp, crab, seaweed, fish, clam). In the absence of such indices, it was necessary to use the price index for total product output. The marine product price index contains both changes in the general consumer price index and changes in the prices of marine products relative to other consumer products. Because of these relative price increases for marine products, the long-term decline in physical productivity is not fully reflected in long-term decline in value of output.

The prices of marine products may have been lower if the production from Tokyo Bay had not decreased and thereby supplies had been more plentiful. Data are not available here to determine if this is the case, and the assumption is made that alternative additional supplies came forth from other areas at no additional cost to replace the lost Tokyo Bay production; that is, there was no significant shift in the supply curve. The relative price increases for marine products, therefore, reflect changes in demand, not supply, patterns.

From Tables 6.1 and 6.2, it is possible to make estimates of the decline in average annual output of marine products over the 1956–72 period and the average

Table 6.2   Value of Marine Product Output, Tokyo Bay, 1956-77, from Current and 1979 Prices

Year	Total value of output (10^9 yen)		Price index, marine product output (1979 = 100) (3)
	Current prices (1)	1979 prices (2)	
1956	8	33	24
1957	9	39	23
1958	6	24	25
1959	8	36	22
1960	11	50	22
1961	12	55	22
1962	9	38	24
1963	10	33	30
1964	7	30	23
1965	10	22	45
1966	13	23	56
1967	14	23	60
1968	11	17	65
1969	15	26	58
1970	12	23	52
1971	12	23	52
1972	15	27	55
1973	15	28	54
1974	16	28	57
1975	15	24	63
1976	18	24	75
1977	29	27	107

annual decline by the end of the period. Also from Tables 6.1 and 6.2, unit market values of the annual outputs (in current and 1979 prices) can be derived.

Table 6.3 shows the gross profit to fishermen in Tokyo Bay for the years 1956–77 in both current and 1979 prices using the marine product price index from Table 6.2. The table also shows the percentage of the value of output (in 1979 prices), which is gross profit. Gross profit is defined as market value less the amortized value of capital costs. Note that costs of fishermen's labor and other operating costs have *not* been deducted from market prices to obtain gross profit. The zero price for fishermen's labor is based on the assumption that, because of tradition and other factors, fishermen were not willing to work at any other occupation or in any other location; hence, their opportunity cost was effectively zero. This is a very strong (and probably unrealistic) assumption, but data on labor and operating costs are not available.

If labor costs are given a shadow price of zero, and other operating costs are neglected, the gross profit data provide a reasonable estimate of the resource value. Hence, declines in gross profit over the 1956–72 period can be taken as declines in resource value. Also, future value of output losses can be computed by using gross profit data.

Table 6.3 Gross Profit to Fishermen from Marine Products, Tokyo Bay, 1956-77, from Current and 1979 Prices

| Year | Gross profit (10^9 yen) | | Percent of output value[a] (1979 prices) (3) |
	Current prices (1)	1979 prices (2)	
1956	5	21	64
1957	6	26	67
1958	5	20	83
1959	6	27	75
1960	8	36	72
1961	10	45	82
1962	6	25	66
1963	7	23	70
1964	5	22	73
1965	7	16	73
1966	10	18	78
1967	11	18	78
1968	9	14	82
1969	11	19	73
1970	9	17	74
1971	9	17	74
1972	11	20	74
1973	11	20	71
1974	12	21	75
1975	11	17	71
1976	13	17	71
1977	18	17	63

[a]Column 2 divided by column 2 from Table 6.2.

Note: Gross profit equals value of marine product output less capital costs. Operating costs, including fishermen's labor costs, are not included.

Table 6.4 Breakdown of Compensation Payments in Current Prices (10^9 yen)

Year	Total payment (1)	Payment for capital facilities (2)
1956	4.0	1.0
1958	5.0	1.9
1960	25.0	8.5
1961	70.0	26.0
1962	10.0	4.0
1963	15.0	3.7
1964	10.0	4.2
1966	13.0	6.0
1967	14.0	6.5
1968	15.0	6.9
1969	150.0	70.2
1970	20.0	7.0
1971	22.0	9.0
1972	35.0	14.4
Total	408.0	169.3

Note: Fictitious but realistic data.

Compensation Data

Beginning in 1956, fishermen were compensated for their lost fishing rights. Table 6.4 shows data on compensation paid by years 1956–72. For completeness, part of the data is fabricated. Payments for the fishery resource were derived in the compensation process by bargaining between fishermen unions and developers. In part the value was determined by estimating the average annual gross profit (value of gross output minus capital costs) over the preceding few years and capitalizing that value at an interest rate of 8 percent.

The Economic Analysis

The problem is to estimate the economic value of the marine product resources destroyed by development in Tokyo Bay during the 1963–77 period. The discount rate is 8 percent.

Two different approaches are used to solve this problem.

Value of Lost Fishery Production

Estimate the value of lost fishery production based on the data in Tables 6.1, 6.2, and 6.3. Data are available from 1956 to 1977. Assume that major fishery-damaging development in Tokyo Bay did not begin until 1963; therefore, 1956–62 represents the predevelopment period and 1963 thereafter is the postdevelopment period.

Several steps are required. Calculate average physical production per year for the 1956–62 period (Table 6.1). This is the predevelopment "expected" yield. Then calculate the marine product output loss for 1963 to 1977. To value these losses calculate the unit value (10^6 yen) per 10^3 ton of marine products for 1963 to 1977 using 1979 prices (Tables 6.1 and 6.2). As mentioned earlier, to determine the gross profit per unit catch, capital and operating costs have to be subtracted. Table 6.3 presents data on gross profit (net of capital and operating costs) for 1956 to 1977. When compared to gross catch value (Table 6.2), the ratio of gross profit to production value is obtained (Table 6.3, column 3). This in turn is used in valuing the annual economic loss from decreased marine production.

After making assumptions about future market prices for marine products, estimate the future annual economic value of lost productivity. Calculate the capitalized value of this loss.

Compensation Paid to Fishermen

Another way to value the lost fishery resource is to examine the amount of compensation paid to fishermen to give up their fishing rights. This compensation includes payments to fishermen for the capitalized unused value of their boats, gear, and other equipment, as well as the capitalized (present) value of the fishing rights. Table 6.4 presents data on total payments and payments for unused capital facilities. The residual compensation, in Table 6.4 found by subtracting column 2 from column 1, would represent the capitalized (present) value of the fishery resource in current prices. Convert these data to 1979 prices, and calculate both a capitalized (present) value and annual value of fishery productivity.

Comparison of the Two Approaches

Compare the results of the two approaches and discuss why the results vary.

The Results

Approach 1, Based on Physical Output Declines

From data in Table 6.1:
1. Compute total average annual output, 1956–62 inclusive.

	10^3 tons
1956	155
1957	150
1958	145
1959	145
1960	202
1961	194
1962	172
Total	$1{,}163 \div 7 = 166 \times 10^3$ tons

2. Assume this (166×10^3 tons) to be the annual average output for years 1963–77 inclusive, assuming *no retirement of fishing rights*.

3. Marine product output losses from retirement of fishery rights for 1963–77 inclusive are average annual output 1956–62 (166×10^3 tons), less actual output for the years indicated. From data in Table 6.1:

Year	Loss
1963	166 − 113 = 53
1964	166 − 104 = 62
1965	166 − 95 = 71
1966	166 − 100 = 66
1967	166 − 73 = 93
1968	166 − 82 = 84
1969	166 − 80 = 86
1970	166 − 96 = 70
1971	166 − 81 = 85
1972	166 − 50 = 116
1973	166 − 52 = 114

Year	Loss
1974	166 − 55 = 111
1975	166 − 44 = 122
1976	166 − 53 = 113
1977	166 − 97 = 69

4. From value of marine product output data (Table 6.2) and total marine product output data (Table 6.1), compute the unit value per 10^3 ton for each year, 1963–77. Use 1979 price data.

Year	Output (10^3 tons)	Value of output (10^9 yen)	Unit value (10^6 yen/10^3 ton)
1963	113	33	292
1964	104	30	288
1965	95	22	232
1966	100	23	230
1967	73	23	315
1968	82	17	207
1969	80	26	325
1970	96	23	240
1971	81	23	284
1972	50	27	540
1973	52	28	538
1974	55	28	509
1975	44	24	545
1976	53	24	453
1977	97	27	278

5. To obtain value of annual losses, apply the unit value per 10^3 ton figures for years 1963–77 to the annual tonnage losses for those years.

Year	Unit value (10^6 yen/10^3 ton)		Production losses (10^3 tons)		Value of production losses 1979 prices (10^9 yen)		Ratio of gross profit to production value	Loss of resource value (10^9 yen)
1963	292	×	53	=	15.4	×	.70	10.8
1964	288	×	62	=	17.9	×	.73	13.1
1965	232	×	71	=	16.5	×	.73	12.0
1966	230	×	66	=	15.2	×	.78	11.9
1967	315	×	93	=	29.3	×	.78	22.9
1968	207	×	84	=	17.4	×	.82	14.3
1969	325	×	86	=	28.0	×	.73	20.4
1970	240	×	70	=	16.8	×	.74	12.4
1971	284	×	85	=	24.1	×	.74	17.8
1972	540	×	116	=	62.6	×	.74	46.3
1973	538	×	114	=	61.3	×	.71	43.5
1974	509	×	111	=	56.5	×	.75	42.4
1975	545	×	122	=	66.5	×	.71	47.2
1976	453	×	113	=	51.2	×	.71	36.4
1977	278	×	69	=	19.2	×	.63	12.1

6. Based on the preceding data (item 5), the average annual production loss for the 1972–77 period can be calculated:

Year	Annual value of resource loss (10^9 yen)
1972	46.3
1973	43.5
1974	42.4
1975	47.2
1976	36.4
1977	12.1
	227.9
Annual Average	38.0 × 10^9 yen

If this annual production loss is capitalized at 8 percent, the present value in perpetuity of this lost resource is 475×10^9 yen.

Approach 2, Using Compensation Payments

1. From raw data on compensation payments made, years 1956–72, subtract the portion of payments made for capital facilities to obtain payments made for the fishery resource.
2. Convert payments for the fishery resource from current prices to 1979 prices, using the price index data given (see column 3, Table 6.2). This result is given in Table 6.5.
3. The third column in Table 6.5 represents the yearly compensation paid for fishery rights surrendered in each year from 1956 to 1972. The total value, 650.4×10^9 yen, represents the capitalized value of these rights. Using an 8 percent discount rate, the annual productivity value of compensation payments is $650 \times .08 = 52 \times 10^9$ yen.

Comparison of the Two Approaches

The results of the two approaches can be compared as follows:

	Capitalized value (10^9 yen)	Annual value (10^9 yen)
Physical output declines	475	38
Compensation payments	650	52

The difference between the two approaches is substantial. Although compensation payments may overstate the value of lost physical marine production, since the fishermen owned the property rights to the fishery, the willingness-to-accept com-

Table 6.5   Conversion of Payment for Fishery Resources from Current
and 1979 Prices

Year	Payment for fishery resources in current prices (10^9 yen) (1)	Price index (1979 = 100) (2)	Payment in 1979 prices (10^9 yen) (3)
1956	3.0	.24	12.5
1958	3.1	.25	12.4
1960	16.5	.22	75.0
1961	44.0	.22	200.0
1962	6.0	.24	25.0
1963	11.3	.30	37.7
1964	5.8	.23	25.2
1966	7.0	.56	12.5
1967	7.5	.60	12.5
1968	8.1	.65	12.5
1969	79.8	.58	137.6
1970	13.0	.52	25.0
1971	13.0	.52	25.0
1972	20.6	.55	37.5
Total	238.7		650.4

pensation measure would appear to be the correct one. The higher compensation-based payments may in part also reflect an attempt to pay for other intangible values lost by the fishermen, such as "traditional way of life" or the sea experience. The value of the reclaimed land for new industrial development is so large that local governments are willing to pay higher fishing rights payments than justified by lost fishery production alone in order to obtain the land.

Discussion

This case, fishery production in Tokyo Bay, has presented an interesting example of how two different approaches can be used to value a given natural resource. The two approaches produce different results, but the results are within 25 percent of each other. Since both the lost fish production approach and the compensation approach rely in part on estimated fishery production, this is not surprising.

Compensation payments were made over a period of years (1956 to 1972), frequently before the true extent of fishery production declines became known. As such, they represent a measure of *willingness-to-accept compensation* on the fishermen's behalf for their lost fishing rights. Because of the fishermen's ownership of the resource property right, such a measure yielded a higher value than would a *willingness-to-pay* measure. In the Tokyo Bay case an example of the latter is how much the fishermen would be willing to pay to retain their fishing rights, an amount indicated by the value of lost production (Approach 1).

Future prices for marine products are difficult to determine. We have approximated them by looking at the recent past. If marine product prices rose rapidly relative to other prices in the future, the value of the lost resource would be greater than calculated. Still, the value of industrial production from reclaimed lands is so large that, on a straight economic benefit-and-cost calculation, fishery production will always lose to industrial development in Tokyo Bay. If society determines that such tidal and inshore areas should be preserved, it should do so for social or environmental reasons and not on the basis of a strict economic analysis.

Another approach to the problem of trading off marine versus industrial uses of the bay would be to examine if there may not be *other* locations, site configurations, or specific site designs for industry, thereby preserving parts or all of the bay and the fishery. These would preserve some or all of the bay's value as an aquatic resource for fishing, recreation, or environmental uses. These economic opportunity costs of preservation are probably very large in this case, but sufficient data are not available to estimate them in this chapter.

Labor costs have not really been considered in this case study. In earlier calculations, not reported here, the use of even a modest opportunity cost (shadow wage) for fishermen's time produced a zero net value. And yet, the fishermen's unions were successful in negotiating compensation payments larger than those estimated based solely on foregone catch, not even including any labor costs. This may be consistent with the fact that the fishermen were "unwilling sellers" and as such demanded a higher-than-market value to give up their occupation.

An alternative approach to valuing the lost marine resource has also been suggested. This approach uses the change in gross profits from fishing in Tokyo Bay over the same time period. Using the data in Table 6.3, the average level of gross profit (in 1979 prices) for the 1956–62 period can be calculated. This value is 28.6×10^9 yen per year (200 ÷ 7). If the gross profit for each year, 1963–77, is then subtracted from this average amount, the annual reduction in gross profit is obtained; that is, a series is calculated as follows:

1963	$28.6 - 23 = 5.6 \times 10^9$ yen
1964	$28.6 - 22 = 6.6$
1965	$28.6 - 16 = 12.6$
:	
1970	$28.6 - 17 = 11.6$
:	
1975	$28.6 - 17 = 11.6$
1976	$28.6 - 17 = 11.6$
1977	$28.6 - 17 = 11.6$

This reduction in gross profits is used as a proxy for the value of the lost marine resource.

If these reductions in gross profit are averaged, the average annual reduction is

6.96×10^9 yen, or, capitalized at 8 percent, 87×10^9 yen. This value is considerably less than the capitalized values calculated earlier (475 to 650×10^9 yen). If the loss of production approach and the gross profit approach are considered, the same value for the lost resource would be obtained under certain specific conditions. More precisely, the lost production approach relies on the following relationship:

$$\Delta r = m_1 p_1 (q_0 - q_1) \tag{6-1}$$

$$= m_1 p_1 q_0 - m_1 p_1 q_1$$

$$= m_1 p_1 q_0 - r_1$$

where r = rent or profit
       m_1 = profit ratio in years 1963–77
       p_1 = post-1962 average price (yen/ton)
       q_0 = pre-1963 annual output (tons)
       q_1 = post-1962 annual output (tons)

The gross profit approach is more simple:

$$\Delta r = r_0 - r_1 \tag{6-2}$$

Thus the two approaches will yield the same answer only if $r_0 = m_1 p_1 q_0$; that is, the pre-1963 output can be sold at later year prices and at the later year profit margins. If this condition is not met, the two estimates of the lost marine resource will vary. In fact, the results calculated earlier showed that the lost production approach yielded a considerably greater value for the lost resource (475×10^9 yen) than the gross profit approach (87×10^9 yen). When the data are examined, we see that whereas the average pre-1963 profit ratio, m_0, is about the same as m_1 (72.7 percent versus 73.3 percent), the pre-1963 average price, p_0, is considerably less than p_1. That is, the average physical loss is valued much higher using later year prices. This helps explain the divergence in estimates of the value of the lost marine resource.

This discussion illustrates how reasonable assumptions can lead to quite different results, even when the same data are used. In reality, additional information is required to arrive at a more precise valuation. Data are not available on the price of the various *components* of the marine product output (see Table 6.1) and hence an average price per ton of output is computed. Although it is reasonable to assume that the price of a ton of fish is *not* the same as a ton of clams or seaweed or shrimp, it is not possible to determine these separate prices. What is really desired is a way to place a value on the marine products from the preempted areas near the shore. This is the true resource cost of development. In Tokyo Bay, these lost marine products are largely shrimp and crabs, seaweed, and clams (see Table 6.1). Therefore what should be valued are the quantities of these products (i) "lost" by development of shallow coastal areas (q_{0i}); post-1962 prices should be used, as well as post-1962 profit margins for the *type of fishery lost*. This calculation was not possible here since the $p_{1i}s$ for the individual marine products (i) are not available in this case study; neither are the m_{1i}, the profit margins for the lost shrimp and crab, seaweed, or clam fishery (i).

7
Evaluation of Lumpinee Public Park in Bangkok, Thailand

Adapted by Somluckrat Grandstaff and John A. Dixon from
materials prepared by Siriwut Eutrirak and Somluckrat Grandstaff

Summary

Sometimes an environmental resource, such as a public park, provides many
benefits to its users but, because no admission fee is charged, no direct expression
of its value is seen. This does not mean that the environmental resource is without
value or that its loss would not impose a welfare loss on society. Lumpinee Park in
Bangkok is such a resource, and this case study examines several techniques that
can be used to place a monetary value on the benefits received by park users and
other individuals.

Two approaches are presented here. First, the *travel-cost approach* uses information on the time and monetary expenses incurred by park visitors to travel to and
from the park to estimate a demand curve for park use. This information in turn is
used to calculate the consumer's surplus enjoyed by park users. A second approach
relies on *hypothetical valuation;* that is, current and potential park users are
interviewed about their willingness to pay for maintaining access to the park.
These techniques are discussed in Chapter 6 of the *Guide* (pp. 216–46).

The results from these two approaches provide information about benefits from
both park use and the existence of the park (for users and potential users). This case
study is not a benefit-cost analysis per se since it focuses only on the benefit side.
However, this information could be used if a proposal were made to develop the
park for some other use. In this event, the benefits of both park use and its
existence would be lost and would thus become a cost—the opportunity cost of
using the park land for development. Conversely, the opportunity cost of not
developing the park for some other use is the value of potential development
benefits foregone (taking into consideration the location of alternative sites for
development). The valuation techniques presented here are commonly used to
value open-access recreational and other environmental resources.

Background Information

Lumpinee is a public park situated in the heart of Bangkok, the capital of Thailand. Over time, increasing demand for space in the city has driven up the price of land and thus raised the opportunity cost of maintaining Lumpinee as a park. Undoubtedly, however, the recreational value of the park has also increased due to the increasing demands for open spaces and recreational amenities. Several attempts were made in the past to put the park into commercial use. Such attempts have been successfully resisted on grounds such as the beauty and the historical values of Lumpinee Park. Inevitably demand to put the park into other uses will persist and unless its recreational and amenity values can be shown to be greater than its commercial value from other activities, it will be increasingly difficult to maintain the park in its present form of land use.

This study evaluates the recreational value of the park. The contribution of this study in economic analysis of natural resources can be viewed at two levels. In a narrow sense, the outcome will provide a base value for the park from the viewpoint of people who use it for recreational purposes (user value) and a value from society's point of view (social value). This will allow comparison with values from other proposed commercial uses of the park. In a broader sense, this methodology for evaluating an extra-market good (one where a nominal or zero charge is made for its use) may be applied in the valuation of other goods with similar characteristics such as national parks or other sites with recreational, historical, or cultural significance.

Environmental Dimensions

Since Lumpinee is an urban park, its value lies primarily in its recreational use. To a lesser extent, it also contributes positively to air quality, aesthetic value, and human health. With increasing population and building densities in the city, however, such environmental values will become relatively more significant with the increase in the relative scarcity of such environmental services.

The Issue and Technique Used

Valuation of any commodity sold through the market is straightforward—usually a multiplication of quantity transacted and its price if the market is not distorted. When market distortions exist, certain adjustments may be necessary to estimate a "shadow price" reflecting the true value of such a commodity.

In the case of a public park where admission is free of charge, the valuation exercise becomes complicated. Indirect methods of measuring the amount (price) visitors are willing to pay for access to the park have to be employed. One valuation technique adopted for this study is the "travel-cost approach." This approach is discussed in Chapter 6 of the *Guide*. The basic assumption of this approach is that the cost in money and time spent traveling to a free, or nominally priced, recreational site is a reflection of people's willingness to "pay" for the site. For nearby residents the travel cost is low, and they will demand more of the good—the use of the site. For more distant residents the travel cost is high, and they demand less of the good. This information is used to derive a demand curve for the site. This technique also assumes that visitors will react to changes in travel cost incurred to visit a recreational site in the same manner that they would react to changes in admission fees they would otherwise have to pay.

To measure the value of Lumpinee Park, the following activities were carried out:

1. Two surveys were conducted to obtain information needed for the valuation.
2. A demand function for the service of the park was estimated.
3. The value of consumer's surplus associated with the demand curve was computed to represent the value of the park in the year of the study.

The major difference between this study and other travel-cost studies carried out in developed countries lies in the nature of the park. Lumpinee is an urban park and was used for short visits; most of the other studies were done for national parks where trips usually involved more travel and visitors spent one or more days at the park. For these studies the travel cost, which accounted for quite a major portion of the total cost of the trip, was thus shown to significantly determine the demand for visits. When a park is situated in the city, actual outlays necessary to travel to the park become less important a determinant than the cost visitors pay in terms of the time it takes them to get to their destination and return. However, the result of the analysis still confirmed an inverse relationship between the travel cost and the number of visits. A user demand function for the visit was thus derived and the value of the park calculated.

Theoretical Framework

On the basis of willingness to pay, two methods were used in estimating the value of Lumpinee Park: the travel-cost approach and the hypothetical valuation approach.

Travel-Cost Approach

The basic model used under this approach depicts the rate of visits per 1,000 population as a function of factors such as the travel cost, the time spent in traveling, substitute sites, and average income. This relationship can be summarized as

$$V_i^0 = f(C_i, T_i, A_i, S_i, Y_i) \tag{7-1}$$

where V_i^0 = visitation rate/1,000 at zero admission fee
           C_i = round trip travel cost between zone i and the park
           T_i = total time for the round trip
           A_i = taste
           S_i = substitute sites available to people in zone i
           Y_i = average income per person in zone i
            i = zones around the park

When admission fees become positive, the model can be modified to include admission fees as one of the determinants of the visitation rate. Equation (7-1) thus becomes

$$V_i^x = f(C_i + x, T_i, A_i, S_i, Y_i) \tag{7-2}$$

where x stands for admission fees. By varying x, $\overline{V}_i^x$, which is the total number of visits by residents in each zone, i, can be found. Each $\overline{V}_i^x$ associated with a particular admission fee of x represents a point on a demand curve for visits to the park from a particular zone. The visitation rate is thus a function of the admission fee x: $\overline{V}^x = g(x)$. If the visitation rates are multiplied by the population in the zone, a demand curve is defined.

The area under this demand curve represents the gross value of consumer's surplus and thus the gross value of the recreational site for one year. This value will be treated, in this study, as the average annual benefit from the park, which can be converted into the present value (PV) of these benefits by use of the capitalization formula

$$PV = \frac{W}{d} \tag{7-3}$$

where d is the discount rate and where W is the integral of the demand curve. Capitalization is a simple way to express the present value of a future stream of benefits. Since the park's recreational benefits can occur indefinitely, the capitalization formula calculates the value of these benefits using a given discount rate.

Given the future increase in population and increasing scarcity of open land, the value of W for all future years may be higher than that for the present year. The present value calculated from the annual benefit for 1980 can thus be treated as the minimum expected present value (base value) of the park.

The model as defined in equations (7-1) and (7-2), however, is subject to the problem of multicollinearity between the travel cost and the time spent in traveling; a longer trip implies greater travel costs. The time variable was thus converted into a monetary value (in terms of income foregone during the trip "on the road") and added to the cost of traveling. Furthermore, the availability of substitute sites was incorporated as a variable. This variable, STC_i, is in the form of travel cost plus time cost to visit alternative recreational sites. Educational level, ethnic background, and religion were used as proxies for taste. Nevertheless, since these factors did not vary significantly between the various origin zones within the limited study area, they were dropped from the model. Using TC_i to denote the total cost (the monetary travel cost and the time cost for a round trip), the tested model took the following form:

$$V_i^0 = f(TC_i, STC_i, Y_i) \tag{7-4}$$

Hypothetical Valuation Approach

This approach is less complicated than the travel-cost approach. In principle, the study area would be divided into concentric rings (zones) around the park, and residents in each zone would be interviewed about their willingness to pay per year to maintain the park in its present form of land use. People interviewed would include both present users and nonusers of the park. For this study, since detailed population information was not available for use in drawing concentric zones, the administrative districts were used instead as a basis for analysis (Figure 7.1). Sampling frequency was greatest in the districts near Lumpinee Park.

The Data

Information on variables outlined in the previous section is not usually recorded on a regular basis. Surveys were conducted to obtain the data needed to estimate the demand for park visits and the amount of people willing to maintain the park. For the travel-cost approach, 187 people were interviewed at the park. For the hypothetical valuation approach, 225 people, spread over the whole study area, were interviewed at their residence about their willingness to pay to maintain Lumpinee Park. In addition, the 187 people interviewed at the park for the travel-cost portion were also asked about their willingness to pay to keep the park in existence.

Survey data were therefore available to value Lumpinee Park using both the travel cost and hypothetical valuation approaches. These two approaches will now be considered in turn.

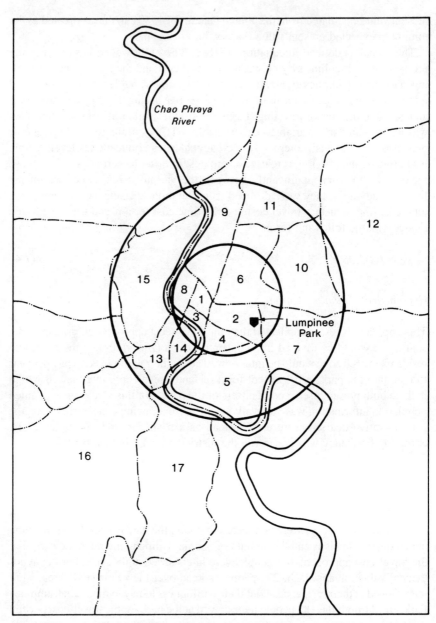

Figure 7.1 Lumpinee Park study area and numbered zones of origin.

The Economic Analysis

Travel-Cost Approach

The travel-cost approach is the first to be examined. The number of visitors was counted during the weekdays and weekends to determine the total number of visitors per week. The first count was done in August 1980, and a second count was done in November 1980. The average number of visitors was 2,455 per day on weekdays and 14,071 per day on weekends (Table 7.1). Estimated visitors per week were thus 40,417. Although questionnaires were filled out for a random sample of 200 users, 13 had to be discarded due to mistakes made during the interview. Of the remaining 187 respondents, 37 percent were weekday visitors and 63 percent were weekend visitors. All 187 respondents were then divided by residence into 17 groups on the basis of administrative districts.

The initial survey was divided into weekday and weekend use for two reasons: to determine if there was a difference in use rates between the two periods, and to determine if the "average" user varied markedly between weekday and weekend. The answer to the first question was a definite yes—Lumpinee Park use is heaviest on the weekend. The second question concerning type of user (and possibly different values) was also evaluated, and it was decided that weekend and weekday users were not statistically different. The entire sample could therefore be grouped to estimate the travel-cost function. If the two groups were very different, such an aggregation could yield a biased result.

Table 7.1 Visitors per Day, Weekday and Weekend

Time	Visitors/day Weekday	Visitors/day Weekend
05.01–07.00	317	4,360
07.01–08.00	253	1,342
08.01–09.00	60	1,141
09.01–10.00	49	695
10.01–11.00	46	304
11.01–12.00	61	321
12.01–13.00	57	404
13.01–14.00	48	227
14.01–15.00	80	295
15.01–16.00	250	878
16.01–17.00	596	2,138
17.01–18.00	638	1,966
Total	2,455	14,071

Note: Counted at all four gates, Lumpinee Park, August 1980.

Table 7.2   Visitation Rate per 1,000 Population per Year for All Zones

Zone	Population	Sample Person	%	Visitation rate/1,000
1	190,450	10	5.3	590
2	235,647	27	14.4	
3	77,112	4	2.1	
4	131,542	23	12.3	
5	380,416	30	16.0	
6	519,869	18	9.6	
7	523,831	37	19.8	
8	123,109	3	1.6	
9	479,659	4	2.1	
10	201,334	4	2.1	
11	388,333	6	3.2	
12	255,555	7	3.7	
13	262,097	1	0.5	
14	140,249	4	2.1	
15	382,621	5	2.7	
16	204,434	1	0.5	
17	113,769	3	1.6	
Total	4,610,027	187	99.6[a]	

[a]Percentages do not add to 100 because of rounding.

Given the information available from the surveys, a demand function for visits to the park can be estimated. This information is then used to estimate a demand curve for park use from each zone as an increasing admissions fee is imposed. At some level demand will be choked off and no one will visit from that zone. These curves from all zones can then be summed horizontally to derive an aggregate demand curve for the park. Another way to derive the aggregate demand curve is to sum the number of visitors from all zones at each level of admissions fee. This approach is used here although both ways give the identical result. Since the present admission fee is zero, the whole area under the demand curve becomes a measurement of the consumer's surplus. Calculation of the value of Lumpinee Park under the travel-cost approach and the hypothetical valuation approach can be carried out as follows:

Using information on the percentage of sampled visitors from each of the 17 zones, total visitors per week, and the population in each zone, the visit rate per 1,000 population in each zone (Table 7.2) can be determined by using the following formula:

$$\text{Visit}/1,000/\text{year} = \frac{\left(\frac{V_i}{n}\right)N \times 52 \times 1,000}{P} \tag{7-5}$$

where V_i = visitors from zone i
             n = sample size = 187
             N = visitors per week = 40,417
             P = total population in zone i

The visitation rate in terms of 1,000 per year for zone 1 is given in Table 7.2. Calculate the yearly visitation rates for all other zones in the same way.

Information on the round-trip monetary travel cost and the average time for each trip was also collected. The time spent traveling was then changed into a monetary value using a representative wage rate and was then added to the travel cost. Average monetary travel cost per round-trip (T_i), the value of average time of traveling per round trip (I_i), and average total cost $(\overline{TC}_i = T_i + I_i)$ for each zone were computed and are presented in Table 7.3. The same information for substitute recreation sites is also presented.

A regression equation was estimated, regressing the visitation rates $(\overline{V})$ calculated in Table 7.2 against average total travel cost $(\overline{TC})$ given in Table 7.3. The following result was obtained:

$$\overline{V} = 1322.88 \ - \ 58.464 \ \overline{TC} \qquad R^2 = .5908 \qquad\qquad (7\text{-}6)$$
$$(6.667)^* \ (-4.653)^* \qquad e_{\overline{TC}} = 1.804$$

The value e stands for the elasticity of visitation with respect to total travel cost, t tests are in parentheses, and * signifies that the results are significant at the 99 percent level.

The total cost per visit from Table 7.3 for each zone was substituted into equation (7-6) to obtain the visits per 1,000 population for each zone at zero admission fee. When the fee became positive, say, baht (฿)2 per visit per person, it was added to the total cost and again substituted into equation (7-6) to solve for the visitation rate per 1,000 people and the total visits from each zone at the new admission fee.

Example zone 1

When admission fee = 0; $\overline{TC}$ = 8.08

$$\overline{V}_1^0 = 1322.88 \ - \ 58.464(8.08) = 850.5$$

Total visits in zone 1 when admission fee = 0 is

$$\frac{850.5 \times 190,450}{1,000} = 161,978$$

Table 7.3 Visitation Rate per 1,000 Population, Average Total Cost to Visit Lumpinee and Other Recreational Sites

Zone	Visitation rate/1,000	Average total cost to Lumpinee			Average total cost to other sites		
		Travel cost (B)	Time (minutes)	Total cost[a] (B/visit)	Travel cost (B)	Time (minutes)	Total cost[a] (B/visit)
1	590	5.00	39	8.08	11.40	109	20.11
2		1.25	31	3.72	15.00	106	23.48
3		6.05	53	10.25	18.00	189	33.12
4		2.13	36	5.04	14.65	110	23.47
5		4.87	47	8.64	11.73	123	21.57
6		5.47	56	10.00	7.39	94	14.93
7		6.17	94	13.66	11.05	135	21.88
8		8.13	107	16.65	9.67	71	15.38
9		6.73	93	14.18	8.75	89	15.89
10		7.43	101	15.50	10.00	154	22.30
11		10.35	125	20.35	5.00	99	12.91
12		10.02	119	19.52	6.43	140	17.66
13		8.61	107	17.16	11.75	137	22.75
14		8.50	106	17.01	11.75	133	22.38
15		10.10	104	18.43	6.60	72	12.35
16		15.09	156	27.59	20.00	125	30.00
17		11.35	129	21.70	20.00	194	35.51

Source: Survey at Lumpinee Park, November 1980.

[a]Total cost equals travel cost plus the quantity B0.08 times travel time in minutes.

When admission fee $= 2$; $\overline{TC} = 10.08$

$\overline{V}_1^2 = 1322.88 - 58.464(10.08) = 733.6$

Total visits in zone 1 when admission fee $= 2$ is

$$\frac{733.6 \times 190,450}{1,000} = 139,714$$

The number of visitors per year for zone 1 at various levels of admission fee are presented in Table 7.4. Following the example, calculate the number of visitors from all other zones by substituting information from Table 7.3 into equation (7-6). The number of visits at various levels of admission fee for any one zone represents the demand function for Lumpinee visits for that zone. By summing up total visits across all zones at a given admission fee, a point on a user demand curve for Lumpinee Park is found. Plot the number of total visitors per year from all zones against the admission fees. Compute the area under this user demand curve. This area represents the user value of the park based on the travel-cost approach for 1980. (Note: To calculate the value of consumer surplus, the area under the demand curve is first divided on the basis of the admission fees. Then each subarea under the curve is computed.)

Hypothetical Valuation Approach

Under this approach, people were directly asked a hypothetical question: If the government could no longer allocate the budget to maintain the park but in fact was considering turning it into other uses, what would be the maximum amount you are willing to contribute per year to keep the park? The summation of all these maximum willingness-to-pay responses, adjusted for the total population in each area, represented the hypothetical value of the park.

Hypothetical valuation techniques must be used with caution because of the potential biases that can occur. These biases are due to the hypothetical nature of the approach—since actual market behavior is not being observed, the possibility exists that respondents' answers may overstate or understate their true willingness to pay. Careful survey design can help control these sources of bias. A discussion of this problem and a description of various possible biases (including those due to information, strategic game playing, bid starting point, and payment vehicle) are found in Chapter 6 of the *Guide* (pp. 252–54).

Two sets of values were obtained from the surveys. The first set represented the user value since the interviews were conducted at the park. The second set of answers came from respondents, including both users and nonusers of the park, who were interviewed at their residences. The answer on the willingness to pay thus reflected more closely the social value of the park, accepting that the max-

Table 7.4 Visits at Various Admission Fees in One Year

Zone	Population	Total cost (B/visit)	Number of visits at various admission fees (B)										
			0	2	4	6	8	10	12	14	16	18	20
1	190,450	8.08	161,978	139,714	117,438	95,169	72,900	50,631	28,362	6,093	--	--	--
2	235,647	3.72											
3	77,112	10.25											
4	131,542	5.04											
5	380,416	8.64											
6	519,869	10.00											
7	523,831	13.66											
8	123,109	16.65											
9	479,659	14.18											
10	201,334	15.50											
11	388,333	20.35											
12	255,555	19.52											
13	262,097	17.16											
14	140,249	17.01											
15	382,621	18.43											
16	204,434	27.59											
17	113,769	21.70											

Total visits per year

imum amount they were willing to pay reflected both direct and indirect benefits received from the park. This statement was confirmed by the fact that 46 percent of the respondents were not current visitors of the park but who still expressed a willingness to pay to keep the park. In evaluating the value of the park based on the hypothetical valuation approach, only potential visitors with effective demand were considered. Potential visitors were defined as people between ages 15–75 who presumably had some income and thus possessed the *ability* to pay, as well as the *willingness* to pay. Out of a population of 4.6 million in the study area, 65 percent of the population was in the age range of 15–75 (i.e., three million persons were considered potential visitors with the ability to pay). They formed the basis for the analysis.

User Value of the Park under the Hypothetical Valuation Approach

The 187 people interviewed for the travel-cost study were also asked for the maximum amount they would be willing to pay per year to keep the park. The amount per year volunteered by the respondents seemed to relate closely with their frequency of visit. Visitors for recreational purposes (83 percent of the sample) offered an average of B168 per year. Visitors for morning and evening exercise purposes (17 percent of the sample) offered an average of B218 per year. The latter group visited the park more frequently; thus, their average willingness to pay per visit became relatively less than the first group (Table 7.5).

Given an average of 40,417 visitors per week (from Table 7.1), the number of visitors per year (visitors per week × 52) was estimated at 2.1 million. However, since most respondents reported frequent visits to the park (see Table 7.5), it seems more appropriate to treat the 2.1 million figure as the number of visits (instead of visitors) per year. This distinction is important since the value of the park will vary greatly depending on the proportion of visitors using the park for recreational and exercise purposes and their average visitation rates.

Assume that the survey was done correctly and reflects the mix of average visitors to the park and their valuation of its benefits. From Table 7.5 the average

Table 7.5   Average Willingness to Pay

Purpose of visit	Visitor (%)	Amount/yr (B)	Visits/yr	Amount/visit (B)
Recreation	83	168.21	25.37	6.63
Exercise	17	218.39	174.29	1.25
Weighted average visits/person/yr			50.68	

Note: Survey at Lumpinee Park, August 1980.

willingness to pay *per visit* is known. Based on this data, estimated yearly visitors, and the visitor mix between recreational and exercise uses, calculate the total willingness to pay of park visitors in 1980.

Social Value of the Park under the Hypothetical Valuation Concept

In the study area, 225 residents were interviewed. Random samples were selected in proportion to the number of people in each of the 17 districts within the concentric rings around the park. The average willingness to pay of those interviewed was grouped into nine monetary ranges. The yearly amount varied from B0 to B500 per year (Table 7.6). This valuation represents a broader "social value" of the park to both users and nonusers. For nonusers it captures part of the option value of the park, that is, the value placed on maintaining the park so that they could use it if they desired.

To calculate the total "social value" of the park, the 3 million residents in the 17 districts sampled were apportioned according to the sample percentage in each of the nine monetary groups shown in Table 7.6; that is, 19.6 percent of the total, or 588,000 people, were assumed to have no willingness to pay. The total willingness to pay (TWP) was then derived according to the following formula:

$$TWP = \sum_{i=1}^{9} AWP_i \left(\frac{ni}{N}\right)(3,000,000) \qquad (7\text{-}7)$$

where AWP_i = average willingness to pay, amounts 1 through 9
n_i = number of respondents willing to pay AWP_i
N = total number of people interviewed

Based on Table 7.6, for example, 10 out of 225 people interviewed were willing to pay B2.5 per year to keep the park; for the entire population, therefore, the total amount all the potential visitors were willing to pay is

$$= 2.5 \times \left(\frac{10}{225}\right) \times 3,000,000$$

$$= B333,333$$

Calculate the value of the park associated with each average level of annual payment (obtained from the survey). Calculate the total value of the park (TWP), the summation of all AWP_is (Table 7.6).

Compare the three estimates of the annual value of Lumpinee Park to users and Bangkok residents; one estimate is based on cost of travel and time, and two estimates are based on hypothetical valuation. Discuss how and why these esti-

Table 7.6   Social Value of Lumpinee Park to Residents

Amount willing to pay/yr[a]		Sample		Population	Social value
Range (Ɓ)	Average (Ɓ)	Person	%	age 15-75 (000)	of park/yr (Ɓ1,000)
0.00	0.0	44	19.6	588	0
0.01- 5.0	2.5	10	4.4	133	333
5.01- 15.0	10.0	59	26.2	787	
15.01- 25.0	20.0	47	20.9	627	
25.01- 35.0	30.0	11	4.9	147	
35.01- 75.0	50.0	21	9.3	280	
75.01-125.0	100.0	20	8.9	267	
125.01-275.0	200.0	9	4.0	120	
275.01-	500.0	4	1.8	54	
Total		225	100.0	3,003[b]	

[a]Amount willing to pay per year above Ɓ275, based on survey information, is assumed to be Ɓ500/person/year.

[b]Column does not add to 3,000 because of rounding.

Note: Survey in study area at Lumpinee Park, November 1980.

mates vary. Calculate the capitalized value of the park based on a 10 percent discount rate.

How could willingness-to-pay figures be used in setting policy? Are there alternative ways these figures can be checked? How sensitive are the results to the actual number of people who use the park, and the frequency with which each person uses the park?

The Results

A number of calculations were called for in the case study. Using the formula (equation 7-5) for calculating the visitation rate per 1,000 people, the visitation rate for all 17 zones is easily calculated. These results are given in Table 7.7. These visitation rates are actually *visits* per 1,000 people, not visitors per 1,000 people, since many individuals make repeat visits during the year.

This information, along with data on total travel costs, is used to estimate equation (7-6). This equation, in turn, is used with data on cost per visit from Table 7.3 to trace out changes in demand for visits with increasing admission fees. These results are given in Table 7.8.

When plotted, these results give the user demand curve illustrated in Figure 7.2. Using the hint given earlier, the area under this curve is calculated using a simple approximation illustrated in Table 7.9. This approximation assumes that the demand curve is linear between any two points; hence, the total area is easily calculated—in this case Ɓ13.2 × 10⁶.

Table 7.7   Visitation Rate per 1,000 Population per Year for All Zones

Zone	Population	Sample Person	%	Visitation rate/1,000
1	190,450	10	5.3	590
2	235,647	27	14.4	1,288
3	77,112	4	2.1	583
4	131,542	23	12.3	1,965
5	380,416	30	16.0	886
6	519,869	18	9.6	389
7	523,831	37	19.8	794
8	123,109	3	1.6	274
9	479,659	4	2.1	94
10	201,334	4	2.1	223
11	388,333	6	3.2	174
12	255,555	7	3.7	308
13	262,097	1	0.5	43
14	140,249	4	2.1	320
15	382,621	5	2.7	147
16	204,434	1	0.5	55
17	113,769	3	1.6	296
Total	4,610,027	187	99.6[a]	

[a]Percentages do not add to 100 because of rounding.

This estimate is based on measured visitation costs and implicit consumer's surplus. A second set of estimates is based on hypothetical valuation of the park by both users and residents in Bangkok.

Based on data in Tables 7.5 and 7.8, the total willingness to pay of park visitors is as follows:

2.275 million "visitors"/visits per year
         83% for recreation
         17% for exercise

Therefore

$$0.83 \times 2.275 \times B6.63 = B12.519 \times 10^6$$
$$0.17 \times 2.275 \times B1.25 = \underline{B\ \ .483 \times 10^6}$$
$$B13.002$$

or B13 million per year, very close to the area calculated for the consumer's surplus calculated in Table 7.9 and illustrated in Figure 7.2.

This measure of willingness to pay was based on actual users. When a wider range of Bangkok residents were interviewed in their homes and not in the park, another hypothetical valuation was derived. These results are based on data in

Table 7.8 Visits at Various Admission Fees in One Year

Zone	Population	Total cost (B/visit)	Number of visits at various admission fees (B)										
			0	2	4	6	8	10	12	14	16	18	20
1	190,450	8.08	161,978	139,714	117,438	95,169	72,900	50,631	28,362	6,093	--	--	--
2	235,647	3.72	260,483	232,929	205,375	177,821	150,268	122,714	95,160	67,606	40,052	12,499	--
3	77,112	10.25	55,800	46,783	37,768	28,750	19,734	10,717	1,700	--	--	--	--
4	131,542	5.04	135,254	119,873	104,492	89,111	73,730	58,349	42,968	27,587	12,206	--	--
5	380,416	8.64	311,085	266,604	222,123	177,641	133,160	88,678	44,197	--	--	--	--
6	519,869	10.00	383,788	323,000	262,213	201,426	140,639	79,851	19,064	--	--	--	--
7	523,831	13.66	274,624	213,373	152,123	90,872	29,621	--	--	--	--	--	--
8	123,109	16.65	43,021	28,626	14,231	--	12,541	--	--	--	--	--	--
9	479,659	14.18	236,884	180,798	124,713	68,627	--	--	--	--	--	--	--
10	201,334	15.50	83,893	60,352	36,810	13,268	--	--	--	--	--	--	--
11	388,333	20.35	51,701	6,294	--	--	--	--	--	--	--	--	--
12	255,555	19.52	46,424	16,543	22,482	--	--	--	--	--	--	--	--
13	262,097	17.16	83,776	53,129	13,260	--	--	--	--	--	--	--	--
14	140,249	17.01	46,058	29,659	4,412	--	--	--	--	--	--	--	--
15	382,621	18.43	93,890	49,151	--	--	--	--	--	--	--	--	--
16	204,434	27.59	--	--	--	--	--	--	--	--	--	--	--
17	113,769	21.70	6,167	--	--	--	--	--	--	--	--	--	--
Total visits per year			2,274,826	1,766,828	1,317,440	942,685	633,593	410,940	231,451	101,286	52,258	12,499	0

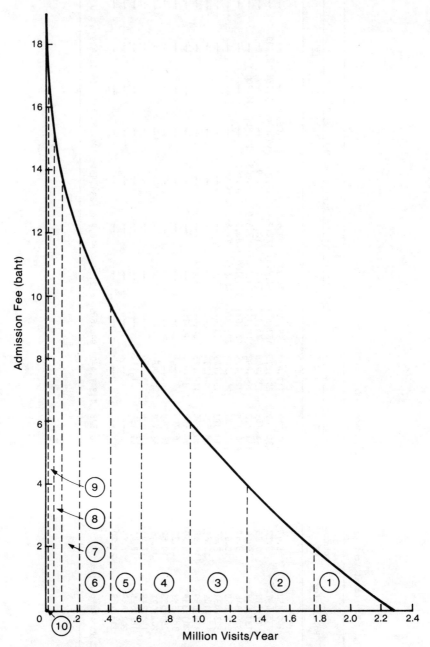

Figure 7.2 User demand curve for Lumpinee visits.

Table 7.9 Calculation of Consumer's Surplus

Section	Computation	Value of consumer's surplus
1	1/2 x 2 x 508,002	508,002
2	(1/2 x 2 x 449,384) + (2 x 449,384)	1,348,152
3	(1/2 x 2 x 374,754) + (4 x 374,754)	1,873,770
4	(1/2 x 2 x 310,094) + (6 x 310,094)	2,170,658
5	(1/2 x 2 x 221,654) + (8 x 221,654)	1,994,886
6	(1/2 x 2 x 179,488) + (10 x 179,488)	1,974,368
7	(1/2 x 2 x 130,169) + (12 x 130,169)	1,692,197
8	(1/2 x 2 x 49,028) + (14 x 49,028)	735,420
9	(1/2 x 2 x 39,759) + (16 x 39,759)	675,903
10	(1/2 x 1 x 12,499) + (18 x 12,499)	231,232
1 - 10	User value of Lumpinee, 1980	13,204,588

Table 7.6 and are presented in Table 7.10. This "social" valuation is much higher—more than 116 million baht in 1980—which may in part reflect the valuation of the park by people who may not actually use it, but who wish to retain the option to do so. This "option value" can be significant for a well-known resource such as Lumpinee Park. A strong possibility of hypothetical bias also exists leading people to overstate their willingness to pay since they feel they may

Table 7.10 Social Value of Lumpinee Park to Residents

Amount willing to pay/yr[a] Range (B)	Average (B)	Sample Person	%	Population age 15-75 (000)	Social value of park/yr (B1,000)
0.00	0.0	44	19.6	588	0
0.01- 5.0	2.5	10	4.4	133	333
5.01- 15.0	10.0	59	26.2	787	7,884
15.01- 25.0	20.0	47	20.9	627	12,545
25.01- 35.0	30.0	11	4.9	147	4,414
35.01- 75.0	50.0	21	9.3	280	14,014
75.01-125.0	100.0	20	8.9	267	26,693
125.01-275.0	200.0	9	4.0	120	24,024
275.01-	500.0	4	1.8	54	26,693
Total		225	100.0	3,003[b]	116,583

[a]Amount willing to pay per year above B275, based on survey information, is assumed to be B500/person/year.

[b]Column does not add to 3,000 because of rounding.

Note: Survey in study area at Lumpinee Park, November 1980.

not be called upon to pay. This bias can be minimized by making both the questioning and the payment vehicle as realistic as possible.

We thus have three measures of the park's value in 1980:

"Consumer's surplus" approach	13.2×10^6
User's hypothetical valuation	13.0×10^6
Social hypothetical valuation	116.6×10^6

Capitalized at 10 percent, these three measures yield a present value of B132, 130, and 1166 million, respectively. Given the 1980 exchange rate (US$1 = B20), this represents a current value of from $6 to $58 million. Clearly Lumpinee Park is a valuable environmental resource and, even though people do not presently pay an admission fee, there is a large area of consumer's surplus or welfare gain associated with the existence of the park.

The techniques discussed here help place minimum values on some of the goods and services provided by Lumpinee Park. As population pressure increases, one would expect that the park will become relatively more valuable.

8
The Nam Pong Water Resources Project in Thailand

Adapted by Maynard M. Hufschmidt
from a paper prepared by Ruangdej Srivardhana

Summary

The Nam Pong Water Resources Project is a large, multipurpose reservoir-irrigation system development in Northeast Thailand. The Ubolratana Dam regulates stream flow, generates electricity, and provides irrigation for a large area near Khon Kaen. This case study examines one management option for controlling erosion in the upstream watershed for the main reservoir. The natural systems assessment approach used is the *conservation of mass approach* described in Chapter 5 of the *Guide* (pp. 129–31); the valuation technique used is the *loss of economic productivity approach* described in Chapter 6 of the *Guide* (pp. 172–75).

The case study examines two options—no watershed management program with an increase in erosion rates, and a comprehensive watershed management program with a decrease in average erosion rates. The costs of the management option are compared to the benefits from management. These benefits are a function of reservoir capacity and include hydroelectric energy generation, irrigation benefits, flood damage reduction, and the reservoir fishery.

The case study uses some simplifying assumptions and some "hypothetical but realistic" data because of data constraints but illustrates how physical measures can be used to evaluate an environmental management option. Benefits in the upstream watershed itself for the management option are not covered in this study.

Background Information

The material presented in this case is based on the output of a five-year research project of the Interim Committee for Co-ordination of Investigations of the Lower Mekong Basin (the Mekong Committee 1979a).

In an effort to understand the environmental effects of this water resources development project, the Mekong Committee in 1976 undertook a major study of the 10-year experience in the Nam Pong Basin since completion of the major storage dam. The research was undertaken in three phases. Phase I (September

141

1976–January 1978) was a comprehensive data collection effort comprising an extensive literature review, a reconnaissance survey of the basin, a postaudit of socioeconomic aspects, and the preparation of an annotated bibliography (SEAT-EC 1978). Phase II (June 1977–November 1979) was a fact-finding exercise to identify social, economic, and ecological changes mainly through collection and analysis of field data.[1] This phase consisted of 13 discrete research tasks covering such topics as hydrology, water quality, water and land use, fisheries, socioeconomics, human and animal health, and insects and pests (Interim Committee 1979b). The two phases are different in both depth of analysis and topics covered. Both, however, provided an invaluable factual background to Phase III of the study.

Phase III, which was started in September 1980, was a two-stage exercise of (1) transferring a specific environmental impact assessment methodology to a team of Thai scientists and (2) applying the methodology to the case of the Nam Pong development project. One of the most important final products to emerge from this exercise was a management-oriented computer simulation model, designed to be a useful supporting tool for policy formulation and decision making for resources management in the Nam Pong Basin. However, Phase III did not present a conventional benefit-cost analysis either of project inputs and outputs or of environmental effects. The final report of Phase III was completed in July 1982.

The River Basin

The Nam Pong river basin is in Northeast Thailand. The river is a tributary of the Nam-Chi river system, and the basin is one of the Mekong's many subbasins. The Nam Pong Basin alone covers an area of approximately 15,000 square kilometers (km^2). The watershed above Ubolratana Dam is about 11,500 km^2 and lies in the provinces of Udon Thani, Loei, and Khon Kaen. Before the construction of the Ubolratana Dam in 1965, much of the watershed area was forested as there had been no extensive clearance for planting upland crops. Glutinous rice was cultivated in the basin's lowland, and there was widespread flooding in the wet season. The only large town in the basin was, and still is, Khon Kaen. The population of the basin has been increasing at about 3 percent per year, and practically all good quality agricultural land has been fully occupied.

About 85 percent of the working population of the Nam Pong Basin earn their

---

1. The Phase II report is composed of 13 working documents. They are, by running number, reports on: 1. Plant Diseases; 2. Livestock Diseases; 3. Land Use; 4. Soil Physics and Chemistry; 5. Survey of Insect Pests, Part A: Rice Insect Pests; 6. Survey of Insect Pests, Part B: Vegetable Insect Pests; 7. Human Health and Nutrition, Diseases, Parasites, and Disease Vectors; 8. Socio-Economic Studies; 9. Survey of Weeds; 10. Hydrological Studies; 11. Water Quality: Physical and Chemical Aspects of the Reservoir; 12. Water Weeds and Studies on Fish, Fish Production, and Productivity; 13. Plankton.

income from farming. Nearly 90 percent of the farmers cultivate their own land for subsistence crops.

The Water Resources Development Scheme

The Ubolratana impounding dam was constructed at Pong Neeb, Nam Pong District in Khon Kaen Province in 1966. Before the dam was completed, the annual average discharge of the Nam Pong River at the dam site, based on 1957–66 stream flow record, was 1,780 million cubic meters (m^3), and the low flow varied from an average of 12 million m^3 in December to practically zero in March or April. The mean annual precipitation in the watershed is about 1,160 milli-meters (mm), with as much as 80 percent of the annual rainfall occurring in May through September.

This rock-filled dam has a crest length of 800 meters (m) and a height of 37 m above the foundation. Its total storage capacity is 2,550 million m^3 at 182 m mean sea level (MSL). The maximum surface of the reservoir is about 410 km^2 with a mean depth of 5.9 m. The water level at maximum permitted drawdown is 174 m MSL (active storage capacity of 1,650 million m^3), where the surface area is reduced to 130 km^2, and the mean depth falls to 3.9 m. The estimated average evaporation loss from the reservoir is 476 million m^3 annually. In the postim-poundment years 1969 to 1980, the average annual inflow to the reservoir esti-mated from rainfall-runoff relationships derived from the 1957–66 stream flow record was 2,698 million m^3.

The Nam Pong Water Resources Development Project has three main objec-tives—to generate electrical energy, to supply water for irrigation, and to alleviate flooding downstream of the dam.

At the beginning of the dam operation, only two turbines of 8.3 megawatts (Mw) each were installed, and later a third turbine of the same capacity was added to meet the rapidly increasing power demand. Average annual generation of hydroelectric energy is now 65 million kilowatt-hours (kwh).

In 1966 the Royal Irrigation Department constructed the Nong Wai diversion weir to divert water into canals on the right and left banks of the Nam Pong River for irrigation. When fully operational, the canals will supply water for 170 km^2 (17,000 hectares [ha]) of dry-season cultivation and 260 km^2 (26,000 ha) for supplementary irrigation in the wet season. An extension of the existing scheme is being developed, which will provide dry-season irrigation to an additional 180 km^2 (18,000 ha) in an area adjacent to the confluence of the Nam Pong and Nam Chi.

Following dam construction and until 1978, only small floods occurred in downstream lowland areas. However, in 1978 and again in 1980 severe floods were experienced downstream from the dam, so that now the alleviation of flood risks has become one of the main concerns of the local administrations.

Water resources development in the Nam Pong Basin has brought about many changes to the area. Many people who formerly lived in the area inundated by the reservoir were relocated to two resettlement areas, which turned out to be problem areas.

Other people were attracted to the watershed area above the reservoir only to discover that making a living there was more difficult than in their original villages. An extremely productive fishery has developed in the reservoir—a benefit that was not anticipated by the project planners. In addition, the reservoir storage provided by the project has made dry-season irrigation possible for an area of approximately 170 km^2 (17,000 ha).

Environmental Dimensions

In the course of producing the original project outputs—electrical energy, flood damage reduction, and irrigation water—the project generated some unforeseen physical, biological, and socioeconomic interactions that led to a number of serious management problems. These problems are related to six distinct subareas of the Nam Pong Basin, as depicted in Figure 8.1. These areas can be described briefly as follows:

I.   *Watershed area:* Rainfed subsistence farming with upland commercial crops such as rice, cassava, sugarcane, and kenaf; lack of alternative employment opportunities; some upland areas still forested; highest birthrate in the basin; population density, 68 persons per km^2; total land area of 11,500 km^2.

II.   *Reservoir area:* Rainfed subsistence farming on land adjacent to the reservoir, and seasonally in the drawdown zone; commercial and subsistence fishing; surveys show health status better than in other subareas; population density, 80 persons per km^2; total land area of 1,000 km^2.

III.   *Downstream and resettlement area:* Rainfed subsistence agriculture and upland commercial crops such as rice, sugarcane, and kenaf; includes two resettlement areas for people displaced by creation of reservoir; kenaf pulp mill, sugar mill; population density, 120 per km^2; total land area of 2,000 km^2, of which about 25 percent is idle. The resettled people are an example of an externality created by the project.

IV.   *Nam Pong/Nong Wai irrigation area:* Supplementary water for wet-season rice and for increasing areas of dry-season crops; highest rural incomes in the basin; off-farm employment available; easy access to city of Khon Kaen; lowest rural birthrate; population density, 200 persons per km^2; total land area of 270 km^2.

V.   *Khon Kaen/urban area:* Urban area with employment in government, commerce, services, and small-scale industry; average income four times the average of rural areas; lowest birthrate and highest population growth rate; density, 1,867 persons per km^2; total land area of 45 km^2.

VI.   *Future extension of irrigation area:* Presently rainfed agriculture, but

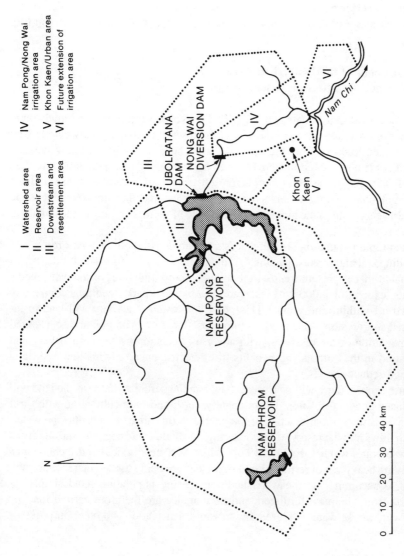

I   Watershed area
II Reservoir area
III Downstream and
    resettlement area

IV Nam Pong/Nong Wai
    irrigation area
V   Khon Kaen/Urban area
VI Future extension of
    irrigation area

Figure 8.1 Major subareas of the Nam Pong Basin.

irrigation scheme under construction; density, 200 persons per km^2; birthrate and income average for rural area; total land area of 180 km^2.

Operation of the project has led to a number of environmental and natural systems effects in each of the six major subareas. In this case, however, attention is given to a single effect: erosion in subareas I and II and its effect on reservoir life.

Management of the Watershed Area:
Erosion and Its Effect on Reservoir Life

This watershed area (subarea I in Figure 8.1) has been subjected to extremely rapid population increase since completion of the reservoir project. Many people who were forced to move from the reservoir area chose to resettle in this watershed area. People also moved in from other areas, so that the total population reached 785,000 in 1980.[2] Furthermore, if present trends of natural increase and net migration continue, the watershed population is estimated to almost double in the next 20 years. This is the highest estimated rate of increase of any of the nonurban subareas.

Such rapid population growth places a severe demand on the area's resources, including soil and forests, leading to rapid depletion of the forest and soils. It was estimated that if present trends were allowed to continue, all of the watershed's forests, except for 2,000 km^2 reserved for a national park, would be completely logged off within nine years.[3] This rapid deforestation activity will lead to increased soil erosion, which will in turn cause increased siltation and accelerated sedimentation of the reservoir, with adverse effects on the reservoir fishery and reduction in the outputs and benefits from electric energy, irrigation, and flood damage reduction.

Furthermore, there will be a great change in the deforested area as the land will be placed under cultivation. Unfortunately, slash-and-burn cultivation with short rotations is the normal practice of the people in this area. As a result, the water, which flows into the reservoir, becomes highly alkaline and degrades the quality of the reservoir's water (SEATEC 1978). Moreover, new agricultural technologies involving heavy use of fertilizers and pesticides are being used to increase productivity to accommodate the watershed's increasing population. Undesirable residuals from chemical fertilizers and insecticides are therefore carried into the reservoir, whose water is reused downsteam for irrigation and other purposes.

2. Estimation done in Phase III of the Nam Pong Environmental Research Project, Interim Committee for Co-ordination of Investigations of the Lower Mekong Basin.

3. Simulation model's result, Basic Scenario, Phase III of the Mekong Committee's Environmental Research Project on the Nam Pong Basin, Thailand, August 1982.

Fishery Production and Project Management

Unexpectedly, the Nam Pong Reservoir has turned out to be a productive fishery with more than 70 edible fish species. The total fish catch per year varies from 1,500 to 4,000 tons, depending on many factors such as the reservoir water level and the fishing effort in the previous year. The fish catch per year is approximately 2,000 tons. This unexpected benefit of the project has contributed a great deal to the well-being of the people in the reservoir shoreline area. Most of the fish are sold for cash income; some less commercially valuable species are used for home consumption.

There is no current policy to govern the fishing practices; thus, there are no limits on the number of fishermen and on types of fishing equipment (e.g., gill net, cast net, harpoon, and bamboo traps). The number of commercial fishermen has increased from 500 in 1969 to 4,000 in 1980. Hence, the fishing effort in the reservoir has become so great that there is danger of serious reduction of the fishery resource, thus decreasing the total catch for fishermen. The Phase III study found that if this overexploitation continues, the catch per unit effort will decline drastically over the next ten years, with the small herbivorous fish species (which have low commercial value) becoming the dominant group. The commercially valuable large carnivore group is expected to decline as a mixed result of the selective fishing and effects of changes in the reservoir ecosystem.

The simulation model of Phase III has also shown an interesting outcome. The current practice of the Fishery Department in its attempt to maintain the reservoir's biomass by annual stocking of the reservoir with fish is not expected to reverse the declining trend of the fish biomass in the future. An effective means to maintain the reservoir's productivity is to control the number of fishermen and the time of access. When the reservoir is low the fish are concentrated in a much smaller volume and are therefore more vulnerable to the fishing effort similarly concentrated over a much reduced surface area. By reducing the number of fishermen and, hence, fishing effort when the reservoir level is low, enough fish biomass can be preserved to maintain a high replacement for the following year.

Assessment and Valuation Approaches

Although the Nam Pong studies identified a number of important natural systems and environmental quality effects of the Nam Pong project, this case will deal with only one: physical effects of erosion in the upstream watershed on the reservoir project. The natural system *assessment* approach that will be used is the *conservation of mass* approach described in Chapter 5 of the *Guide.* The *valuation* approach to be used is the *loss of economic productivity* approach, in which market prices are assumed to exist for the resource inputs and project outputs involved.

Assessment of Physical Effects of Erosion

Human activity in the watershed, along with natural processes such as rainfall and runoff, generates soil erosion. The eroded soil moves downstream through the drainage channels, tributaries, and streams into the reservoir. Stream bank erosion and movement of bedload in streams are also involved in this transport of sediments into the reservoir. As the reservoir area is filled, the *effective* reservoir storage diminishes. This reduction of effective reservoir storage leads directly to reductions in physical outputs of kilowatt-hours of energy generated, cubic meters of irrigation water provided, downstream control of flood flows, and fish catch.

Computation of Annual Erosion Rates

Annual erosion rates are a function of a number of variables including types of land use. For each type of land use, erosion rates can be computed by using the Universal Soil Loss Equation (see pp. 138–42 of the *Guide*). In this equation annual soil loss per unit area (*A*) is a function of a rainfall factor (*R*), soil erodibility factor (*K*), slope length factor (*L*), slope gradient factor (*S*), cropping management factor (*C*), and erosion control practice factor (*P*). In symbolic form this is

$$A = R \times K \times L \times S \times C \times P$$

Total annual soil loss for the entire watershed is estimated by multiplying the unit area soil loss (*A*) for each type of land use by the total area (hectares) in each land-use type.

The Universal Soil Loss Equation was originally developed primarily to estimate annual soil loss from agricultural cropland in temperate climates. An adaptation of the equation to fit the Nam Pong watershed was made in Phase III of the Mekong Committee Study.

Sediment Transport Process

Much of the eroded material is deposited on lower-lying land and in the reservoir tributaries and only a fraction of it reaches the reservoir. On the other hand, stream bank and channel erosion and tributary bedload also contribute to the sedimentation of the reservoir. Accordingly, the magnitude of annual reservoir sedimentation (*S*) is a function of annual soil loss (*E*) from the upstream watershed, stream bank or channel erosion (*C*), tributary bedload (*B*), and the sediment delivery ratio (*R*). The applicable equation is $S = (E + C + B)R$. The sedimentation (*S*) expressed in terms of weight (tons) can be converted into volumes (cubic meters); this study assumes that one ton of sediment is equal to 0.67 m^3.

Effects on Reservoir and the Outputs

The volume of sediment entering the reservoir reduces the total storage capacity of the reservoir. Because a portion of this total storage capacity is "dead" storage that cannot be used for electric energy or irrigation water supply, the reduction in *effective* (i.e., useful) storage capacity from sedimentation is only a fraction of the reduction in total storage capacity. This fraction (U) must be specified in the data.

Reduction in effective reservoir capacity can be translated directly into reductions in hydroelectric energy, irrigation water supply, and flood control effects, and somewhat less directly into fishery production.

Valuation of Economic Effects of Reservoir Sedimentation

Annual economic losses caused by reservoir sedimentation can be estimated by computing the economic value of the reduction in reservoir outputs for electric energy, irrigation water, flood control, and fish production using applicable market prices. Associated with computation of annual economic losses is the computation of the remaining economic benefits from reduced outputs from the reservoir.

Additional Effects

A complete analysis of the physical and economic losses of erosion would include on-site losses in agricultural productivity and other land-use values, local flood losses along tributary streams arising from sedimentation of stream channels, and losses to fish production because of suspended sediments in streams and reservoir. These additional effects are not included here.

Overall Economic Valuation

For overall economic valuation, a period of economic analysis must be selected, and the annual values of gross project benefits (and project costs where applicable) must be identified, and then discounted to obtain a *present value* of net benefits (gross benefits minus costs), using a selected discount rate. By this means, a *present value* of the reduced economic benefits from the project can be calculated.

The Data

Erosion and Reservoir Sedimentation

According to the Final Report of Phase III, Nam Pong Study (1982), the 1979 land-use status of subareas I and II above Nam Pong Reservoir is as shown in Table 8.1. In the absence of effective watershed management and land-use controls, all of the

Table 8.1   Land-Use Status in the Watershed above Nam Pong Reservoir in 1979

| | Area (km^2) | | |
Land-use type	Subarea I	Subarea II	Total
Forest land	4,670	0	4,670
Reforested area	10	0	10
Rice field	3,240	410	3,650
Cassava	480	14	494
Sugarcane	60	0	60
Kenaf	420	33	453
Miscellaneous crops	1,800	23	1,823
Community land	320	424	744
Fish pond	0	0	0
Idle land	500	96	596
Total	11,500	1,000	12,500

remaining forested area, except for 2,000 km^2 in a forest reserve, would be deforested and put to agricultural use. With no controls, even the forest reserve land would suffer some deterioration.

In contrast, with effective watershed management and soil conservation measures, the upland forest areas would be preserved in forest use, deforested lands with high erosion potential would be reforested, and erosion control measures would be installed and maintained on agricultural, community, and other land. The details of the watershed management plan are not given in the Final Report of Phase III.

For technical reasons, the erosion rate data with and without a management plan and the cost-and-benefit data have been "made up" and are *not* based on data from the Nam Pong reports. The data can be termed "realistic but synthetic." It is assumed that the initial decision to build the Nam Pong Reservoir has already been made and hence the with and without the reservoir option is not considered here.

In order to simplify the problem further, the Universal Soil Loss Equation step has been omitted and composite erosion rates (A) have been computed for the entire watershed as shown here.

In the absence of watershed management, annual erosion rates per hectare over the entire 1,250,000 hectares (12,500 km^2) of subareas I and II are assumed to increase linearly from 40 tons/ha/year in the base or year 0 to 80 tons/ha/year in year 10 and to remain constant at that rate until the final or year 50 of the analysis. Although the physical life of the reservoir is more than 100 years, a 50-year period was arbitrarily chosen for this analysis for two reasons: (1) the Phase I evaluation used a 50-year period and (2) 50 years is of sufficient duration to capture most benefits and costs when any positive discount rate is used. In fact, at a discount rate of 10 percent, most of the benefits and costs are captured in the first 30 years.

With an effective management plan, however, the base year annual erosion rate of 40 tons/ha is assumed to decrease linearly to 30 tons/ha/year by year 10, and to maintain constant at that low rate through year 50 (see Figure 8.2).

Watershed erosion can be translated into reservoir sedimentation by means of the following formula:

Annual erosion rate (tons per hectare) × 1,250,000 hectares
× 1.56 (channel and bedload erosion factor) ×
0.2 (sediment delivery ratio), or
Annual watershed erosion (tons) × 0.312 = annual reservoir
sedimentation (tons)

For purposes of translating weight to volume, it is assumed that one ton of sediment has a volume of 0.67 m³.

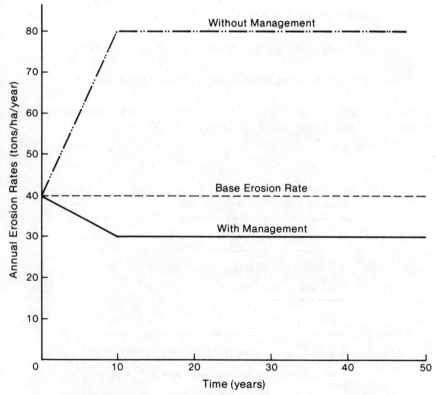

Figure 8.2 Annual erosion rates, with and without management.

Reservoir Sedimentation Capacity Data

The total storage capacity of the reservoir is 2,550 million m³, of which 1,650 million m³ is *effective* storage capacity (i.e., above the "dead" storage pool). The volume of reservoir sedimentation is assumed to reduce the total storage capacity by an identical amount, but the *effective* storage capacity by only 75 percent of the volume of sedimentation (the remaining 25 percent of sedimentation being deposited in the "dead" storage pool). Thus the fraction U to be applied to obtain reduction in effective storage is 0.75. Given the initial (1983) effective storage capacity of 1,650 million m³, once the cumulative reductions in effective storage capacities have been computed for the years 1–50, the remaining effective storage capacities can be calculated.

Gross annual benefits (based on modification of data contained in the SEATEC report) are assumed to be a linear function of effective storage capacity. Gross annual benefits for an effective storage capacity of 1,650 million m³ are assumed to be 300 million baht (Table 8.2). For effective storage capacities of less than 1,650 million m³, gross annual benefits (B) in 10^6 baht are assumed to be

$$B = 300 - 0.2 \ (1{,}650 \times 10^6 \ \mathrm{m}^3 - y) \qquad (8\text{-}1)$$

$$\text{or} \quad B = 300 - 0.2 \ (\text{change in effective storage capacity})$$

where y = remaining effective storage capacity in million m³

Under this formulation, gross annual benefits become zero when remaining effective storage capacity drops to the low level of 150 million m³.

Table 8.2   Average Annual Project Benefits,
Assuming Full Development in 1982

	10^6 B[a]
Hydroelectric energy	70
Irrigation	161
Flood damage reduction	31
Reservoir fishery	38
Total	300

Source: Adapted from SEATEC Report (1978:12-34).

[a]The exchange rate in 1982 was about US$1 = 22 baht.

Cost Data

There are no watershed management costs for the first scenario because no specific watershed management is involved. For the second scenario, costs of watershed management measures are estimated to be 100 million baht per year for the first ten years (1983–92) and 50 million baht per year for the remaining 40 years (1993–2032).

As an aid in computation, discounting factors are given for the 6 percent and 10 percent discount rates in Table 8.3. In addition, the following discount factors can be used to compute present values of costs:

	0%	6%	10%
For summation of years 1–10	10	7.36	6.15
For summation of years 11–50	40	8.40	3.76

Table 8.3   Discount and Annuity Factors

RATE 6%   RATE 10%

Year	DISCOUNT FACTOR How much 1 at a future date is worth today	PRESENT WORTH OF AN ANNUITY FACTOR How much 1 received or paid annually for X years is worth today	DISCOUNT FACTOR How much 1 at a future date is worth today	PRESENT WORTH OF AN ANNUITY FACTOR How much 1 received or paid annually for X years is worth today	Year
1	943 396	943 396	909 091	909 091	1
2	889 996	1 833 393	826 446	1 735 537	2
3	839 619	2 673 012	751 315	2.486 852	3
4	792 094	3 465 106	683 013	3.169 865	4
5	747 258	4 212 364	620 921	3.790 787	5
6	704 961	4 917 324	564 474	4 355 261	6
7	665 057	5 582 381	513 158	4.868 419	7
8	627 412	6 209 794	466 507	5 334 926	8
9	591 898	6 801 692	424 098	5.759 024	9
10	558 395	7 360 087	385 543	6.144 567	10
11	526 788	7 886 875	350 494	6.495 061	11
12	496 969	8 383 844	318 631	6 813 692	12
13	468 839	8 852 683	289 664	7 103 356	13
14	442 301	9 294 984	263 331	7 366 687	14
15	417 265	9 712 249	239 392	7 606 080	15
16	393 646	10 105 895	217 629	7 823 709	16
17	371 364	10 477 260	197 845	8.021 553	17
18	350 344	10 827 603	179 859	8 201 412	18
19	330 513	11 158 116	163 508	8 364 920	19
20	311 805	11 469 921	148 644	8 513 564	20
21	294 155	11 764 077	135 131	8 648 694	21
22	277 505	12 041 582	122 846	8 771 540	22
23	261 797	12 303 379	111 678	8 883 218	23
24	246 979	12 550 358	101 526	8 984 744	24
25	232 999	12 783 356	092 296	9 077 040	25
26	219 810	13 003 166	083 905	9 160 945	26
27	207 368	13 210 534	076 278	9 237 223	27
28	195 630	13 406 164	069 343	9 306 567	28
29	184 557	13 590 721	063 039	9 369 606	29
30	174 110	13 764 831	057 309	9 426 914	30
31	164 255	13 929 086	052 099	9 479 013	31
32	154 957	14 084 043	047 362	9 526 376	32
33	146 186	14 230 230	043 057	9 569 432	33
34	137 912	14 368 141	039 143	9 608 575	34
35	130 105	14 498 246	035 584	9 644 159	35
36	122 741	14 620 987	032 349	9 676 508	36
37	115 793	14 736 780	029 408	9 705 917	37
38	109 239	14 846 019	026 735	9 732 651	38
39	103 056	14 949 075	024 304	9 756 956	39
40	097 222	15 046 297	022 095	9 779 051	40
41	091 719	15 138 016	020 086	9.799 137	41
42	086 527	15 224 543	018 260	9.817 397	42
43	081 630	15 306 173	016 600	9.833 998	43
44	077 009	15 383 182	015 091	9.849 089	44
45	072 650	15.455 832	013 719	9.862 808	45
46	068 538	15 524 370	012 472	9.875 280	46
47	064 658	15 589 028	011 338	9 886 618	47
48	060 998	15 650 027	010 307	9.896 926	48
49	057 546	15 707 572	009 370	9 906 296	49
50	054 288	15 761 861	008 519	9 914 814	50

Source: Gittinger (1973:13 and 21). Reprinted by permission of The World Bank and The Johns Hopkins University Press.

The Economic Analysis

Given the data presented in the previous section, the problem is to evaluate in physical and economic terms two alternative management scenarios for the Nam Pong Reservoir. One scenario involves no watershed management at all; as a consequence, erosion rates increase until the 10th year and remain high thereafter during the 50-year period of analysis. On the other hand, there are no watershed management costs. The second scenario contains a well-developed watershed management plan, which lowers erosion rates until the 10th year and keeps them at this lower level for the remaining 40 years of the 50-year period. However, installation and operating costs are substantial under this plan.

The specific assignment is to compute, for each scenario, (1) the remaining effective reservoir capacity for each of the 50-year period; (2) the gross benefits for each of these years; and (3) the present value of the annual gross benefits and of the annual costs of the reservoir management program for the 50 years, using discount rates for 10, 6, and 0 percent.

Physical data on erosion rates for each scenario, watershed area, and translation and conversion factors contained in the previous section are to be used to compute remaining effective reservoir capacities. Gross benefits are computed by using the formula translating remaining effective reservoir capacity into gross benefits. Watershed management cost data are used along with data on annual gross benefits to compute annual net benefits. The table of present value factors at 6 percent and 10 percent for 50 years can be used to help compute the present values of the 50-year annual net benefit streams. The two scenarios are to be compared in terms of present value of net benefits at each of the three discount rates.

Based on the results, what conclusions can be drawn as to the economic feasibility of the watershed management plan? How would reductions in the cost of watershed management affect the economic feasibility of the plan for the different discount rates? What level of watershed management expenditures would be "economically" justifiable at different discount rates? How would "on-site" watershed management benefits in terms of increased value of agricultural crops on watershed lands affect the economic feasibility of the plan?

The Results

Scenario 1: No-Management Plan

Starting with year 1, the annual erosion rate per hectare increased 4 tons/ha each year for 10 years from the base-year rate of 40 tons/ha. Thus the rate is 44 tons/ha in year 1, 48 tons/ha in year 2, and 80 tons/ha in year 10. For years 11 through 50, the rate is constant at 80 tons/ha, all as shown in item 1 of Table 8.4.

Using the information shown under "The Data," this chapter, the reduction in

Table 8.4 Cumulative Annual Reductions of Effective Reservoir Capacity and Gross Annual Benefits, Nam Pong Reservoir, with No-Management Program for the Watershed: Scenario 1

Item						Year							
	0	1	2	3	4	5	6	7	8	9	10	~	50
1. Annual erosion rate (tons/ha)	40	44	48	52	56	60	64	68	72	76	80	~	80
2. Factor to convert annual erosion rate to annual reservoir sedimentation (10^6 m^3)[a]	0.261	0.261	0.261	0.261	0.261	0.261	0.261	0.261	0.261	0.261	0.261	~	0.261
3. Factor to convert annual reservoir sedimentation to reduction in effective reservoir capacity	0.75	0.75	0.75	0.75	0.75	0.75	0.75	0.75	0.75	0.75	0.75	~	0.75
4. Annual reduction in effective reservoir capacity (10^6 m^3)	0	8.62	9.41	10.19	10.97	11.76	12.54	13.33	14.11	14.89	15.68	~	15.68
5. Cumulative reduction in effective reservoir capacity (10^6 m^3)	0	8.62	18.03	28.22	39.19	50.95	63.49	76.82	90.13	105.82	121.15	~	748.35
6. Annual gross benefits (baht million)[b]	300.00	298.28	296.39	294.36	292.16	289.81	287.30	284.64	281.97	278.84	275.77	~	150.33

[a]Watershed area of 1,250,000 hectares x 1.56 (channel and bedload erosion factor) x 0.2 (sediment delivery ratio) x 0.67 (cubic meters/ton) x $1/10^6$ = 0.261 x 10^6 m^3.

[b]Annual gross benefits = benefits in base year (300.00 baht million) − 0.2 (cumulative reduction in effective reservoir capacity, 10^6 m^3 [item 5]).

Table 8.5 Cumulative Annual Reductions of Effective Reservoir Capacity and Gross Annual Benefits, Nam Pong Reservoir, with Management Program for the Watershed: Scenario 2

Item	Year											
	0	1	2	3	4	5	6	7	8	9	10	50
1. Annual erosion rate (tons/ha)	40	39	38	37	36	35	34	33	32	31	30	30
2. Factor to convert annual erosion rate to annual reservoir sedimentation (10^6 m^3)[a]	0.261	0.261	0.261	0.261	0.261	0.261	0.261	0.261	0.261	0.261	0.261	0.261
3. Factor to convert annual reservoir sedimentation to reduction in effective reservoir capacity	0.75	0.75	0.75	0.75	0.75	0.75	0.75	0.75	0.75	0.75	0.75	0.75
4. Annual reduction in effective reservoir capacity (10^6 m^3)	0	7.64	7.45	7.25	7.06	6.86	6.66	6.46	6.27	6.07	5.88	5.88
5. Cumulative reduction in effective reservoir capacity (10^6 m^3)	0	7.64	15.09	22.34	29.40	36.26	42.92	49.38	55.65	61.72	67.60	302.80
6. Annual gross benefits (baht million)[b]	300.00	298.47	296.98	295.53	294.12	292.75	291.42	290.12	288.87	287.66	286.48	239.43

[a] Watershed area of 1,250,000 hectares x 1.56 (channel and bedload erosion factor) x 0.2 (sediment delivery ratio) x 0.67 (cubic meters/ton) x 1/10^6 = 0.261 x 10^6 m^3.

[b] Annual gross benefits = benefits in base year (300.00 baht million) − 0.2 (cumulative reduction in effective reservoir capacity, 10^6 m^3 [item 5]).

effective reservoir storage capacity for each year (1 through 50) is computed as follows:

1. Annual erosion rate per hectare is multiplied by the area of the watershed in hectares (1,250,000).
2. This product is multiplied by the channel and bedload erosion factor 1.56 and the sediment delivery ratio 0.2, thus translating watershed erosion into reservoir sedimentation.
3. This product is multiplied by the factor (0.67) converting tons to m³.
4. This product is multiplied by the factor (0.75) translating volume of reservoir sediment to reduction of effective reservoir storage capacity. These computations are shown in Tables 8.4 and 8.5.

From these data on annual reduction of effective reservoir storage capacity (item 4, Table 8.4), one can compute the cumulative reduction in such capacity (item 5, Table 8.4).

Equation (8-1) shows that annual gross benefits (*B*) from operation of the reservoir is a function of the remaining effective storage capacity for the year in question. The functional relationship is given as

$$B = 300 - 0.2 \, (1,650 - y) \tag{8-2}$$

where B = annual gross benefits in 10^6 baht
and y = remaining effective storage capacity in 10^6 m³

This equation can be rewritten as

$B = 300 - 0.2$ (cumulative reduction in effective storage capacity),

or

$$B = 300 - 0.2 \, (\text{item 5, Table 8.4}) \tag{8-3}$$

The results of these calculations are shown in item 6, Table 8.4, and in the second column of Table 8.6.

The annual discount factors for 6 percent and 10 percent shown in Table 8.3 are used to compute present values of annual benefits for each of the 50 years. Total present values for the entire 50-year period are $4,095 \times 10^6$ baht for a 6 percent discount rate and $2,701 \times 10^6$ baht for a 10 percent discount rate. Undiscounted benefits for the 50 years are $11,398 \times 10^6$ baht. These values are shown in Table 8.6.

Scenario 2: With Watershed Management Plan

The computations of annual and cumulative reductions in reservoir storage and gross annual benefits are the same as for Scenario 1. The only difference is that the annual erosion rates decline from the base-year rate of 40 tons/ha. The decline is at

Table 8.6   Present Value of Gross Benefits, Nam Pong Reservoir, under
Scenario 1: with No Watershed Management (10^6 baht)

Year	Annual benefit	Present value of benefits at	
		6% discount rate	10% discount rate
1	298.28	281.40	271.17
2	296.39	263.79	244.94
3	294.36	247.14	221.15
4	292.16	231.42	199.55
5	289.81	216.58	179.94
6	287.30	202.55	162.18
7	284.64	189.31	146.08
8	281.97	176.91	131.54
9	278.84	165.05	118.26
10	275.77	153.99	106.31
11	272.56	143.58	95.53
12	269.42	133.90	85.84
13	266.28	124.83	77.14
14	263.14	116.39	69.24
15	260.00	108.50	62.24
16	256.86	101.10	55.89
17	253.72	94.23	50.19
18	250.58	87.78	45.08
19	247.44	81.78	40.46
20	244.41	76.21	36.32
21	241.27	70.98	32.60
22	238.14	66.08	29.24
23	235.00	61.52	26.25
24	231.87	57.27	23.53
25	228.73	53.29	21.11
26	225.59	49.58	18.93
27	222.46	46.14	16.97
28	219.32	42.90	15.20
29	216.19	39.91	13.62
30	213.05	39.09	12.21
31	209.91	34.49	10.94
32	266.78	32.05	9.80
33	203.64	29.77	8.78
34	200.51	27.66	7.84
35	197.37	25.68	7.03
36	194.23	23.83	6.27
37	191.10	22.13	5.62
38	187.96	20.53	5.02
39	184.83	19.06	4.49
40	181.69	17.66	4.02
41	178.55	16.37	3.59
42	175.42	15.17	3.21
43	172.28	14.06	2.86
44	169.15	13.02	2.60
45	166.01	12.07	2.27
46	162.87	11.16	2.04
47	159.74	10.34	1.81
48	156.60	9.55	1.61
49	153.47	8.82	1.44
50	150.33	8.16	1.28
Total	11,397.99	4,094.78	2,701.23

the rate of 1 ton/ha/year until the 10th year, when the rate of 30 tons/ha is attained. This rate is maintained for the remaining 40 years of the 50-year period of economic analysis. The data and computations are shown in Table 8.5.

As in the first scenario, the gross benefits for each of the 50 years are discounted at the 6 percent and 10 percent discount rates. The sums of present values for the 50 years are $4,431 \times 10^6$ baht at 6 percent, $2,837 \times 10^6$ baht at 10 percent, and $13,517 \times 10^6$ baht undiscounted. These results are shown in Table 8.7.

Watershed management costs must be deducted from these gross benefits to obtain net benefits for Scenario 2. We previously noted that watershed management costs are 100 million baht for each of the first 10 years and 50 million baht for each of the remaining 40 years. Using the appropriate discount factors shown under "Cost Data," this chapter, the following present value of costs in baht are obtained:

	0%	6%	10%
Years 1–10	$1,000 \times 10^6$	736×10^6	615×10^6
Years 11–50	$2,000 \times 10^6$	420×10^6	188×10^6
Entire 50 years	$3,000 \times 10^6$	$1,156 \times 10^6$	803×10^6

Net benefits for Scenarios 1 and 2 can now be compared. For Scenario 1, the no-management option, net benefits are as stated earlier. For Scenario 2, net benefits are found by subtracting discounted management costs from discounted gross benefits (measured in 10^6 baht):

		0%	6%	10%
Scenario 2	Gross benefits	13,517	4,431	2,837
	Gross costs	−3,000	−1,156	−803
	Net benefits	10,517	3,275	2,034

Comparing Scenarios 1 and 2 net benefits in 10^6 baht shows that Scenario 1, the no-management option, has greater net benefits:

		Discount rate		
		0%	6%	10%
Scenario 1	Net benefits	11,398	4,095	2,701
Scenario 2	Net benefits	10,517	3,275	2,034

Discussion

On the basis of the data provided, Scenario 1—no management—has greater net benefits at all three discount rates. This means that, in terms of the narrowly defined Nam Pong Reservoir benefits only, the watershed management plan is not economically feasible. It appears that at a 0 discount rate only $2,119 \times 10^6$ baht

Table 8.7 Present Value of Gross Benefits, Nam Pong Reservoir, under Scenario 2: with Watershed Management (10^6 baht)

Year	Annual benefit	Present value of benefits at	
		6% discount rate	10% discount rate
1	298.47	281.58	271.34
2	296.98	264.31	245.42
3	295.53	248.13	222.03
4	294.12	232.97	200.88
5	292.75	218.77	181.77
6	291.42	205.45	164.55
7	290.12	192.96	148.89
8	288.87	181.24	134.76
9	287.66	170.27	122.00
10	286.48	159.97	110.44
11	285.30	150.30	100.00
12	284.12	141.21	90.52
13	382.94	132.64	81.97
14	281.77	124.63	74.19
15	280.59	117.09	67.17
16	279.42	109.98	60.80
17	278.24	103.34	55.04
18	277.06	97.05	49.84
19	275.89	91.18	45.11
20	274.71	85.65	40.82
21	273.54	80.48	36.96
22	272.36	75.58	33.45
23	271.18	70.99	30.29
24	270.01	66.69	27.41
25	268.83	62.64	24.81
26	267.66	58.84	22.46
27	266.48	55.27	20.33
28	265.30	51.89	18.39
29	264.13	48.76	16.64
30	262.95	45.78	15.07
31	261.78	43.01	13.64
32	260.60	40.39	12.35
33	259.42	37.93	11.18
34	258.25	35.61	10.10
35	257.07	33.44	9.15
36	255.90	31.40	8.27
37	254.72	29.50	7.49
38	253.54	27.69	6.77
39	252.37	26.02	6.13
40	251.19	24.42	5.55
41	250.02	22.93	5.03
42	248.84	21.52	4.55
43	247.66	20.21	4.11
44	246.49	18.98	3.72
45	245.31	17.83	3.36
46	244.14	16.72	3.05
47	242.96	15.72	2.75
48	241.78	14.75	2.49
49	240.61	13.84	2.26
50	239.43	13.00	2.04
Total	13,516.96	4,430.55	2,837.34
Watershed management costs	3,000.00	1,156.00	803.00
Net benefits	10,516.96	3,274.55	2,034.34

(13,517 − 11,398) of watershed management expenses could be economically justified.

If watershed management costs were reduced to 75 million per year for the first 10 years and 31.25 million per year for the next 40 years, present value of costs would be as follows:

	0%	6%	10%
Years 1–10	750,000	552,000	461,250
Years 11–50	1,250,000	262,500	117,500
	2,000,000	814,500	578,750

Net benefits for the two scenarios would be:

	0%	6%	10%
Scenario 1 (no management)	11,398	4,095	2,701
Scenario 2 (with management)	10,517	3,275	2,034

When costs are reduced to 37.5 million per year for the first 10 years and 15 million per year for the next 40 years, the results are as follows:

Present value of costs

	0%	6%	10%
Years 1–10	375	276	230.6
Years 11–50	600	126	56.4
	975	402	287.0

Net benefits

	0%	6%	10%
Scenario 1 (no management)	11,398	4,095	2,701
Scenario 2 (with management)	12,542	4,029	2,550

If the costs for the first 10 years are reduced even further, the net benefits of the with-management option, Scenario 2, will just exceed the net benefits of the no-management option, Scenario 1. It appears, therefore, that at a 6 percent discount rate, an annual expenditure rate for watershed protection of about 37 million baht per year for the first 10 years and 15 million per year for the remaining 40 years would be justified in terms of Nam Pong Reservoir benefits.

If on-site crop production benefits were computed and found to be sizable, then additional investments in watershed management can be justified. As mentioned earlier, there is also the strong possibility that other benefits from erosion control and reservoir life prolongation exist but have not been included in the benefit function. An earlier discussion mentioned the changes in reservoir water quality due to watershed land-use activities that included use of fertilizer and pesticides for agricultural production. These effects have not been included in the analysis. As a result, the benefits placed on watershed management may be taken as a minimum, not a maximum, value. This in turn would support a decision to undertake watershed protection measures at a level equal to or in excess of the cost just mentioned—37 million baht per year for the first 10 years and 15 million per year for the remaining 40 years.

References

Gittinger, J. P., ed. *Compounding and Discounting Tables for Project Evaluation.* Baltimore: Johns Hopkins University Press, 1973.

Interim Committee for Co-ordination of Investigations of the Lower Mekong Basin. *Environmental Management and Water Resource Development in the Nam Pong Basin of Northeastern Thailand,* November 1979a.

———. *Nam Pong Environmental Management Research Project Working Documents no. 1–13,* 1979b.

———. *Nam Pong Environmental Management Research Project: Final Report for Phase III,* 1982.

SEATEC Consulting Engineers. *Study of Environmental Impact of Nam Pong Project,* January 1978.

9
Selected Policy Options for Fuelwood Production and Use in the Philippines

Adapted by John A. Dixon from materials
prepared by Eric L. Hyman (additional background
materials contributed by K. Freerk Wiersum)

Summary

Fuelwood collection is a basic activity for households and certain cottage industries in many of the countries in the Asia-Pacific region. This case study examines benefits and costs of selected policy options for increasing fuelwood supplies or decreasing fuelwood demand in the Ilocos region in northern Luzon in the Philippines. On the supply side, a benefit-cost analysis is done on a government-sponsored treefarming project. In order to reduce the demand for fuelwood, two demand-side options also are considered—the introduction of an improved, more energy-efficient woodstove, and the substitution of a kerosene stove for a traditional woodstove.

Fuelwood is important because it satisfies a basic need for the rural poor, but overcutting of trees for fuelwood can have environmental impacts. Given the complicated interactions between humans, forest lands, land-use practices, and fuelwood collection, it is difficult to state precisely that a 20 percent decrease in fuelwood collection will result in an x percent improvement in forest land use or a y percent decrease in deforestation or erosion. The analysis presented here illustrates techniques for evaluating each policy option with respect to certain economic and environmental factors. Ideally, these options could then be incorporated into a larger benefit-cost analysis of a forest land management program that would aim to meet many of the complex forest land use needs at one time. This case study does not attempt to analyze the wider energy planning exercise that would be needed to understand accurately the various alternatives available in Ilocos Norte. The wider analysis would examine such things as what mix of industries, and what sorts of fuel, make the most sense in the particular setting.

Background Information

Wood, burned directly or converted to charcoal, is the fourth largest source of energy in the world, after petroleum, coal, and natural gas. Furthermore, woodfuel use statistics often greatly underestimate true consumption because most wood is gathered directly by users rather than being purchased. The shortage of woodfuels leads to economic welfare losses, as well as environmental degradation from overcutting of trees.

The Philippines is in the middle range of Southeast Asian countries in terms of per capita woodfuel consumption; fuelwood comprises 41 percent of total energy in kilograms per coal equivalent (Knowland and Ulinski 1979). At the same time, with the present lack of good forest management practices, the Philippines has a low sustainable forest yield (Hyman 1983b).

This case study examines various policy options for meeting the demand for fuelwood and rural energy supplies in one province of the Philippines, Ilocos Norte. Ilocos Norte is located in the upper northeast portion of Luzon and has a land area of 370,000 hectares. Except along the coastal fringe, it is primarily mountainous. Degraded second-growth forest of noncommercial species occupies 54,500 hectares, often on sloping lands. Since Ilocos Norte has only 24,500 hectares of old-growth forest, most of which is inaccessible or of low quality, there is little logging for domestic or export production of timber or pulpwood. Nevertheless, tree cutting rates are high due to local demands for fuelwood, polewood, and construction wood. There are 270,000 hectares of noxious Imperata grasslands, open lands, and developed areas (Argete, pers. com. 1982), partly caused by slash-and-burn agricultural practices in the uplands.

The population of Ilocos Norte in 1980 was about 395,000 and about three-quarters of all households were in rural areas (Philippine National Census and Statistics Office 1980). In addition to food crop production, cash crops are also grown, of which the major ones are tobacco and cotton.

Fuelwood is an important form of rural energy in Ilocos Norte. Nearly 97 percent of all households cook with fuelwood at least part of the time. The average household fuelwood consumption is 65 kilograms (kg)/week/family; in addition, rural households burn small amounts of charcoal and agricultural residues. Large amounts of fuelwood are also needed for tobacco curing. The fuelwood required for curing amounts to about 17 percent of the total household fuelwood needs.

Fuelwood is obtained either from public or private lands. On private lands some farmers have responded to the demand for fuelwood by establishing woodlots or by planting trees along farm boundaries. The major tree species in such woodlots are Giant Ipil-Ipil (*Leucaena leicocephala*) and Kakawate (*Gliricidia sepium*). Farmers have developed several methods for managing these woodlots or other private tree resources, but no statistics are available about their total area and production capacity (Wiersum 1982). Similarly, no reliable data are available about the importance of public forest lands for providing fuelwood.

Although the present regional resource basis for fuelwood is known imprecisely and the few existing studies about the local fuelwood situation mainly have been consumption surveys rather than supply-and-demand studies, there are several reasons the future fuelwood production capacity of the area is in doubt. First, the production capacity of most public forest lands is threatened by conversion to nonforest land uses. Second, the future demand for fuelwood will rise in response to population growth and increases in tobacco production. Third, there exist several plans in Ilocos Norte for the establishment of large-scale projects such as charcoal-using pig iron blast furnaces and dendro-thermal power plants, which will increase the demand for fuelwood tremendously. As planned, these projects are assumed to provide their own wood energy resources from associated plantations. Because of slow progress in planting and high rates of mortality, however, it seems reasonable to expect that commercialization will result in at least some degree of substitution of fuelwood from the existing traditional fuelwood sector to this new modern fuelwood sector (Wiersum 1982; Hyman 1984a).

Various policy options exist to meet future fuelwood demand by the traditional sector in Ilocos Norte. Three such options include treefarming, adoption of more efficient woodstoves, and use of kerosene as a substitute fuel. This case study presents various valuation techniques that can be used to evaluate these options and permit a more informed decision about these alternatives.

Environmental Dimensions

The environmental dimensions of this case study are difficult to quantify. While it is known that Ilocos Norte is subject to a heavy demand for fuelwood and is already extensively deforested, the relationship between these two processes is not known precisely. As already mentioned it is not known how much fuelwood is actually derived from the public forest lands and how much from private lands. Although fuelwood cutting is often considered a major factor in deforestation on public lands, other causes of deforestation may include the search for new agricultural lands, illegal logging of timber, and indiscriminate burning. These latter two causes are often of prime importance in the initial clearing of forests, with fuelwood cutters only removing the last remaining trees and shrubs (Wiersum 1982).

The environmental effects of degradation of forests and deforestation are also varied and site-specific. Conventional wisdom holds that deforestation increases flood peaks in lowland areas, decreases dry-season stream flow, and increases erosion. Although the hydrological impacts of deforestation are now being reexamined, there is little doubt that unsustainable land-use practices and removal of forest cover can lead to increased soil erosion and downstream siltation, especially during the critical period immediately after cutting. Ilocos Norte may be particularly susceptible to these environmental effects because the province receives little rainfall for eight months of the year and heavy rainfall during the rest of the year. In the long run, soil erosion can be controlled by appropriate cultivation techniques or by using various forms of ground cover. Another possible economic loss from the overcutting of remaining tree stands for fuelwood is the foregone production potential for future timber and other forest products—products that may have alternative uses with a higher market value than firewood or charcoal.

Regardless of the exact environmental consequences of deforestation, there is general agreement in Ilocos Norte on several facts: (1) there is a rural energy shortage; (2) fuelwood is the most common rural fuel, and its use will increase for both continued household use and for new commercial purposes; (3) deforestation decreases the production capacity for fuelwood; (4) deforestation is often the symptom of unsustainable land-use practices that lead to negative environmental consequences on-site and off-site; and (5) reforestation of denuded lands may assist to ensure a future resource base for fuelwood production, as well as to control environmental degradation.

The Approach Used

This case study is based on data from a large survey of the demand for fuelwood and an analysis of nine options for meeting that demand (Hyman 1985). This use of a large-scale survey is different from the survey-based techniques presented in Chapter 6 of the *Guide*. Rather than relying on surveys to determine values for an environmental good or even the value of fuelwood, this study used surveys to determine the magnitude of fuelwood demand and the various factors that affect this demand.

In analyzing woodfuel energy consumption, the following aspects were considered important:

1. The characteristics of the users;
2. The tasks energy performs;
3. The cost in money, traded goods, or effort in collecting and growing wood;
4. The potential for substitution of alternative fuels, their costs, and availability;
5. Characteristics of the fuel such as renewability, storability, ease of transport, convenience, versatility, and requirements for auxiliary equipment; and
6. Environmental impacts of fuelwood acquisition and use including deforestation, cleanliness, health effects, and real and perceived safety of combustion.

In addition, the original study was designed to produce information that could be used in the formulation of policies regarding woodfuels rather than just the creation of another data base. Some of the policies that were included as relevant are:

1. Government-sponsored programs for growing trees on public lands by individuals or groups;
2. Loans for growing trees on private lands;

3.   The use of agroforestry practices, combining both agricultural crops and trees instead of purestand treefarming;
4.   Dissemination of improved woodstoves that are more fuel efficient, low cost, and compatible with cultural preferences;
5.   More fuel-efficient methods of energy use for traditional, small-scale industrial purposes such as tobacco curing;
6.   Encouragement to substitute other fuels (such as bamboo, kerosene, LPG, and electricity);
7.   Adoption of more efficient charcoal production processes; and
8.   Regulations designed to maintain the maximum sustained yield for the short-run or long-run balance between supply and demand.

Additional policies, which may be of importance in addressing the fuelwood situation but which could not be included in the original study, include:

1.   Improvement of management practices for existing smallholder woodlots;
2.   Information campaigns; and
3.   Improved distribution and marketing of fuelwood.

The survey reached 802 rural and urban households—1 percent of the number in the province (Hyman, in press). Another sample consisted of 359 cottage industry firms including tobacco curers, blacksmiths, bakeries, restaurants, and producers of sugarcane wine, molasses, salt, and pottery (Hyman 1984a). The demand surveys investigated consumption and uses of wood and charcoal fuels. These questionnaires elicited data on time spent in collecting firewood; species preferred; proportion and source of firewood bought, traded, or collected for free; proportion grown for own use; and prices paid. All the amounts of fuelwood were converted into actual weights because of lack of standardization of commonly used units. Special emphasis was placed on preferences for types of woodstoves and attitudes toward tree growing in order to develop policies directed at solving the woodfuels shortage.

Some questions in the consumption survey also were directed toward consumption of other biomass fuels such as bamboo, coconut shells and husks, rice hulls and stems, bagasse, and animal dung, as well as conventional fuels such as LPG, kerosene, and electricity, to determine the extent to which these currently serve as substitutes for fuelwood.

Another survey dealt with participants in two government projects designed to encourage treefarming (Hyman 1983d; 1984b). The questionnaires for the fuelwood treefarmers were quite different from those for fuelwood consumers. The questions in the treefarming surveys covered background of the treefarmer; size and quality of the treefarm site; initiation of the project; tree spacing; staging of planting and harvesting; labor requirements for clearing land, planting, taking care of trees, and harvesting them; tree growth and mortality; economic returns; use of co-products such as leaves, fruits, and nuts; market for the output; extension of treefarming beyond the project area; treefarmers' evaluations of the program and participating institutions; problems and good points of the project; and willingness to participate again in a similar project. Another survey covered fuelwood sellers and charcoal makers (Hyman 1983a). The methodology used in the preceding surveys is discussed in Hyman (1983c). Another source of information on wood energy survey methodologies is FAO (1983). Where resources permit, data also should be collected on the extent and production capacity of the various existing fuelwood resources.

This case study examines several supply-side or demand-side policy options for dealing with the fuelwood problem. The main supply-side approach to providing fuelwood is through treefarming projects, whether carried out by the private sector or by the government. Demand-side options are aimed at reducing firewood demand by either introducing more efficient wood-burning stoves or by substituting other fuels such as kerosene.

Techniques Used for Shadow Pricing Fuelwood

Some fuelwood is collected by household members and some is bought in the market. Thus, market prices are available for valuing purchased fuelwood, although there is considerable variation in prices. However, a shadow price must be estimated for collected, own-consumption fuelwood. Several methods for deriving the shadow price of fuelwood are possible. The first method applies *hypothetical valuation* techniques, such as direct questioning or bidding games, to estimate maximum willingness to pay (*WTP*) for resource supply or minimum willingness-to-accept compensation for resource deprivation (see Chapter 6 of the *Guide*). Respondents tend to express low *WTP* values because in rural areas fuelwood has been a free good historically. Furthermore, *WTP* is bounded by the low ability to pay of the poor. Strategic bias may also be a problem since individuals may have incentives to underreport their true valuation of fuelwood.

The second method, the one adopted here, bases the shadow price on *revealed preferences*. It assumes that the value people place on woodfuel must at least equal their costs in collecting it as a free good, including travel time to collection sites and related transportation costs. Thus, travel time is valued at its opportunity cost in terms of foregone labor. Based on relative productivity and opportunity cost factors, a child's labor time is valued at one-half of the adult wage rate. If there is extensive surplus labor due to underemployment or unemployment, the opportunity cost of labor time in collecting fuelwood may be low. Transportation costs are very low because household members usually travel on foot to collect fuelwood unless they are relatively affluent and grow fuelwood on lands that they own.

In the *alternative cost* or opportunity cost method, the cost of the *next cheapest* (and realistic) energy substitute is taken as the benefits of woodfuel supply. Agricultural residuals or charcoal are now likely to be the next cheapest alternative.

Where it is used, animal dung may be valued in terms of the extra agricultural output that would be obtained if it were used as a fertilizer. In some areas, dung may not have other uses than burning due to difficulties in transportation or waterlogging.

In theory each of the three approaches mentioned above would give the same result for the value of fuelwood if the economy and its prices reflected economic scarcity and if consumers perceived the "true" value of fuelwood (and hence could accurately value it in a hypothetical valuation exercise). In practice the results will vary and will present a range of values.

The hypothetical valuation, *WTP* approach, is hampered by unfamiliarity of consumers with valuation of nominally "free" goods. The revealed preference approach is potentially stronger but heavily dependent on an accurate estimate of the value of labor time. Potentially these two approaches may give the same result. The alternative cost approach does not directly examine the value of the resource in question and may not be a reliable method if the next cheapest alternative is extremely costly. Market prices, although the best example of revealed preference, may be unrepresentative because of the small, limited market for fuelwood. Nonetheless, the techniques should give a useful range of values for the overall analysis.

For policy options that substitute other fuels for fuelwood, the energy supply benefits are valued as the product of the quantity of fuelwood saved as a result of the substitution and the market or shadow price of fuelwood. Estimates of environmental effects of the various options also are made and values assigned.

In sum, this example is not a traditional, self-contained project evaluation. Rather, it presents one way in which various policy options have been addressed and valued and how some of the environmental dimensions have been included. For each of the policy options, net present value (*NPV*) is calculated by estimating and discounting the annual stream of direct benefits (B_d) and direct costs (C_d), and environmental benefits (B_e).

The Data

Based on the survey results and other Philippine sources, the following data are used (at the time of the survey US\$1 = P8):

1. The discount rate is set at 15 percent per annum.
2. The rural adult wage rate is P15 per day (8 hours of work); child labor is valued at half the wage rate of adult labor. This wage rate includes cash and the cash equivalent of in-kind allowances such as food.
3. There are 771 kg of air-dried Giant Ipil-Ipil (a type of leguminous tree) per solid cubic meter of wood.
4. Treefarming inputs and costs, based on median values from the survey data, are presented in Table 9.1.

Table 9.1 Inputs and Costs of Government-Sponsored Treefarming in Ilocos Norte Using Giant Ipil-Ipil (per ha)

Operation or activity	Year	Labor requirement (man-days equivalent)	Input cost (₱)
1. Land clearing and preparation	1	35	
2. Seedlings (5,000/ha at a 1 x 2 meter spacing)	1	-	0.35/ seedling
3. Lining, digging, and planting seedlings	1	35	
4. Seedling replacement in year 2 based on 20% mortality in year 1	2	-	0.35/ seedling
5. Replanting seedlings	2	5	
6. Fertilizer purchases	1		42
	2		61
7. Fertilizer application	1	7	
	2	3	
8. Weeding and brush removal	1	10	
	2	13	
9. Maintenance	3 to 8	4	
10. Weeding and single coppice ratoon	5	4	
11. Harvesting	5 and 9	$1.6/\text{solid m}^3$	
12. Social cost of loan administration	1		110
13. Social cost of nursery development	1		735
	2		147
14. Social cost of collecting loan payment	5, 6, 7, 8		60

5. Kerosene stoves cost ₱70; improved woodstoves cost ₱85; domestic kerosene costs ₱4.67 per liter. (This is not a subsidized price. If kerosene were subsidized, or taxed, these price distortions would have to be removed in an analysis of social benefits and costs.)

6. Land quality benefits from a well-managed forest cover are derived from (1) the accumulation of leafy and woody materials for decomposition into humus and (2) the preservation of topsoil and nutrients as a result of

reduced erosion rates. This study assumes that the incremental productivity of better soil is at least equal to the cost of purchasing and applying the fertilizer that would be needed to maintain soil fertility in the absence of tree cover. This would require 50 kg of fertilizer (at ₱2.32 per kg) and 10 man-days per hectare per year. Thus, the annual *land quality benefits* of a forest cover exceed ₱266 per hectare for those policy options involving tree planting.

In this example, other environmental benefits such as watershed benefits or climatic benefits are not quantified. However, lower-bound estimates could be made for them. If a case can be made on economic grounds for an option based on underestimated benefits, that is all that has to be shown.

The Economic Analysis

Three policy options for dealing with the rural energy problem in Ilocos Norte can be evaluated using the information given. A 9-year time horizon is adopted to reduce the arithmetic in these examples. The first task is to estimate the shadow price of fuelwood based on the labor required to collect it. The survey found that an average family collected 65 kg per week for its own consumption using four hours of adult labor and four hours of child labor. This information will be used in problems 1, 2, and 3.

1. Expanding treefarming is one option for decreasing fuelwood collection pressure on existing forests. In government-sponsored projects the planting of Giant Ipil-Ipil is encouraged. These trees can be harvested for fuelwood in year 5. If the stumps are left standing (the ratoon system), they will sprout back and can be harvested at 4-year intervals three or four times without significantly reducing the yields. At a close spacing and assuming no tree mortality, pure stand yields are 123 m^3/ha at each harvest. Assume that tree mortality is 25 percent even after replanting dead seedlings in year 2.

Using the shadow price of fuelwood, calculate the *NPV* of a 1-ha treefarm based on the data given here and in Table 9.1. Recalculate the *NPV* including the values of environmental benefits from soil conservation (point 6 in the preceding section). Assume that these benefits begin in year 2 of treefarm establishment.

How sensitive are the results to the inclusion of environmental benefits? How much would the *NPV* change if the discount rate were 5 percent? 20 percent? Would the *NPV* increase or decrease if the time horizon were extended to include a total of five harvests (years 5, 9, 13, 17, and 21)?

2. The use of an improved woodstove is another policy option. These stoves would consume less fuel and thereby reduce pressure on existing fuelwood sources. Assume that the efficiency of a traditional stove is 0.075 (that is, only 7.5 percent of the available energy is used in cooking) and that the new stove's efficiency is 0.20. Using the old stove, a family would need 65 kg of wood per

week. Calculate the annual energy supply benefits of each new woodstove adopted.

The new stoves have a 9-year life and cost ₱85 to purchase, and there is a 1-time cost of ₱100 per stove for the administration required to introduce, demonstrate, and market the new stoves. These costs both occur in year 1. Calculate the *NPV* per woodstove.

What would the *NPV* be if the new stove's efficiency were 0.10? How large are the soil conservation benefits associated with the reduced deforestation as a result of the improved woodstoves? Explain how you calculated these benefits.

3.   Kerosene stoves are another policy option. Kerosene would have to be imported but the widespread use of kerosene stoves would decrease fuelwood consumption for home cooking, which is the single largest source of fuelwood demand.

The kerosene stove costs ₱70 in year 1, and there is also the ₱100 administrative cost of implementing a policy of substituting these stoves. Since this is a substitution, the energy supply benefits are the value of fuelwood replaced (65 kg per week) less the cost of the kerosene (2.25 liters per week at ₱4.67 per liter).

Calculate the *NPV* for the substitution of a kerosene stove over a 9-year period excluding environmental benefits. Recalculate the *NPV* including environmental benefits. Assume that the introduction of a kerosene stove leads to a 100 percent substitution of kerosene for previously used fuelwood. In fact, many households prefer the taste of some foods cooked over wood; therefore, the actual substitution of kerosene for fuelwood may be somewhat less.

If a kerosene stove had an expected useful life of 12 years, how would you adjust this analysis? In what direction would the *NPV* change if some parts of the stove have to be replaced in year 7?

The Results

Shadow Price of Fuelwood

This preliminary calculation estimates the value of fuelwood based on the labor time used to collect it. This is probably a minimum value as it does not include any scarcity value of fuelwood nor is it related to the cost of the next best alternative fuel source. The average family surveyed collected 65 kg per week of fuelwood and used both adult and child labor. Valuing the time spent in collection by the appropriate wage rate gives the following:

$(4/8)₱15 + (4/8)₱7.5 = ₱11.25$ imputed labor cost

This is equivalent to ₱11.25/65 = ₱0.173 per kilogram. In terms of solid, air-dried Giant Ipil-Ipil, this is equivalent to ₱133 per cubic meter (771 × ₱0.173 = ₱133). This calculation assumes that there are alternative productive opportunities available for adults and children at the specified wage rate. If such opportunities are not available or the true opportunity costs were higher or lower than assumed here, the shadow price of fuelwood would also change.

Treefarming

Treefarming can be evaluated using an *NPV* approach. The costs of treefarming are derived from the data given in Table 9.1 and include costs for labor and materials (activities 1 to 11) and social or administrative costs (activities 12, 13, 14). The various activities or operations occur in different years. Table 9.2 lists the costs and benefits for each year. For each activity, the labor requirement has to be converted to pesos and input costs (seedlings, fertilizer) must also be calculated.

Social costs are calculated from activities 12, 13, and 14 in Table 9.1. Similarly, input (material) costs are just seedlings and fertilizer and all such costs occur in years 1 and 2. For example, in year 1 seedlings cost P1,750 (5,000 × P0.35) and fertilizer costs P42.

Labor costs occur in all years. For example, in year 1 labor is required for land clearing and preparation (35 man-days), seedling planting (35 man-days), fertilizer application (7 man-days), and weeding and brush removal (10 man-days). This totals 87 man-days valued at P1,305 (87 × P15). In succeeding years, the following amount of labor is required:

Year	Man-days
2	21
3	4
4	4
5	155.6 (8 + 147.6)
6	4
7	4
8	4
9	147.6

Table 9.2 Direct Costs and Benefits from Treefarming (P/ha)

	Costs			Fuelwood	Net	Net present value
Year	Labor	Materials	Social costs	benefits	benefits	(15% discount rate)
1	1,305	1,792	845	0	-3,942	-3,428
2	315	411	147	0	-873	-660
3	60	0	0	0	-60	-39
4	60	0	0	0	-60	-34
5	2,334	0	60	12,270	9,876	4,910
6	60	0	60	0	-120	-52
7	60	0	60	0	-120	-45
8	60	0	60	0	-120	-39
9	2,214	0	0	12,270	10,056	2,859
	Total					3,472

The fuelwood is harvested in years 5 and 9. A purestand would yield about 123 m^3 per hectare; but, even with replanting, there is some mortality (estimated at 25 percent). Therefore, the fuelwood harvest totals 123 × .75 = 92.25 m^3. Harvesting requires 1.6 man-days of labor per cubic meter; total labor required is thus 92.25 × 1.6 = 147.6 man-days. The man-days are then converted to pesos at the stipulated wage rate, ₱15 per day. No costs have been assigned to tools used for harvesting or fieldwork.

The benefits of fuelwood farming are the value of wood produced (direct benefits) and the environmental quality benefits of maintaining land under forest cover or reforesting land. Such benefits may include reduced erosion or increased forest production from "protected" forest lands previously used for fuelwood collection. The direct benefits occur in years 5 and 9. Each year, 92.25 m^3 of fuelwood are harvested. Converted to kilograms and valued at fuelwood's shadow price, the value per hectare in each year is ₱12,270.

When the net benefits in each year are discounted using a 15 percent discount rate and summed, the *NPV* is found. In this case, it is ₱3,472 per hectare (Table 9.2). If the environmental quality benefits also are included, the positive *NPV* becomes even larger. In this example, the environmental benefits consist solely of effects on land quality, valued at ₱266 per hectare. These benefits begin in year 2 and continue for each succeeding year. Discounted, these benefits increase the *NPV* by ₱1,038 for a total *NPV* of ₱4,510.

If only direct costs and benefits are included (Table 9.2), the *NPV* at a 5 percent discount rate is ₱9,317 per hectare of treefarms. With a 20 percent discount rate, it is ₱1,860 per hectare. At higher discount rates, the *NPV* will turn negative quickly since the large initial expenses involved in tree stand establishment outweigh future benefits. The inclusion of other environmental benefits not quantified in this example would increase the *NPV*.

Since most of the costs are incurred in planting, additional coppice rotations (years 10 and on) would increase the *NPV* because the harvest benefits are much larger than the costs of harvesting and weeding.

Improved Woodstove Option

Properly operated and maintained, a new woodstove design could improve fuel efficiency from 7.5 percent to 20 percent, or more than two-and-one-half times. Fuelwood consumption would therefore decrease since now 7.5/20 or .375 as much wood will supply the energy required to cook a given amount of food. The woodfuel saving is thus .625 of the previously used amount or 0.625 × 65 kg = 40.6 kg. At ₱0.173 per kg, this is a saving of ₱7 per week or ₱365 per year.

Over a 9-year period the annual benefits of the new stove are ₱365. The costs are the ₱85 purchase price and ₱100 for promotional and administrative costs. Both costs occur in year 1. The *NPV* over nine years at a 15 percent discount rate is about

₱1,581. The introduction of improved woodstoves appears to be very attractive based on fuel savings alone. If the new stove's fuel efficiency were only 10 percent, the annual fuel saving falls to ₱146, and the first-year cash flow is negative (₱146 − ₱185). The *NPV* over nine years falls to ₱536 or one-third of the previously calculated amount.

Measuring the environmental benefits is a little more complicated. If one assumes that the decreased fuelwood demand reduces the cutting of forests for fuelwood production, one can use the value previously assigned for these benefits (₱266 per ha) and determine what part of a hectare would *not* be cut if the new stove was introduced. If annual yields on existing forest areas were similar to yields in treefarming areas ($25 \text{ m}^3 \times 770 \text{ kg/m}^3 = 19{,}250 \text{ kg/ha}$), the annual woodfuel benefits of about 2,111 kg ($40.6 \text{ kg} \times 52$) are equal to 0.11 of an hectare (2,111/19,250) or about ₱30 in annual environmental benefits per improved woodstove. In reality, natural forest yields are substantially lower than managed treefarms and therefore the environmental benefits from each kilogram of wood saved are greater. In addition, there are other benefits from reduced erosion and increased production of other forest products when fuelwood needs are reduced. If the natural forest's annual increment were only $5.75 \text{ m}^3/\text{ha}$, the environmental benefit would be ₱126 per year. At a 15 percent discount rate, the present value of annual benefits of ₱126 for years 2 to 9 amounts to ₱491.

Kerosene Stove Option

The kerosene stove is assumed to eliminate the need for fuelwood; 65 kg valued at ₱11.25 are saved per week or ₱585 per year. Annual fuel costs are ₱546 (2.25 liters × ₱4.67 per liter × 52 weeks). In addition, the stove costs ₱70 and there is a one-time administrative cost to the government of ₱100 per stove adopted. The direct benefits and costs are very close. In the first year, net benefits are negative (₱585 − ₱546 − ₱170 = − ₱131). In subsequent years, the net benefits are marginally positive, ₱39. Discounted over nine years at a 15 percent discount rate, the *NPV* is only about ₱36. If environmental benefits are included, however, this option becomes more attractive. Reasoning as before for the woodstove example, the annual land quality benefits would be ₱46 per ha (3,380/19,250 × ₱266). This increases the *NPV* by ₱180.

The kerosene stove option should be evaluated with caution. The volatile world petroleum market can lead to rapid changes in the price of kerosene. In addition, in the Philippines most kerosene is imported and foreign exchange is scarce. Therefore, one could apply a shadow price of 1.2 to foreign exchange costs as the Philippine National Economic and Development Authority does in evaluating plans. In fact, due to several major devaluations of the peso since the time of this analysis, the price of kerosene has increased substantially relative to fuelwood.

In addition, a stove may last longer than nine years (thereby increasing the *NPV*) or it may require repairs and replacement parts (thereby lowering the *NPV*). The expected working life of the stove will help determine the appropriate time horizon of the analysis.

Discussion

This case study is an example of how economic valuation techniques can provide additional information to a decision maker on the various options available. The separate options evaluated are all possible components of a forest resource management program. The treefarming example illustrates one of the possible approaches to how the *supply* of fuelwood (and energy) can be changed, while the woodstove and kerosene substitution examples are policies that would reduce the *demand* for fuelwood.

Based on this analysis, one cannot say that treefarming is definitely better than introducing new woodstoves. Both options would appear to be attractive and, if implemented, would both increase fuel supply and decrease demand. This could help to alleviate the rural energy shortage and take some pressure off existing forested areas. In practice, both types of options have been hindered by implementation problems in many areas.

The results of this analysis are very sensitive to the imputed shadow price of fuelwood. If this shadow price were greatly different from the P0.173 per kg calculated, the different options might appear more or less attractive. The only other option discussed here that appears clearly unattractive is the use of kerosene stoves. High fuel costs make this option economically unattractive although some people will opt for kerosene stoves because of convenience or other factors.

Further sensitivity analysis should be done to see how the results change given different assumptions about other key variables such as the price of kerosene, treefarm yields, opportunity cost of labor, and expected life of new stoves.

References

Argete, E. Remote Sensing Division, Philippine Natural Resources Management Center. Personal communication, 1982.

FAO. *Wood Fuel Surveys*. Forestry for Local Community Development Series, Rome, 1983.

Hyman, E. L. "Analysis of the Woodfuels Market: A Survey of Fuelwood Sellers and Charcoal Makers in the Province of Ilocos Norte, Philippines." *Biomass* 3 (1983a):167–97.

———. "Forestry Administration and Policies in the Philippines." *Environmental Management* 7, 6 (1983b):511–24.

———. "How to Conduct a Rural Energy Consumption Survey in a Developing Country." *Renewable Sources of Energy* 1 (1983c):137–49.

———. "Loan Financing of Smallholder Treefarming in the Provinces of Ilocos Norte and Ilocos Sur, the Philippines." *Agroforestry Systems* 1, 3 (1983d):225–43.

————. "The Demand for Woodfuels by Cottage Industries in the Province of Ilocos Norte, Philippines." *Energy—The International Journal* 9 (1984a):1–9.

————. "Providing Public Lands for Smallholder Agroforestry for Fuelwood Production in the Province of Ilocos Norte, Philippines." *Journal of Developing Areas* 18, 2 (1984b):177–90.

————. "FUELPRO: Description and Application of a Linear Programming Model for Analyzing Economic, Social, and Environmental Impacts of Woodfuel Policy Alternatives." In *Systems Analysis in Forestry and Forest Industries,* ed. M. Kallio, A. Andersson, A. Morgan, and R. Seppala. Amsterdam: North Holland Press, 1985.

————. "The Demand for Woodfuels by Rural and Urban Households in the Province of Ilocos Norte, Philippines." *Energy Policy,* in press.

Knowland, B., and C. Ulinski. *Traditional Fuels: Present Data, Past Experience and Possible Strategies.* Washington, D.C.: U.S. Agency for International Development, 1979.

Philippine National Census and Statistics Office. *Integrated Survey of Households Bulletin,* No. 48. Manila, 1980.

Wiersum, K. F. "Fuelwood as a Traditional and Modern Energy Source in the Philippines." Philippines, Multiple-Use Forest Management Project Working Paper No. 6. Manila: FAO, 1982.

10
Systematic Analysis of Water Pollution Control Options in a Suburban Region of Beijing, China

Adapted by Maynard M. Hufschmidt
from a report prepared by Fu Guowei, Zhang Lansheng,
Cheng Shengtong, and Nie Guisheng

Summary

This case study examines a number of water pollution control options for achieving a series of goals for the use of surface water flows in the southeastern region of Beijing. A simulation model is developed that is basically a conservation-of-mass-and-energy approach described in Chapter 5 of the *Guide* (pp. 129–35). This model is then used to test eight discrete alternatives—the present state and seven other river control plans.

Alternative costs are largely construction and operations, maintenance, and replacement (OMR); benefits include those from increased agricultural production and energy output, as well as other costs foregone. Since river waters are used for a variety of uses including irrigation, power plant cooling, and drinking water, if the water quality is sufficiently improved so that other pollution abatement measures are not required, those "foregone costs" can be counted as benefits.

Many other environmental quality effects have not been included. Reduced pollution will result in benefits from better visual and odor quality of the river, increases in fish and other water life, and potential development of recreation-related uses. This study details many of the physical properties of the river and some basic control measures; a more complete analysis would examine a broader management plan and include more nonmarket environmental quality effects. Because of limitations on data, time, and resources, such a study has not been done here.

Background Information

The southeastern suburban region of Beijing extends to the Tong Hui (TH) River in the north, the Liang Shui (LS) River in the south, the West Ti Tian Yin in the west, and the North Canal in the east. The total area of the region is approximately 500 square kilometers (km^2).

The region's climate is both semidry and semiwet depending upon the monsoon. Average annual rainfall is about 640 millimeters (mm), more than 70 percent of which is concentrated in June, July, and August. The average annual evaporation over water surfaces is nearly 2,000 mm, or 3.5 times the rainfall amount; that over land area is 284 mm, or about one-half of the rainfall amount.

The surface water of the region originates from the North Canal, consisting mainly of the Tong Hui River and the Liang Shui River with the Tong Hui Channel connecting them. The Tong Hui River formerly was a canal 20 km in length. It is located close to the urban area of Beijing and near the embassy sector with many important industrial enterprises, such as steam power plants, along the riverside. It supplies water not only for these industrial uses, but for irrigation of agricultural crops; at the same time it functions as a discharge channel for wastewater, sewage, and storm runoff for the urban districts and adjacent regions.

The Liang Shui River is also highly polluted as it has become a receiving body for sewage, storm runoff, and irrigation return flows. The outflow of the Liang Shui River enters the Bohai Sea; enroute it intersects with the North Canal in several places, and sewage water is mixed with the canal waters. Because the North Canal is one of the drinking water sources of Tian Jin City, there have been some cases of contamination of drinking water supply in that city.

The sewage water in this region has been used for irrigation of agricultural lands for as long as 17 years. Such irrigation has led to significant increases in agricultural productivity; however, it also gave rise to environmental pollution because only a small part of the sewage has been treated. For example, the use of water from the Liang Shui River for irrigation once caused the contamination of several hundred acres of wheat, the spreading of ascariasis (parasitic roundworm) among the children in the region, and the pollution of subsurface water of the irrigated area.

Two principal water needs of the region are clean water for drinking and industrial uses, and for sewage disposal facilities.

Regional Water Resources

This case study concentrates on the problems of surface water pollution and does not deal with issues of underground water sources. The region's surface water sources may be classified into three parts as follows:

1. *Inputs from outside the region,* which consist of Tong Hui River with an average annual stream flow of 2.52×10^8 cubic meters (m^3); Liang Shui River with an average annual stream flow of 1.73×10^8 m^3; and the combined miscellaneous sources and discharges from the urban district sewage system of 1.52×10^8 m^3/year. These flows from outside the region amount to 5.77×10^8 m^3/year.
2. *Sewage water from the region,* which consists of sewage (both domestic

and industrial) from a regional sewage collection system, as well as sewage discharged directly to the Tong Hui and Liang Shui rivers and the Tong Hui Channel, amounting to 2.09×10^8 m^3/year.

3. *Runoff from precipitation*, which amounts to about 0.63×10^8 m^3/year.

These surface water resources amount to about 8.49×10^8 m^3/year and are connected in different manners with the Tong Hui River and the Liang Shui River. Various functions of these two rivers are used to meet requirements of the region.

Environmental Dimensions

Pollution Sources and Pollutants

Pollution sources of the region are of several different types, including industrial, domestic, agricultural, and surface runoff. Sources from urban districts outside the region include domestic sewage of millions of residents, as well as wastewater from more than 400 factories. These outside sources are combined with the wastewater from 79 factories in the industrial area of the upper Tong Hui River. These sewage waters enter into the region through the Gao Bei Dian (GBD) Sewage System (see Figure 10.1). About half of the inflow is fed into the GBD wastewater treatment plant; after primary treatment, it is used for agricultural irrigation through the Tong Hui Channel into the Liang Shui River. The other half of the sewage flows without treatment through the GBD Sewage System into the Tong Hui River, forming one of the important pollution sources of that river. Of the sewage water from urban districts, about 40 percent is domestic sewage and the remainder is wastewater from paper manufacturing, electroplating, chemical, textile and printing, and dyeing plants of various scales.

The industrial area of about 280 factories of various sizes produces nearly 120 industrial pollutants in waste discharges, totaling about 50,000 tons per year.

Methodology

The methodology described in this study starts by defining the entire system, its components and boundaries, and then specifies the different subsystems to be simulated to arrive at the status of water quality under the condition that no pollution control measures are undertaken. This may be considered the present condition of the regional system.

The study then develops an overall model for systems analysis in order to evaluate and analyze quantitatively the water quality consequences and the associated costs and benefits of various alternative physical measures in various combinations. The study then combines various pollution control measures into "plans" for each of the two main rivers. This leads to identification of several "states" of control, which are combinations of "plans" for each of the two rivers.

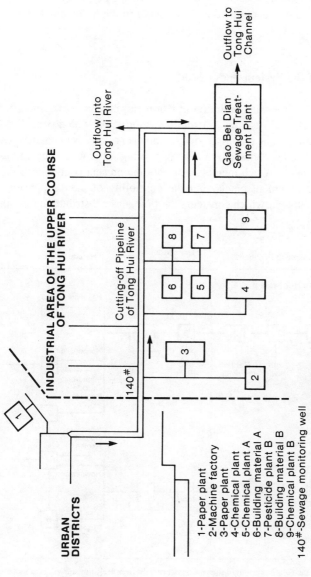

INDUSTRIAL AREA OF THE UPPER COURSE OF TONG HUI RIVER

URBAN DISTRICTS

Outflow into Tong Hui River

Cutting-off Pipeline of Tong Hui River

140#

Outflow to Tong Hui Channel

Gao Bei Dian Sewage Treatment Plant

1-Paper plant
2-Machine factory
3-Paper plant
4-Chemical plant
5-Chemical plant A
6-Building material A
7-Pesticide plant B
8-Building material B
9-Chemical plant B
140#-Sewage monitoring well

Figure 10.1 Sewage system of Gao Bei Dian.

For each of these states of control, a simulation analysis is made using the pollution source-transportation-treatment model to estimate the water quality consequences, economic costs and benefits, and savings of energy.

The methodology is outlined in more detail in the following sections.

The Data

Definition of the System under Study

The regional surface water pollution situation may be shown as a simplified system with three major subsystems: (1) *source of pollution,* which considers only the present condition of the pollution sources and the possibility of clean water separation from polluted water, and recycling of cooling water for reuse; (2) *transportation and treatment,* which includes not only the present condition of the sewage pipelines and treatment plants, but the possibility of their expansion; and (3) *natural environment,* which considers the time-space distribution of pollutants in

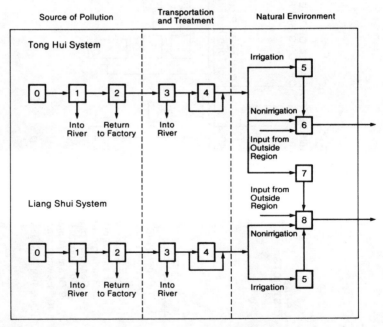

Figure 10.2 Surface water system of the southeastern suburb of Beijing, showing flows of wastewater.

Notes: 0 - source of pollution; 1 - separation of clean water and sewage; 2 - circulation of clean water; 3 - interceptor sewer; 4 - treatment plant; 5 - irrigation; 6 - Tong Hui River; 7 - Tong Hui Channel; 8 - Liang Shui River.

the region's surface water bodies. The system is illustrated in Figure 10.2, showing the flow of wastewater from its source, through the transporting pipelines to the treatment plant, and finally to the natural environment, including irrigation fields and the Tong Hui and Liang Shui rivers, which flow beyond the system boundary.

Model for Stream Flow

The behavior of the three main sources of surface water and their relationships may be expressed collectively by inputs and outputs of water flow at various points along the rivers. Thus it is necessary to evaluate the present state of the overall balance of water flow in the region, and on this basis to calculate the water flow balance of these two rivers respectively.

Because of the specific conditions of the region, the Tong Hui and Liang Shui rivers are divided into five and ten sections respectively (see Figure 10.3). For convenience of calculation, lateral inflows and outflows of water for each section are assumed to concentrate at the upstream end of each section (nodal point) for industrial and agricultural water. For runoff from precipitation, losses due to evaporation, and riverbed leakage, inflows and losses are assumed to concentrate equally at the upstream and the downstream nodal points of each section.

The model for stream flows for each section (or reach) is shown in Figure 10.4. In each reach, there is an inflow (Q_{in}) and outflow (Q_{out}), the outflow being the sum of the inflow and the net result of the additions and subtractions. Additions are the precipitation, surface runoff, and amount of effluents discharged to the river reach. The subtractions are the evaporation, seepage, irrigation use, and other water withdrawals from that reach.

Simulating this model for all of the reaches will result in an overall estimate of the yearly flow rates for the two rivers. The monthly average stream flow rate also can be calculated for the two rivers, by using the following formula:

$$Q_i = \alpha_i \overline{Q}_w \qquad (10\text{-}1)$$

where Q_i = stream flow rate for month i
   α_i = flow rate variation coefficient for month i
   $\overline{Q}_w$ = average yearly stream flow rate of the river

Model for Biochemical Oxygen Demand (BOD) Load

In this study, organic matter has been chosen as the object of analysis, because it is the major pollutant in the region's surface water. Other pollutants, such as heavy metals, are assumed to have been treated in various treatment plants or in factories, and therefore are not considered explicitly. The organic waste matter is comprehensively represented by BOD in this study.

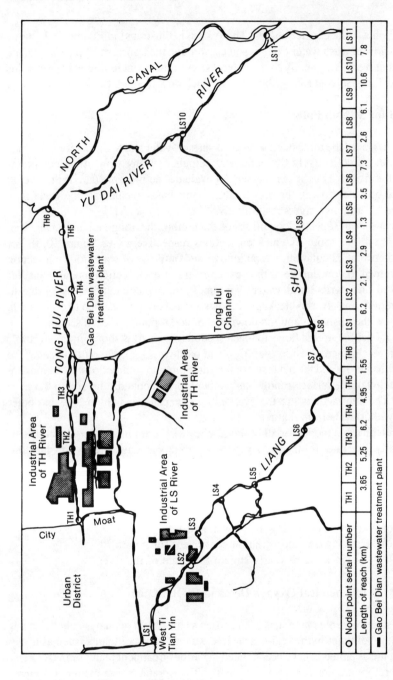

Nodal point serial number	TH1	TH2	TH3	TH4	TH5	TH6	LS1	LS2	LS3	LS4	LS5	LS6	LS7	LS8	LS9	LS10	LS11
Length of reach (km)	3.65	5.25	6.2	4.95	1.55		6.2	2.1	2.9	1.3	3.5	7.3	2.6	6.1	10.6	7.8	

■ Gao Bei Dian wastewater treatment plant

Figure 10.3 The river system of the southeastern suburban region of Beijing, including division into river reaches.

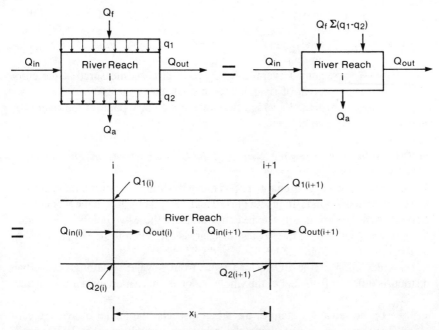

Figure 10.4 Stream flow showing water flow balance of each reach and associated nodal points of the river.

Notes: q_1 - quantity of the surface runoff of rain water (m^3/sec/m)
q_2 - quantity of the evaporation and leakage of river water (m^3/sec/m)
Q_f - quantity of industrial sewage inflow (m^3/sec)
Q_a - quantity of agricultural withdrawal (m^3/sec)
x_i - length of river reach in meters (m)

and,

$$Q_{1(i)} = Q_f + \frac{\Sigma(q_1 - q_2)}{2} = Q_f + \frac{(q_1 - q_2)x_i}{2}$$

$$Q_{2(i)} = Q_a$$

$$Q_{out(i)} = Q_{in(i)} + Q_{1(i)} - Q_{2(i)} = Q_{out(i+1)}$$

BOD Load from Upstream River Water

The upstream waters of both rivers receive some industrial and domestic sewage from urban districts; hence, there is a definite pollutant load at the entry point of the rivers into the system, the value of which is quite small in comparison with the inputs from the whole region. Due to data constraints on the upstream BOD load, the model uses average annual BOD concentrations for each river, namely,

$$Q_{L_{(y)}} = \overline{L}_{(y)} \times \overline{Q}_{w(y)} \tag{10-2}$$

where $Q_{L_{(y)}}$ = total annual input of BOD_5 at entry point of river (kilograms)

$\overline{L}_{(y)}$ = annual average BOD_5 concentration measured at the entry point of river (kilograms/10^6 cubic meters)

$\overline{Q}_{w(y)}$ = annual average flow rate at the entry point of the river (10^6 cubic meters)

BOD Load Input from Sewage Systems of the Urban Districts and the Region

There are many sewage discharge points along the Tong Hui River, most of them located near nodal points Tong Hui (TH) 2 and TH3; therefore, in the model these sewage discharges are assumed to be concentrated at these two points. With regard to the Liang Shui River, the sewage discharges are taken to be concentrated at nodal points Liang Shui (LS) 2, LS3, and LS5.

The calculation of the BOD_5 load input from sewage systems of the urban districts is different from that of the whole region because more data are available:

1. For the sewage system of the urban districts, the model of average concentration is also used in calculating the monthly average BOD_5 load, namely,

$$Q_{L_{(m)}} = \overline{L}_{(m)} \times \overline{Q}_{w(m)} \tag{10-3}$$

where $Q_{L_{(m)}}$ = monthly average BOD_5 load
$\overline{L}_{(m)}$ = monthly average BOD_5 concentration
$\overline{Q}_{w(m)}$ = monthly average river flow rate

2. For industrial sewage discharged into the river separately from various factories in this region, the BOD load of the discharge is calculated from organic matter content in the sewage water of the different factories and its equivalent oxygen demand. The amount of organic matter in the sewage equals the difference between the raw material input and the final product output. The equivalent oxygen demand of organic matter in the sewage can be estimated by reference to handbooks.

Thus, the monthly average BOD_5 load of the industrial sewage water discharged into any given section of the river follows the model with constant total BOD_5 quantity, or

$$Q_{L_{(m)}} = \frac{Q_{L_{(y)}}}{Q_{(y)}} \times Q_{(m)} \tag{10-4}$$

where $Q_{L(m)}$ = monthly BOD load (kilograms)
$\quad\quad\quad Q_{L(y)}$ = total annual BOD load (kilograms)
$\quad\quad\quad Q_{(y)}$ = total annual sewage flow (10^6 cubic meters)
$\quad\quad\quad Q_{(m)}$ = monthly sewage flow (10^6 cubic meters)

Model for Self-purification of the River

Decomposition of organic waste occurs in the river course. The dissolved oxygen (DO) held by the water reacts with the organic matter; thus, to some extent, purification of waste takes place. The Streeter-Phelps Model is used to depict this phenomenon for the river course as follows:

$$L_{i+1} = L_i e^{-k_1 t}$$

$$C_{i+1} = C_s - (C_s - C_i)e^{-k_2 t} + \frac{k_1 L_i}{k_1 - k_2}(e^{-k_1 t} - e^{-k_2 t}) \quad (10\text{-}5)$$

where L_{i+1} = BOD_5 concentration at the downstream nodal point of river
$\quad\quad\quad\quad$ reach i with x kilometers in length (mg/l)
$\quad\quad L_i$ = BOD_5 concentration at the upstream nodal point of river
$\quad\quad\quad\quad$ reach i (mg/l)
$\quad\quad C_{i+1}$ = dissolved oxygen at the downstream nodal point of the
$\quad\quad\quad\quad$ reach (mg/l)
$\quad\quad C_i$ = dissolved oxygen at the upstream nodal point of the reach
$\quad\quad\quad\quad$ (mg/l)
$\quad\quad C_s$ = saturated dissolved oxygen (mg/l)
$\quad\quad k_1$ = oxygen-consuming coefficient of the river water per day
$\quad\quad k_2$ = oxygen-recovering coefficient of the river water per day
$\quad\quad t$ = time for water to flow through the river reach of the x
$\quad\quad\quad\quad$ kilometers in length (day), $t = x/\overline{U}_x$
$\quad\quad \overline{U}_x$ = average speed of water (km/day)

Recurrence Formula for Water Quality

On the basis of the preceding models, the river course may be simplified into a model that can be used for recurrent calculation of BOD and DO for all the sections and nodal points. The model, shown in Figure 10.5, uses the materials-balance approach to derive the relationship of the values of stream flow, BOD_5, and DO at point i to their values at point $i+1$ in the river course.

The terminology used and the relationship between values at point i and values at point $i+1$ are analogous to the stream flow model shown in Figure 10.4.

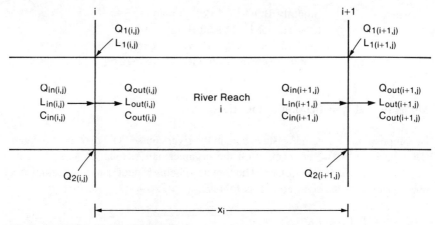

Figure 10.5 BOD and DO models for river reach i and its nodal points i and $i + 1$, for month j.

Notes: 1. All side inputs enter after the nodal points i and $i + 1$.
2. All side outputs leave before the nodal points i and $i + 1$.
3. DO of all side inputs equals zero.
4. In case any side input or output consists of two or more components, each should be identified by its specific water quality in order to calculate the correct BOD_5 load under corresponding flow rate.

Water Quality Indices

Values of stream flow, BOD, and DO vary from one river section to another. Thus, for each section, water quality is indicated by its BOD and DO contents.

Summary indicators would be indices that reflect the overall quality of the entire river course. Such indices, which can be interpreted as the combined effect of the models defined earlier, indicate the general surface water quality in the region, assuming that no pollution control measures are undertaken. These indices, which are computed as average values for each of the two rivers, can be computed as average monthly and average annual and maximum concentrations of BOD,and average annual and minimum concentrations for DO in milligrams per liter.

Pollution Source-Transportation-Treatment Model

From the entire system shown in Figure 10.2, we can establish a model composed of the pollution source, transportation, and treatment. This model will be simulated under the conditions where pollution control measures are undertaken.

In addition to calculating the overall water quality of each river, we can also arrive at the estimates of economic costs (capital and OMR), benefits (largely irrigation), and savings on energy under each alternative state for which this model is simulated. The model is defined as follows (see also Figure 10.6):

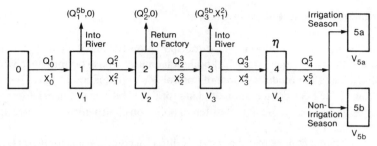

Figure 10.6 Model of system for pollution source, transportation, and treatment.

Notes: 0 - source of pollution; 1 - separation of clean water and sewage; 2 - recirculation and reuse; 3 - interceptor sewer; 4 - treatment plant; 5a - irrigation; 5b - river.

Q_i^j = the flow of subsystem i to subsystem j (m³/day)
X_i^j = the concentration of BOD in the flow of subsystem i into subsystem j (kg/m³)
V_i = corresponding values of annual economic losses and gains for subsystem i (10,000 yuan/year)
Q_1^{5b} = the flow of clean water into the river after being separated from wastewater
Q_2^0 = the flow of recycled clean water after being separated from wastewater
Q_3^{5b} = sewage flow discharged directly into river rather than routed to the sewage treatment plant
X_4^5 = BOD concentration of sewage discharged into river, which comes from source of pollution—transporting and handling systems or that of the sewage irrigation
η = treating rate of treatment plant

From water quantity equilibrium

$$Q_4^5 = Q_3^4 = Q_2^3 - Q_3^{5b} = Q_1^2 - Q_3^{5b} = Q_0^1 - Q_1^{5b} - Q_3^{5b} \qquad (10\text{-}6)$$

From water quality equilibrium

$$X_4^5 = X_3^4(1 - \eta) = X_2^3(1 - \eta) = X_1^2(1 - \eta) \qquad (10\text{-}7)$$

$$= X_0^1(1 - \eta)\frac{Q_0^1}{Q_1^2} = \frac{X_0^1}{mn}(1 - \eta)$$

m = ratio of the amount of clean water reused to that of the mixture of polluted and clean water
n = estimated coefficient of actual separable water

The magnitudes of flow and BOD and DO concentrations obtained from the simulation have been converted into monthly average values in kilograms.

Alternative States of Pollution Control

Having defined the pollution source-transportation-treatment model, it is now necessary to identify the "states" of pollution control whose performance will be simulated using the model. A *state* of control is a combination of *plans* for each river (i.e., state *i* is a combination of plan *j* for the TH River and plan *k* for the LS River). A *plan* is a combination of different pollution control measures for a single river—either TH or LS.

Seven different control measures and six different control plans for the TH River are shown in Table 10.1. There is not a "do-nothing" option since the GBD treatment plant exists and treats about half of the sewage water passing through it.

In the same manner, five control measures and five control plans (including the "do-nothing" option) for the LS River were identified and are shown in Table 10.2.

From the plans for the two rivers, seven alternative "states," or alternatives of pollution control, for the whole region have been chosen for this study (see Table 10.3).

Table 10.1 Control Measures and Plans for the Tong Hui River

	Control plan					
Control measure	1	2	3	4	5	6
1. Cutting off sewage overflow from the GBD sewage treatment plant	X	X	X	X	X	X
2. Cutting off other scattered sewage inflows to the river	0	X	X	X	X	X
3. Separating 60% of clean water from the sewage mix	0	0	0	X	X	X
4. Recycling 50% of clean water separated in the region	0	0	0	0	X	X
5. Primary treatment for irrigation or discharge to LS River	X	X	0	X	X	0
6. Primary treatment for irrigation or discharge to Bo Hei Sea, bypassing the LS River	0	0	X	0	0	0
7. Secondary treatment for irrigation or discharge to TH River	0	0	0	0	0	X

Note: The control measures adopted and included in a plan are denoted by the "X" sign. Thus, control plan 1 consists of control measures 1 and 5.

Table 10.2   Control Measures and Plans for the Liang Shui River

Control measure	Control plan				
	0	1	2	3	4
1. Cutting off sewage discharged into the river	0	X	X	X	X
2. Separating 80% of clean water from the sewage mix	0	0	X	X	X
3. Recycling 50% of clean water separated in the region	0	0	0	X	X
4. Primary treatment for irrigation or discharge to LS River	0	X	X	X	X
5. Secondary treatment for irrigation or discharge to LS River	0	0	0	0	X

Note: The control measures adopted and included in a plan are denoted by the "X" sign. Thus, control plan 1 consists of control measures 1 and 4.

The Economic Analysis

Given the eight alternatives ("states")—including the present "no-change" state—defined in Tables 10.1 and 10.2 and summarized in Table 10.3, the problem is (1) to estimate the economic costs and benefits and to compute the present value

Table 10.3   Combinations of Control Plans for the Tong Hui and Liang Shui Rivers Forming Alternative States of Pollution Control for the Region

LS River control plan	TH River control plan					
	1	2	3	4	5	6
0	State 1					
1		State 2	State 3			
2				State 4		
3					State 5	State 6
4						State 7

Note: The state 1 alternative of pollution control for the whole region consists of plan 1 for the TH River and plan 0 (the "do-nothing" plan) for the LS River; state 2 alternative consists of plan 1 for the LS River and plan 2 for the TH River; and so on.

of net benefits of each alternative, and (2) to rank the eight alternatives in order of preference, taking into account the contribution to improving the water quality of the TH and LS rivers. Use discount rates of 3, 6, and 10 percent.

Construction and Operation, Maintenance, and Replacement (OMR) Costs for Various Control Measures Grouped by Alternative States

	Cost	
	Construction (10^4 yuan)	OMR (10^4 yuan/yr)
Present State		
TH River		
Sewage treatment plan	965	16.9
Alternative 1		
TH River		
Primary treatment for irrigation or discharge to LS River	2,753	33.9
LS River		
—	—	—
Alternative 2		
TH River		
Cutting off sewage inflow	2,973	—
Primary treatment	5,140	63.4
LS River		
Cutting off sewage inflow	500	—
Primary treatment	1,069	13.1
Alternative 3		
TH River		
Cutting off sewage inflow	2,973	—
Primary treatment (bypass LS)	5,140	63.4
LS River		
Cutting off sewage inflow	500	—
Primary treatment	1,069	13.1
Alternative 4		
TH River		
Separation of clean water	528	—
Cutting off sewage inflow	2,973	—
Primary treatment	4,111	50.8
LS River		
Separation of clean water	164	—
Cutting off sewage inflow	500	—
Primary treatment	749	9.3
Alternative 5		
TH River		
Separation of clean water	528	—
Recycling of water	214	86.0
Cutting off sewage inflow	2,973	—
Primary treatment	3,596	44.4
LS River		
Separation of clean water	164	—
Recycling of water	33	13.2
Cutting off sewage inflow	500	—
Sewage treatment	749	9.3

	Cost	
	Construction 10^4 yuan	OMR 10^4 yuan/yr
Alternative 6		
TH River		
Separation of clean water	528	—
Recycling of water	214	86.0
Cutting off sewage inflow	2,973	—
Sewage treatment	6,254	170.3
LS River		
Separation of clean water	164	—
Recycling of water	33	13.2
Cutting off sewage inflow	500	—
Sewage treatment	749	9.3
Alternative 7		
TH River		
Separation of clean water	528	—
Recycling of water	214	86.0
Cutting off sewage inflow	2,973	—
Sewage treatment	6,254	170.3
LS River		
Separation of clean water	164	—
Recycling of water	33	13.2
Cutting off sewage inflow	500	—
Sewage treatment	1,286	35.0

All capital costs are assumed to be spent at a uniform rate over a two-year period. OMR costs begin in year 3 and run through year 22 (project life = 20 years following completion).

Economic Benefits of Various Control Measures

The economic benefits consist of benefits from (1) recycling clean water, (2) use of treated sewage for irrigation, and (3) improvement in quality of water used for cooling in the power plant.

Benefits from recycling water for industrial use are based on the resources saved by avoiding the need to provide clean water from another (presumably least-costly) alternative source. These resource savings consist of avoidance of construction and operation, maintenance, and replacement costs. Values of these savings are shown in Table 10.4.

Benefits from sewage use for irrigation are based on (1) the resources saved by not having to provide irrigation water from the cheapest available alternative source, and (2) the savings obtained from avoiding use of chemical fertilizers. Irrigation water benefits are computed by estimating the volume of sewage flow used for irrigation and multiplying by a unit cost for irrigation water. Savings in fertilizer costs are computed by multiplying the estimated volume of sewage flow used for irrigation by the equivalent fertilizer value per unit of sewage flow, and

Table 10.4 Economic Benefits for Alternative States of the System

Alternative state	Recycling benefits		Sewage irrigation benefits (10^4 yuan/yr)	Power plant cooling water benefits (10^4 yuan/yr)
	Construction savings (10^4 yuan)	OMR savings (10^4 yuan/yr)		
Present	0	0	426	0
1	0	0	457	0
2	0	0	510	270
3	0	0	510	270
4	0	0	455	270
5	4,638	376	455	270
6	4,638	412	346	270
7	4,638	418	324	270

then multiplying by the unit cost of chemical fertilizer. Values for the seven alternative states are shown in Table 10.4.

Benefits from improvement in power plant cooling water are computed by estimating the increased electric energy generated by measuring the increase in thermal efficiency of the power plant and multiplying this amount by a unit value in terms of yuan per kilowatt-hour. Values are shown in Table 10.4.

The economic life of the control measures in each of the alternatives is taken as 20 years.

Water Quality Effects of the Alternative States

Computer simulation analyses of the Tong Hui and Liang Shui river systems for each of the eight alternative "states" yield information on the monthly average values of water quality of the six reaches of the Tong Hui River and eleven reaches of the Liang Shui River. Water quality is measured in terms of BOD_5 and DO. These data are summarized into indices of annual average and maximum BOD_5 levels, and annual average and minimum DO levels, for each of the two rivers. Higher levels of BOD_5 indicate poorer water quality, and lower levels of DO indicate poorer water quality. These data are shown in Table 10.5.

The Results

The analysis of the cost and benefit data is made on the basis of discount rates of 3, 6, and 10 percent. Capital investment is assumed to take place over a 2-year period, with capital costs divided equally for each year. Annual OMR costs and benefits are assumed to begin in year 3 and continue at constant levels through year 22.

Table 10.5   Summary Indices of Water Quality Conditions in Tong Hui and Liang Shui Rivers for the Present State and the Seven Alternatives

Alternative state	BOD (mg/1)				DO (mg/1)			
	TH River		LS River		TH River		LS River	
	Ave.	Max.	Ave.	Max.	Ave.	Min.	Ave.	Min.
Present	36.1	188.7	31.3	83.3	1.9	0	1.5	0
1	10.1	17.3	32.3	83.3	3.2	1.6	1.5	0
2	3.1	5.4	20.5	61.8	5.2	2.4	2.1	0
3	3.1	5.4	12.2	51.8	5.2	2.4	2.5	0
4	3.2	5.3	18.2	60.7	5.0	2.2	2.3	0
5	3.2	5.3	18.2	59.6	5.2	2.4	2.3	0
6	5.8	19.8	12.2	55.7	4.4	1.4	2.4	0
7	5.8	19.8	6.7	13.0	4.4	1.4	3.7	1.6

Note: The Japanese "E" standard of desirable surface water quality for BOD_5 is 10 mg/1.   The comparable China standard is 4 mg/1.

Table 10.6 summarizes capital and OMR costs and their present values at each of the three discount rates for each alternative.

Table 10.7 summarizes the gross benefits for each of the alternatives and presents information on the present values of the gross benefits at each of the three discount rates. Gross annual benefits are shown for each of the alternatives. In addition, for alternatives 5, 6, and 7, a capital cost saving of $4,638 \times 10^4$ yuan is shown as a benefit. This represents the capital costs saved by recycling water for industrial use and not having to provide it from another source (Table 10.4). This saving is assumed to be gained in years 1 and 2, with the amount divided equally between the years. These amounts are then discounted to the present (year 0) to obtain the present value of the capital savings benefits.

Table 10.8 presents information on the present value of net benefits (gross benefits less capital and OMR costs) at the three discount rates.

Finally, in Table 10.9 the alternatives are ranked according to the present value of net benefits shown in Table 10.8, and according to the effects on water quality in the TH and LS rivers shown in Table 10.5. A summary ranking is also provided based upon the judgment of the analyst.

All information on costs, benefits, and water quality contained in these tables and the summary rankings shown in Table 10.9 are based on the data provided. However, the summary ranking in the last column of Table 10.9 involves subjective valuation of the benefit and water quality information by the analyst. The data clearly show alternative 5 is the best choice. It has the largest value of positive net benefits regardless of discount rate, and in terms of water quality it has the highest value of DO and is marginally close to the lowest BOD value in the TH River. Only in terms of BOD and DO in the LS River does alternative 5 fall short, but even here its performance is in the middle range.

Table 10.6 Present Value of Capital and OMR Costs for the Alternatives with Discount Rates of 3%, 6%, and 10% (time period = 22 years; 10^4 yuan)

Alternative state	Total capital cost (x)	Annual OMR cost (y)	Present value at								
			3%			6%			10%		
			Capital cost[a]	OMR cost[b]	Total	Capital cost[c]	OMR cost[d]	Total	Capital cost[e]	OMR cost[f]	Total
Present	965	16.9	923	237	1,160	885	172	1,057	837	119	956
1	2,753	33.9	2,634	475	3,109	2,524	346	2,870	2,389	239	2,628
2	9,682	76.5	9,263	1,073	10,336	8,875	781	9,656	8,402	538	8,940
3	9,682	76.5	9,263	1,073	10,336	8,875	781	9,656	8,402	538	8,940
4	9,024	60.1	8,634	843	9,477	8,272	614	8,886	7,831	423	8,254
5	8,757	153.0	8,378	2,146	10,524	8,028	1,562	9,590	7,599	1,077	8,676
6	11,415	279.0	10,921	3,913	14,834	10,464	2,848	13,312	9,905	1,963	11,868
7	11,952	305.0	11,435	4,277	15,712	10,956	3,113	14,069	10,372	2,146	12,518

[a]$(x/2)1.9135$

[b]$y(15.936917 - 1.913470)$

[c]$(x/2)1.8334$

[d]$y(12.0416 - 1.8334)$

[e]$(x/2)1.735$

[f]$y(8.771540 - 1.735537)$

Table 10.7   Present Value of Gross Benefits for the Alternatives with
Discount Rates of 3%, 6%, and 10% (time period = 22 years; 10^4 yuan)

Alternative state	Total benefits		Present value of benefits[a]		
	Capital	Annual	3%	6%	10%
Present	−	426	5,974	4,349	2,997
1	−	457	6,409	4,665	3,215
2	−	680	9,535	6,942	4,784
3	−	680	9,535	6,942	4,784
4	−	725	10,167	7,401	5,101
5	4,638	1,101	15,440	11,239	7,746
			4,437	4,252	4,023
			19,877	15,491	11,769
6	4,638	1,028	14,416	10,494	7,233
			4,437	4,252	4,023
			18,853	14,746	11,256
7	4,638	1,012	14,192	10,331	7,120
			4,437	4,252	4,023
			18,629	14,583	11,143

[a]Computed as follows: Capital benefits assumed to be gained--one-half in
year 1, one-half in year 2.   Annual benefits assumed to begin in year 3 and
terminate in year 22.   These annual streams of benefits are discounted at 3,
6, and 10 percent.

Table 10.8 Present Value of Net Benefits for the Alternatives (10^4 yuan)

Alternative state	3%	6%	10%
Present	4,814	3,292	2,041
1	3,300	1,795	587
2	−801	−2,714	−4,156
3	−801	−2,714	−4,156
4	690	−1,485	−3,153
5	9,353	5,901	3,093
6	4,019	1,434	−612
7	2,917	514	−1,375

Table 10.9 Ranking of Alternatives in Order of Preference

Rank	In terms of PV net benefits	In terms of water quality BOD		In terms of water quality DO		In terms of both benefits and water quality
		TH	LS	TH	LS	
1	5	2	7	5	7	5
2	PS	3	6	2	3	6
3	6	4	3	3	6	7
4	1	5	4	4	5	PS
5	7	6	5	6	4	1
6	4	7	2	7	2	4
7	2	1	PS	1	1	2
8	3	PS	1	PS	PS	3

◖--Signifies ties.

PS--Present state.

The choice of second and third best alternatives is not clearcut. Alternatives 6 and 7 show good water quality performance but have negative net benefits at the 10 percent discount rate, ranking only fourth and fifth in terms of net benefits at the 6 percent and 10 percent discount rates. On the other hand, the present state and alternative 1 both have positive net benefits at all three discount rates, and rank second and third in terms of the 6 percent and 10 percent discount rates. However, these alternatives provide very poor water quality in both of the rivers and rank the lowest in this respect.

On the basis of these analyses, summary rankings of second and third were given to alternatives 6 and 7, with the present state and alternative 1 given summary rankings of fourth and fifth. Alternatives 4, 2, and 3 were given the lowest rankings because they had negative net benefits at all three discount rates and performed poorly in terms of water quality.

The rankings of the alternatives did not change as discount rates were changed. In this case, the discount rate was *not* a factor in choice among alternatives.

Index